Effective Teaching

Evidence and Practice

Daniel Muijs and David Reynolds

P·C·P

Paul Chapman
Publishing

First published 2001

 Paul Chapman Publishing
A SAGE Publications Company
6 Bonhill Street
London EC2A 4PU

SAGE Publications Inc
2455 Teller Road
Thousand Oaks, California 91320

SAGE Publications India Pvt Ltd
32, M-Block Market
Greater Kailash - I
New Delhi 110 048

British Library Cataloguing in Publication data

A catalogue record for this book is available from the British Library

ISBN 0 7619 6880 6
ISBN 0 7619 6881 4 (pbk)

Library of Congress catalog record available

Typeset by Dorwyn Ltd, Rowlands Castle, Hants
Printed in Great Britain by Athenaeum Press, Gateshead

Effective Teaching

School of Educational Studies

Contents

Acknowledgements

We would like to thank our wives, family and parents for their support during writing and life in general; Professors Eugene Schaffer, Charles Teddlie, Sam Stringfield and Bert Creemers for introducing us to teacher effectiveness research; the Gatsby Charitable Foundation, for supporting our research; all teachers and heads who have welcomed us into their classrooms and schools; and, finally, all the students we have met during our research, and who we hope will be the ultimate beneficiaries of the knowledge contained in this book and in all our other educational research.

Introduction: The Importance of Teacher Effectiveness

In the last 20 years there has been a worldwide movement of researchers, practitioners and policy-makers that has begun to study what makes more 'effective' schooling (Teddlie and Reynolds, 2000). Starting in the USA and the UK in the 1970s with the work of Brookover *et al.* (1979) and Rutter *et al.* (1979) respectively, the field has moved on to encompass issues to do with school improvement, the evaluation of schools, international comparisons of effective school characteristics and the particular problems of 'ineffective' school regimes.

We have written this book because we believe that it is now time for the school effectiveness movement to look at the classroom 'level', or teachers in classes, with the same mission, clarity and focus with which it has studied schools. All the evidence that has been generated in the school effectiveness research community shows that classrooms are far more important than schools in determining how children perform at school (see Teddlie and Reynolds, 2000, ch. 3). Yet, of course, overall the number of studies conducted internationally in the 'effective schools' tradition greatly exceeds those in the 'effective teacher' tradition. Research into teacher effectiveness in the USA has been much less prevalent in the 1990s than in the 1980s. Research into teacher effectiveness in the UK has scarcely developed as a specialty in the last 30 years.

The quantity of school effectiveness and teacher effectiveness research is not the only issue. School effectiveness research has achieved considerable popularity among policy-makers and practitioners, and indeed there is considerable evidence that the research literature has influenced policies pursued by government directly (Reynolds and Sullivan, 1999). No such notice has been taken of the literature, such as it is, on teacher effects, partly because the assumption is that various Office for Standards in Education (OFSTED) reports have closed down the issue and partly, no doubt, because policy-makers have an unhealthy obsession with the school level and the headteachers who lead at that level.

The absence of any national discourse about, and a strong research effort on, teacher effectiveness is surprising and itself needs explaining. What factors may be responsible for this? First, there is a view that teaching is an 'art', not a science, and that therefore it is personal factors and qualities, often idiosyncratic and difficult to influence by educational policies, which are the key factors. It goes without saying that such a view – linked in the case of Britain to other beliefs about 'gifted amateurs', 'muddling through' and, indeed, to the whole problem of the two cultures and Britain's placing of education within the humanities tradition – is clearly wrong and probably condemns societies where it is prevalent to having only those small number of excellent teachers who inherit the 'art', rather than the larger number who could acquire the applied science of a teaching methodology.

Second, there is a belief in some societies like Britain that we do not need a discourse about teaching because teaching is such a simple 'technology' that it does not need elaboration.

Third, we have been held back from a discourse about teachers and teaching by our unwillingness to confront the issue of inter-teacher variation. School effectiveness research when it began had to struggle against a widespread unwillingness to permit school-against-school comparisons. Although a knowledge of which individuals and indeed departments are effective is an essential building block of our educational knowledge on 'good practice', the fact that effective teachers have to be studied in contrast to ineffective teachers has clearly been politically and interpersonally difficult to handle.

Fourth, school effectiveness researchers have themselves been partially responsible for this state of affairs, since because critics of schools said 'schools make no difference', researchers celebrated the school level, not the classroom level, in their attempted rebuttals.

This is not an exhaustive list of reasons: the absence of any tradition in countries like Britain in the fields of 'learning and instruction' within educational psychology is also important, as has been the focus upon the goals of education within educational discourse. The tendency of some in the discipline of school effectiveness to waste their time playing politics has also not helped (the historically more successful American teacher effectiveness community has been notable for *not* playing politics, for sticking to the matter in hand and for consequently generating what is probably the world's most robust knowledge base).

However, our unwillingness to address issues to do with teaching has been shown to be costly by a number of recent events. First, continued reports from bodies such as OFSTED have shown a very wide variation in teacher behaviours, competence and in consequent outcomes, although it must be stated that these judgements rest more on an experiential than on a research-orientated knowledge base. Second, British school effectiveness research has increasingly been showing that the range of variation *within* schools dwarfs the range of variation between schools (Fitz-Gibbon, 1996) and that the influence of the teacher and of the learning level considerably exceeds that of the school. Indeed, the more one looks at the relative effects of schools as against teachers, the more one is given plausible explanations for why so many of our educational reforms have not thus far been successful. We have, by intervening at the school level rather than at the learning level, been 'pulling levers' that have small effects on their own and which may not have generated any 'ripple through' to affect the key level of the classroom.

Third, the cost of our inability to address issues concerning teaching and the learning level has been shown by those countries which do have this knowledge base intervening productively in children's lives in ways unknown to others. Bob Slavin's (1996) *Education for All*, a literacy programme of awesome power which generates cohorts of children in which few possess reading ages below their chronological age, was based soundly on teacher effectiveness research, as is the highly successful Dutch School Improvement Project.

In this book, therefore, we aim to give an accessible introduction to research in this relatively neglected field. The book is divided into three parts. In Part 1 we will discuss generic teaching skills, in Part 2 issues in teaching specific skills or students, and in Part 3 we will discuss the teaching of specific subjects and the issue of assessment and observation of teaching in classrooms.

Part 1, research on generic teaching skills, contains eight chapters looking at research on what can be termed 'the basics of teaching'. The first three chapters rely heavily on the effective teaching school of research mentioned above. In Chapter 1 the main studies and research methods used in effective teaching research are summarized, and the method identified as the most effective way of teaching basic skills, the direct instruction method, is discussed. In Chapter 2 research on interactive teaching, an essential component of direct instruction and of most other effective teaching methods, is summarized. This research has produced detailed findings on such matters as the cognitive level of questions, what to do when pupils give a wrong answer and how long to wait for a pupil to answer a question. In Chapter 3 we will look at the main elements needed to effectively implement individual practice by students, as well as at the advantages and disadvantages of small group work during practice sessions.

In the next two chapters we discuss the extensive body of research on classroom and behaviour management, which form part of the basic repertoire of any effective teacher. In Chapter 4, classroom management, we will discuss such matters as how to avoid disruption when starting or ending the lesson, or during transitions between lesson parts and when giving homework assignments, and why and how to establish clear rules and procedures. In Chapter 5 we will discuss research on how to deal with pupil misbehaviour when it does occur, including the most effective ways to use rewards and punishments in the classroom.

In Chapter 6 we look at classroom climate, including such matters as how to create a pleasant classroom climate and the importance of teacher expectations. In Chapter 7 we discuss homework, including the main types of homework in use, its main goals, what research has to tell us about the effectiveness of homework as a learning tool and how this may differ by grade, and how to use homework effectively. In the final chapter of Part 1 the research on developing students' higher-order thinking will be reviewed, and we will look at three main approaches: the heuristic approach, the metacognitive approach and the formal operations-based approach to teaching thinking skills.

In Part 2 we will focus on strategies aimed at reaching particular goals or students. Developing students' social skills is the subject of Chapter 9, in which research will be reviewed on the importance of peer relations to children's development, characteristics that may lead to children being unpopular with peers, how social skills can be taught or enhanced and what parents can do to help develop their children's social skills. Another important social outcome is enhancing students' self-esteem, which is discussed in Chapter 10. This is a subject which has received a lot of attention in recent decades, and we will look at what research has found on the relationship between these concepts and school achievement, whether students' age and gender affect their self-concept and what teachers can do to improve their students' self-concept and self-esteem.

In the next three chapters we look at ways of teaching specific student groups. First, in Chapter 11, we review what is known about teaching students with a variety of special needs, such as learning disabilities, autism, hearing problems, behavioural difficulties, attention disorders, Tourette's syndrome and mental retardation, as well as the findings on including students with special needs in the regular classroom. A different group of students with special needs are gifted students. In Chapter 12 we will look at how to identify gifted students and the advantages and disadvantages of different methods of catering for gifted students such as ability grouping, curricular enrichment, co-operative learning and acceleration. Research on teaching in the early years is reviewed in Chapter 13, in which we will discuss differing views on how to teach in pre-school, how best to promote childrens' school-readiness in pre-school settings, the importance of play and what children learn from it. Finally, in Chapter 14 various ways of dealing with individual differences between students are discussed, including the use of selection, streaming and setting, individualized instruction and various theories on different learning styles such as Gardner's (1983) theory of multiple intelligences.

In the final part (Part 3) we will look at the teaching of particular subjects and other specific classroom techniques such as assessment and classroom observation. One of the most contentious issues in education over recent years has been the teaching of literacy. In Chapter 15 we will discuss the two methods which have caused so much controversy, phonics and whole language, and review the research on how children learn to read and what the best way to teach them this crucial skill is. Chapter 16 focuses on another crucial basic skill, numeracy. We look at research on how children learn mathematics, and at the implications of this and other research on mathematics teaching. In Chapter 17 we discuss the role of information communication technology (ICT) in the classroom, reviewing the main ways in which ICT can help student learning, some ways of using ICT in the classroom and some of the problems and pitfalls of ICT use.

The last two chapters focus on assessment (Chapter 18) and classroom observation (Chapter 19). Assessment is an area which has received a lot of attention from researchers, and we will review the main characteristics of standardized tests, the advantages and disadvantages of using teacher-made tests, the advantages and disadvantages of multiple choice and open essay-style questions, and the most common forms of alternative assessment. The use of peer classroom observation is the subject of the last chapter. We will see why classroom observation can be a powerful staff development tool, and give some examples of classroom observation instruments that are used in practice.

We hope that we have provided an overview of research in a wide range of areas related to teaching in an accessible but thorough way. Obviously, it is not possible to treat all these aspects in detail in this volume, and we have probably gone for breadth rather than depth. Hopefully, though, we will have stimulated the reader to go and look for more information in the references provided.

PART 1
GENERIC TEACHING SKILLS

1

Direct Instruction

Advance Organizers

In this chapter you will learn:

- What direct instruction means.
- The evidence for the effectiveness of this strategy.
- Why this strategy is effective.
- What specific behaviours have been found to enhance student learning.
- Some models of direct instruction.
- How direct instruction ties in with learning theory.
- Limitations and criticisms of the direct instruction model.

History of research into direct instruction

In this and the following chapters we will discuss what research has to say about one of the most widely used and most effective teaching methods: direct instruction. Direct instruction, also known as active teaching or whole-class teaching, refers to a teaching style in which the teacher is actively engaged in bringing the content of the lesson to students by teaching the whole class directly.

Whole-class teaching has been employed in schools for a long time, but the effectiveness of whole-class teaching methods has not been scientifically studied until recently. Interest in this style of teaching took off with the 'teacher effectiveness' school of research, which started in the late 1960s, following the failure of attempts to explain differences in the performance of teachers by looking at their personality. In contrast, the teacher effectiveness researchers decided to look at the actual behaviours of teachers in classrooms, observing actual lessons and linking the behaviours they observed to student outcomes such as scores on standardized tests. This research school started in a period in which policy was moving towards 'child-centred' strategies in many countries (e.g. the USA and the UK), which often degenerated into lessons in which students spent most of their time working from worksheets on their own, while the teacher would sit at her or his desk marking the work of students.

The early teacher effectiveness researchers in the USA, who looked at teacher behaviours using classroom observation, gradually started to find patterns which indicated that more effective teachers (that is, teachers

3

whose students made stronger gains on standardized achievement tests) tended to actively teach the whole class, spending significantly more time than ineffective teachers explicitly lecturing, demonstrating or interacting with the class than less effective teachers (Rosenshine, 1979). As well as actively teaching the whole class for more of the time, effective teachers used a number of behaviours that will be identified in this and the next three chapters.

After this initial research had identified a number of behaviours that were effective, researchers decided to put theory into practice by training teachers to use these effective methods and testing whether this would actually make a difference to student achievement. One of the first and most important of these programmes was the Missouri Mathematics Effectiveness Study conducted by Good and Grouws (1979) in the late 1970s. In this study 40 teachers were divided into two groups. One group of teachers received training in the effective direct instruction behaviours identified in previous research, while the other group continued to teach as before. It was found not only that the 'trained' group did indeed use the strategies they were taught, but that their students made more gains on the test than did those taught by the control teachers. A similar study was conducted by Fitzpatrick (1982) for English teaching, and he also found that these behaviours could successfully be taught to teachers, and that teachers using them were more able to engage students in their classrooms.

A number of studies outside the USA reported the same positive findings for whole-class teaching methods. In the UK, three major (non-experimental) studies of teacher effectiveness have been conducted in the last few decades. The first of these, Galton's ORACLE project, found that teachers labelled as 'Class Enquirers' generated the greatest gains in mathematics and language, but that this finding did not extend to reading. By contrast, the group of 'Individual Monitoring' teachers made among the least progress. It is important to note that the more successful 'Class Enquirers' group spent four times as much time using whole class interactive teaching than the 'Individual Monitors' (Galton and Croll, 1980; Croll, 1996).

The second important British teacher effectiveness study is the Junior School Project of Mortimore *et al.* (1988), based upon a four year cohort study of 50 primary schools, which involved collection of a considerable volume of data on children and their family backgrounds ('intakes'), school and classroom 'processes' and 'outcomes' in academic (reading, mathematics) and affective (e.g. self-conception, attendance, behaviour) areas. This study reported 12 factors that were associated with effectiveness both across outcome areas and within specific subjects such as mathematics. Significant positive relationships were found with such factors as structured sessions, use of higher-order questions and statements, frequent questioning, restricting sessions to a single area of work, involvement of students and the proportion of time utilized in communicating with the whole class. Negative relationships were found with teachers spending a high proportion of their time communicating with individual students (Mortimore *et al.*, 1988), which once again suggests that use of whole-class teaching is beneficial to students.

Most recently, a classroom observation study of over 100 mathematics teachers in England and Wales also found that the effective behaviours we will discuss below were able to distinguish effective from ineffective teachers, and that it was teachers who spent more time teaching the whole class as opposed to teaching individual students whose students showed stronger gains in mathematics achievement (Muijs and Reynolds, 1999).

Studies in continental Europe tend to support this viewpoint (Creemers, 1994). However, a review of Dutch research found disappointing results, with teaching factors such as whole-class teaching, achievement orientation and time spent on homework being positively related to student outcomes at the primary level in, respectively, three, four and four studies out of 29 (and negatively related in none), while differentiation and co-operation were negatively related to outcomes in two and three studies, respectively, and positively related to outcomes in none (Scheerens and Creemers, 1996). However, where significant results are obtained, they tend to support the conclusions of the American and British studies (Westerhof 1992; Creemers, 1994).

More evidence comes from international comparative research, such as the 'Worlds Apart' report (Reynolds and Farrell, 1996) in the UK, which compared teaching methods in England with those employed in countries that did better in international studies of students' achievement (like the Third International Mathematics and Science Study), such as Singapore. The authors found that one of the main factors that distinguished these more successful countries from England was a more widespread use of whole-class interactive teaching.

There are several reasons why this whole-class approach has been found to be more effective than individualized learning approaches. One of these is that studies have found that whole-class teaching actually allows the teacher to make more contacts with each individual student than individual work. And, as we will discuss further on in this book, interaction between students and the teacher is a crucial aspect of successful teaching and learning. Students have also been found more likely to be on task during whole-class sessions than during individualized instruction. This is mainly because it is easier for the teacher to monitor the whole class while teaching than to monitor individual students. Whole-class teaching also allows the teacher to easily change and vary activities and to react quickly to signs that students are 'switching off', either through lack of understanding of the content or through boredom. It also allows mistakes and misconceptions made by students to be illustrated to the whole class. Furthermore, some other arrangements, in particular those in which different students or groups of students are doing different activities within the classroom, are more complex, and therefore more difficult to manage effectively than a whole-class setting in which students are mainly doing the same thing (Brophy and Good, 1986; Rosenshine and Stevens, 1980).

This, however, does not mean that teachers should spend the whole lesson teaching the whole class. Individual or group practice remains an essential part of the lesson if student learning is to be maximized, as students have to have the opportunity to reinforce their learning. How to manage this section of the lesson effectively will be discussed in Chapter 3.

The main elements of effective direct instruction

It is not enough merely to teach the whole class in order to have a lesson involving effective direct instruction. A number of conditions need to be met in order to maximize the effectiveness of these. These will be discussed here.

Clearly structured lessons

The lesson should have a clear structure, so students can easily understand the content of the lesson and how it relates to what they already know. Many researchers recommend starting the lesson with a review and practice of what was learnt during the previous lesson, for example by going over homework, as this will allow the teacher to find out to what extent students have grasped the content of previous lessons, and therefore to what extent this content will need to be *retaught*.

The objectives of the lesson should be made clear to students from the outset, with examples such as 'today we are going to learn about . . .', or through writing the objectives on the board or on a flipchart. During the lesson the teacher needs to emphasize the key points of the lesson, which may otherwise get lost in the whole. A certain amount of repetition will certainly do no harm here. At the end of the lesson the main points should once again be summarized either by the teacher, or preferably by the students themselves, e.g. through asking them what they have learnt during the lesson. Subparts of the lesson can usefully be summarized in the same way during the course of the lesson. Teachers must also clearly signal transitions between lesson parts such as the start of a new topic or practice of the previous topic. All this not only ensures that students will remember better what they have learnt, but will help them to more easily understand the content as an integrated whole, with recognition of the relationships between the parts.

It is also recommended that teachers build a certain amount of redundancy into the lesson, in the form of repeating and reviewing general rules and key concepts, in order to facilitate student retention and understanding of the topic. This is particularly important for more demanding topics or rules. Teachers would also do well to explain such demanding topics using a variety of media and methods, in order to help students with different learning styles (Rosenshine and Stevens, 1986; Brophy, 1992; Borich, 1996; Reynolds and Muijs, 1999a).

Clear, structured presentations

Within this overall structure, it is recommended that material should be presented in small steps pitched at the students' level, which are then practised before going on to the next step. This allows students to gain a sense of mastery over the content and will stop them getting bored or losing the thread of the lesson. Information should be presented with a high degree of clarity and enthusiasm. Teachers need to focus on one point at a time, avoid digressions and avoid ambiguous phrases or pronouns.

There are a number of ways to enhance the clarity of presentations. Two traditional models of presenting a topic are the *deductive* model and the *inductive* model. In the deductive model, the presentation starts with general principles or rules and goes on to more detailed and specific examples. An example of this is teaching comparative democracy. One could start with the general principle of what democracy means, and then attempt to apply this to the political system of a variety of countries. In the inductive model, the presentation starts with (real-life) examples and moves on to general rules or principles. Using the same examples, one could look at the system of government in a number of different countries, and then work out some general principles of what makes for democratic government.

Borich (1996) suggests a number of other methods for structuring content. The first of these is the *part-whole format*. A topic is introduced in its most general form, and then divided into easily distinguishable (and digestible) subparts. The teacher should make sure that the subparts are clearly and explicitly related to the whole. Borich gives the example of teaching the possessive by first explaining what a possessive is, and then dividing it into rules for 'of' phrases (the daughter of . . .) and 's' phrases (the holiday of). A second method is *sequential ordering*. With this method the content/rule is taught in the order in which it occurs in the real world.

The sequential ordering method is often used in teaching mathematical rules. Another example is teaching how the steel-making process works, by going through the different stages from iron ore to finished product. It is also possible to use *combinatorial relationships*. In this method the teacher brings together the various decisions or elements that influence the use of rules, facts or sequences in a single format. For example, in teaching law one could draw together all the influences on the process of making a particular law. Finally, in the *comparative relationships* method different elements are placed side by side so that learners can compare and

Links to learning theory

While direct instruction was developed mainly from empirical research and less from theory, the main behaviours identified as effective can clearly be linked to two main learning theories, *Behavioural Learning Theory* and *Cognitive Information Processing Theory*.

Behavioural Learning Theory, which was developed by psychologists such as Pavlov, Skinner and Bandura from the 1920s onwards, emphasizes *change in behaviour* as the main *outcome* of the learning process. Behavioural theorists concentrate on directly observable phenomena using a strict positivistic scientific method borrowed from the natural sciences. The most radical behaviourists, such as B. F. Skinner, considered all study of non-observable behaviour ('mentalism', according to pioneering behaviourist Watson) to be unscientific. In recent years, however, most researchers and psychologists in the behaviourist tradition, such as Bandura, have expanded their view of learning to include expectations, thoughts, motivation and beliefs.

The theory was first developed using laboratory tests of the learning behaviour of dogs and rats. Main tenets are that one can condition learning by providing positive reinforcement to teach desired behaviours and negative reinforcement to deter unwanted behaviours. Bandura's theory of observational learning is particularly relevant to direct instruction models. This contains four stages:

1. *Attentional phase*: the first phase of learning is paying attention to a particular model. Students will tend to pay more attention if the model is perceived as successful, attractive, interesting and popular.
2. *Retention phase*: once the students' attention has been captured (e.g. by the teacher), the teacher must model the behaviour he or she wishes the students to imitate, and then give them a chance to practise that behaviour. An example of this type of teaching would be the modelling of handwriting.
3. *Reproduction*: during the reproduction phase learners try to match their behaviour to that of the model, e.g. after having learnt a timetable, can the students independently reproduce it?
4. *Motivational phase*: the final step in Bandura's model is motivation. Students will imitate a model because they think that this will increase their chances of receiving reinforcement. This phase in the classroom can consist of praise or the awarding of grades, so students know what it is the teacher wants them to do, and also that doing so carries rewards.

This theory is clearly connected to modelling and to the 'teaching a small step–practice–review' model used in direct instruction. The methodological emphasis of the teacher effectiveness researchers – looking at observable behaviours and linking them to achievement – is clearly a stimulus-response model of the type used in behavioural psychological research.

Cognitive Information Processing Theory is a more recent development, inspired by the evolution of computing technology.

Especially important in this theory is the role of memory in learning processes. The memory consists of three parts: the sensory buffer, the working memory and the long-term memory.

The memory works as follows: one's experiences (tactile, visual or auditory) are registered in the sensory buffer, and then converted into the form in which they are employed in the working and long-term memories. The sensory buffer can register a lot of information, but can only hold it briefly. Some parts of the information in it will be lost, other parts will be transmitted to the working memory. The working memory is where 'thinking gets done'. It receives its content from the sensory buffer and the long-term memory but has a limited capacity for storing information, a fact that limits human mental processes. The working memory contains the information that is actively being used at any one time.

The long-term memory has a nodal structure, and consists of neural network representations, whose nodes represent chunks in memory and whose links represent connections between those chunks. As such, nodes can be equated with concepts, and links with meaningful associations between concepts. Together these form schemata, or clusters of information. Activating one item of the cluster is likely to activate all of them.

Information processing theory thus emphasizes the importance of helping students to memorize content, by connecting new knowledge to the schemata already in existence, and aiding students by providing them with clear structures to form new schemata. This is clearly connected to the need for structure and clarity in presentations, which are particularly stressed in direct instruction. The use of advance organizers (which can sometimes take the form of schemata themselves) is based on this theory of learning.

contrast them. One could, for example, compare two different beliefs in religious studies in this way.

Pacing

Pacing of the lesson is an important, but not wholly uncontroversial part, of effective direct instruction. Initially, researchers suggested that lessons need to be fast-paced. The advantages of this were seen to lie in maintaining momentum and interest of students, and in allowing a relatively large amount of content to be processed. However, it has been found that while this seems to be the best way to teach lower-level basic skills and younger students, in higher grades and for more demanding content the pacing needs to be slower to allow students more time to develop understanding. It is recommended that lessons designed to teach basic skills are paced in such a way that during weekly or monthly reviews students are able to respond correctly in 90–95 per cent of cases.

Modelling

A useful procedure to follow when teaching certain topics is to explicitly model a skill or procedure. Modelling means demonstrating a procedure to learners. This can be more effective than using verbal explanations, especially with younger learners or those who prefer a visual learning style. Modelling follows this sequence: the teacher (or another person who is perceived to be an expert) demonstrates the behaviour by doing it, linking the behaviour to skills or behaviours that learners already possess. She or he needs to go through the different parts of the behaviour in a clear, structured and sequential way, explaining what she or he is doing after each step. Then learners need to memorize the steps seen, and imitate them (Ausubel, 1968).

Use of conceptual mapping

A strategy that can help to structure the lesson in students' minds is the use of conceptual mapping. A conceptual map is a framework that can be presented to students before the topic of the lesson is presented, providing the student with an overview linking different parts of a topic and with a ready-made structure (or schema). This helps students to store, package and retain the concepts, and to link different lessons to one another. This is especially useful for more complex topics, which take several lessons to cover. An example of this is the conceptual map for a history topic in Figure 1.1.

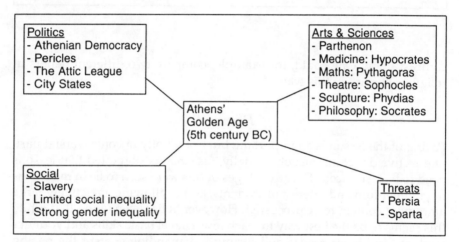

Figure 1.1   Conceptual map: the Golden Age of ancient Athens

Interaction and individual/group practice

Two crucial parts of the direct instruction lesson are interactive questioning and individual or group practice. As there is a lot of research on both these elements, these will be discussed separately in the next two chapters.

Some examples of direct instruction

Several models of direct instruction have been developed over the years. We will discuss a number of them here, in order to provide a clearer view of what direct instruction means in practice. One of the first models to be put into practice was the Active Teaching Model, developed for the Missouri Mathematics Effectiveness Project (Good, Grouws and Ebmeier, 1983). On the basis of extant research findings a primary school teaching model was designed, which teachers were trained to implement. Lessons were to be structured as follows:

1. Daily review (+/– 8 minutes, except on Mondays):
   (a) Review of concepts and skills associated with yesterday's homework.
   (b) Collect and deal with homework assignment.
   (c) Ask several mental computation exercises.
2. Development (+/– 20 minutes) (introducing new concepts, developing understanding):
   (a) Briefly focus on prerequisite skills and concepts.
   (b) Focus on meaning and promoting student understanding by lively explanations, demonstrations, etc.
   (c) Assess student competence:
       i Using process and product questions (active interaction).
       ii Using controlled practice.
   (d) Repeat and elaborate on the meaning portion as necessary.
3. Seatwork (+/– 15 minutes):
   (a) Provide uninterrupted successful practice.
   (b) Momentum – keep the ball rolling – get everyone involved, then sustain involvement.
   (c) Alerting – let students know their work will be checked at the end of each period.
   (d) Accountability – check the student's work.
4. Homework assignment:
   (a) Assign on a regular basis at the end of each maths class except Fridays.
   (b) Should involve about 15 minutes of work to be done at home.
   (c) Should include one or two review problems.
5. Special reviews:
   (a) Weekly review:
       i Conduct during the first 20 minutes on Mondays.
       ii Focus on skills and concepts covered during the previous week.
   (b) Monthly review:
       i Conduct every fourth Monday.
       ii Focus on skills and concepts covered since the last review.

As mentioned above, this programme was highly successful, and a slightly revised secondary version of the Active Mathematics Teaching model was also found to be effective. Programmes based on the same teacher-effectiveness principles, but with modifications suited to the particular contexts, have been implemented on a smaller scale in the USA, such as Griffin and Barnes's (1986) Comprehensive Teaching Programme (CTP), which also showed good results (Schaffer, 1997).

One of the most ambitious applications of direct instruction models is currently taking place in England, in the form of the National Literacy and National Numeracy Strategies. These were developed as a result of worries about the performance of English students in these two subjects, and have been strongly inspired by research showing the effectiveness of direct instruction. Figure 1.2 illustrates the structure of the 'Literacy Hour', a daily hour of teaching reading and writing that all English primary schools are recommended to use.

As can be seen in Figure 1.2, this lesson plan follows a typical direct instruction model, starting with two whole-class sessions, followed by individual and group practice, with a whole-class review section at the end. This is a highly prescriptive model, and it has to be remarked that there is no research evidence to support an exact time spent on whole-class teaching and individual/group work in each lesson.

The English 'National Numeracy Strategy' for the teaching of primary mathematics likewise was inspired by the direct instruction model, but

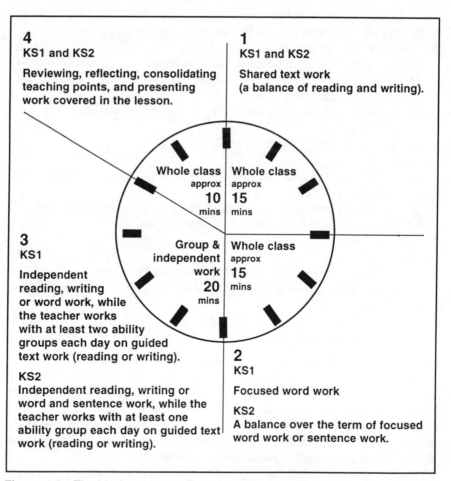

Figure 1.2 The Literacy Hour in English primary schools

Source: http:/www.standards.dfee.gov.uk/literacy/literacy hour

takes a less prescriptive approach, outlining general teaching strategies rather than setting out a strictly delineated time for each part of the lesson.

The advice to teachers given in this strategy, however, clearly shows the influence of direct instruction. Thus, on the education ministry (Department for Education and Employment – DfEE) website, teachers are advised to 'spend as much time as possible in direct teaching and questioning of the whole class, a group of students, or individuals'. It is further stated that 'Direct teaching and good interaction are as important in group work and paired work as they are in whole-class work but organizing students as a 'whole class' for a significant proportion of the time helps to maximize their contact with you so that every child benefits from the teaching and interaction for sustained periods' (DfEE, 1999). Suggested teaching guidelines illustrate this influence further:

- *Directing:* sharing your teaching objectives with the class, ensuring that students know what to do, and drawing attention to points over which they should take particular care, such as how a graph should be labelled, the degree of accuracy needed when making a measurement, or how work can be set out . . .
- *Instructing:* giving information and structuring it well: for example, describing how to multiply a three-digit number by a two-digit number, how to interpret a graph, how to develop a mathematical argument . . .
- *Demonstrating:* showing, describing and modelling mathematics using appropriate resources and visual displays: for example, showing how to scribe numerals, showing how to measure using a metre stick or a protractor, demonstrating on a number line how to add on by bridging through 10, using a thermometer to demonstrate the use of negative numbers . . .
- *Explaining and illustrating:* giving accurate, well-paced explanations, and referring to previous work or methods: for example, explaining a method of calculation and discussing why it works, giving the meaning of a mathematical term, explaining the steps in the solution to a problem, giving examples that satisfy a general statement, illustrating how the statement $7 - 3 = 4$ can represent different situations . . .
- *Questioning and discussing:* questioning in ways which match the direction and pace of the lesson and ensure that all students take part (if needed, supported by apparatus or a communication aid, or by an adult who translates, signs or uses symbols), listening carefully to students' responses and responding constructively in order to take forward their learning, using open and closed questions, skilfully framed, adjusted and targeted to make sure that students of all abilities are involved and contribute to discussions, allowing students time to think through answers before inviting a response . . .
- *Consolidating:* maximising opportunities to reinforce and develop what has been taught, through a variety of activities in class and well-focused tasks to do at home, asking students either with a partner or as

a group to reflect on and talk through a process, inviting them to expand their ideas and reasoning, or to compare and then refine their methods and ways of recording their work, getting them to think of different ways of approaching a problem, asking them to generalise or to give examples that match a general statement . . .

- *Evaluating students' responses:* identifying mistakes, using them as positive teaching points by talking about them and any misconceptions that led to them, discussing students' justifications of the methods or resources they have chosen, evaluating students' presentations of their work to the class, giving them oral feedback on their written work . . .
- *Summarising:* reviewing during and towards the end of a lesson the mathematics that has been taught and what students have learned, identifying and correcting misunderstandings, inviting students to present their work and picking out key points and ideas, making links to other work in mathematics and other subjects, giving students an insight into the next stage of their learning . . .

(DfEE, 1999)

Both the literacy and numeracy strategies, although still in the relatively early stages of implementation, have received positive evaluations from the school inspectorate, OFSTED (2000), and examination performance in English primary schools has rapidly improved since the introduction of these strategies, although the extent to which this reflects the changed methods is as yet unclear.

All the examples above are essentially 'three-part lessons' starting with a whole-class session, followed by individual/group practice and a final whole-class session at the end of the lesson. This is not the only model possible in direct instruction. Alternatives have been developed, such as short whole-class presentations followed by individual practice, which is followed by the next short whole-class session, etc. There is no evidence that this is either more or less effective than the three-part lesson strategy.

Summary

In this chapter we have learnt more about one of the most widely used and also most effective teaching strategies at the disposal of teachers: direct instruction.

This strategy, in which the teacher actively brings the content of the lesson to students, was developed through classroom observation research, in which teacher behaviours were linked to student achievement on standardized tests. A number of common factors were found in different studies from a number of countries.

One of these was that actively teaching the whole class is more effective than letting individual students work on their own during most of the lesson. Within the whole-class teaching part of the lesson, a number of behaviours have been identified as effective.

Weaknesses and limitations of direct instruction

While, as illustrated above, direct instruction is one of the most effective teaching strategies available, it is not necessarily the best strategy to use in all circumstances.

Direct instruction has been found to be the best method to teach rules, procedures and basic skills, especially to younger students (Brophy and Good, 1986). However, when the goals of the lesson are more complex or open-ended (e.g. developing students' thinking skills, or discussing the merits of different electoral systems), the structured and teacher-directed approach that characterizes direct instruction is not the most effective model. More open-ended models may be more appropriate for achieving these goals (Joyce and Weill, 1996).

The effectiveness of direct instruction also seems to depend on the characteristics of the students taught. The highly structured approach seems to be particularly effective for students from disadvantaged backgrounds, or students starting from a low level of achievement in a particular subject. For example, in a recent study in England and Wales, relationships between student achievement and direct instruction-style teacher behaviours were twice as high in schools with a high or average percentage of students from deprived backgrounds, than in schools with a low percentage of students from deprived backgrounds. This suggests that these students are more in need of explicit teaching. However, it must be remarked that positive relationships were also evident in low-deprivation schools (Muijs and Reynolds, 2000c).

A further problem with direct instruction is that the role of students may become too passive, leading to overdependence on the teacher and underdevelopment of independent learning skills (Gipps and McGilchrist, 1999).

The evidence on direct instruction is also skewed towards primary age students and the subjects of mathematics and English. More research in other subjects and in secondary schools is needed to see whether this method is supported in those settings as well.

Further, it has to be remarked that it is entirely possible to use effective direct teaching strategies to teach undemanding and unchallenging content, or to teach in a way that does not suitably connect material. Finally, in some cases direct instruction can degenerate into ineffective lecture-style ('chalk and talk') lessons with little interaction with students.

Therefore, when deciding whether or not to use a direct instruction model must depend on the goals of the lesson, and must be linked to good subject knowledge and suitable lesson content in order to be effective.

First, the lesson as a whole needs to be well structured, with the objectives of the lesson clearly laid out, key points emphasized, and main points summarized at the end.

Material needs to be presented in small steps which need to be mastered before going on to the next step. Teachers need to focus on the main points and not digress. Each step itself needs to be well structured and clear.

The pace of the lesson needs to be fast for lower-level skills, while leaving more time for reflection when the goal of the lesson calls for higher-levels skills.

Use of advance organisers and modelling can help aid lesson clarity.

Examples of direct instruction models were given, one of the first being the Missouri Mathematics Effectiveness model, and two of the most recent being the English National Literacy and Numeracy Strategies.

Limitations of direct instruction were discussed, which included differential utility for different groups of students and the fact that it is more suited to teaching basic skills than to teaching higher order thinking skills.

Self-study questions

1. How does the decision on whether or not to use direct instruction relate to the goals of the lesson?
2. Describe the main elements that make for effective presentations.
3. How does direct instruction relate to learning theories?
4. In what way is the English National Numeracy Strategy a direct instruction model?
5. Can you design a direct instruction lesson to teach a topic of your choice?
6. What is direct instruction?
7. What are the main limitations of the direct instruction approach?

2

Interactive Teaching

Advance Organizers

In this chapter we will:

- Review research on the importance of interaction in direct instruction.
- Discuss why interaction is so important to students' learning.
- Review the main elements of effective questioning techniques as identified by research, such as the right mix of higher and lower-level questions, the best way to react to right and wrong answers and the use of prompting.
- Review class discussion and its relationship to questioning.
- Discuss how to avoid disadvantaging girls and shyer students.

Introduction

As we saw in the previous chapter, in order to be effective direct instruction has to be far more than lecture-style delivery of content to students. Almost all researchers agree on the importance of interaction between teachers and students, and the studies reviewed in the previous chapter pointed not only to the importance of spending a substantial part of the lesson teaching the whole class, but also of teaching in an interactive way.

For example, in their study of primary school students in England Mortimore *et al.* (1988) found positive effects for the use of frequent questioning, of communicating with the class and of the use of 'higher-order' questions/statements. Another recent study in England and Wales also demonstrated the importance of interaction to effective teaching, again factors such as using a high frequency of questions, use of open-ended questions, asking students to explain their answers and using academic questions being significantly related to student achievement, and interactive teaching overall being one of the factors most strongly related to student outcomes (in mathematics) (Muijs and Reynolds, 1999). Similarly, Veenman (1992) found this to be a crucial element of direct instruction in his research in the Netherlands.

American researchers had already demonstrated the importance of interaction in their research prior to this. Rosenshine and Furst (1973) found the use of a wide variety of questions to be a crucial factor in their research from the 1960s and early 1970s. This was confirmed in later studies, such as those mentioned in the previous chapter (Good, Grouws and Ebmeier, 1983; Brophy and Good, 1986; Rosenshine and Stevens, 1986; Brophy, 1992; Creemers, 1994).

American researchers have done more than merely demonstrate the importance of interactive teaching, however, and have studied in detail what makes for effective interaction and questioning techniques. These findings will be discussed in the next section.

How does questioning help student learning?

Questioning is an effective and important part of the lesson for a variety of reasons.

First, questioning allows the teacher to check her or his students' understanding of the lesson. This is of prime importance, as it gives the teacher the information she or he needs to decide whether or not certain topics need to be retaught, and at what level to pitch the lesson. This immediate feedback to the teacher of how well students have grasped the topic is one of the advantages of whole-class interactive teaching over more individual methods, where feedback on students' understanding to the teacher is slower (Brophy and Good, 1986).

Questioning allows students to practise and master the topic taught before having to go on to the next topic. Being able to correctly answer questions also enhances a student's feeling of mastery, which will in turn enhance the student's self-esteem and make her or him more receptive to learning in future (Gagne, Yekovick and Yekovick, 1993).

Another way that questions, in particular higher level questions, can aid learning is through what is known as 'scaffolding'. The term 'scaffolding' derives from research by the Russian psychologist Lev Vygotsky (1973). He believed that students learn through interaction with others, and that learning takes place in what he termed the 'zone of proximal development', which he considered to be the area beyond what a student can learn on her or his own, but within which she or he can learn with the help of others who can provide 'scaffolds' for the student's learning. These others can either be adults or other students, who must, however, possess some additional knowledge to that of the student. It is clear that interactive teaching can play an important role in the scaffolding process, with the teacher providing the challenge that students need to progress to a higher stage of learning through testing, high-level questions.

Answering questions also allows students to clarify their own thinking and understanding of the concept taught, and makes them verbalize their thinking, especially if they are asked to explain the method or knowledge they used to work out a particular answer. This will help them develop verbal skills they will need not only in school but in the workplace as well.

What does effective interaction entail?

Due to its widely acknowledged importance, questioning is one of the most widely studied elements in teaching research. Therefore we know quite a bit about what effective questioning entails. This evidence, taken from the research discussed earlier (Rosenshine, 1980; Bennett *et al.*, 1981;

Brophy and Good, 1986; Rosenshine and Stevens, 1986; Cooper, Heron and Heward, 1987) will be discussed here.

When and how often to use questioning

As one of the most important elements of effective instruction, questioning should take up a large part of the lesson. In the previous chapter we mentioned that a lot of researchers believe the lesson should start with a review of what was learnt previously. This is the first part of teaching where interaction and questioning are crucial as they are the best way of checking students' retention of material taught earlier. Once new content is presented in small steps each step should be followed by *guided practice*, to allow students to practise what they have learnt, and to allow teachers to check how well students have understood the lesson. This will help the teacher to decide whether all or part of it needs to be retaught. The same goes for the review at the end of the lesson. While it is possible for the teacher to list what was learnt in the lesson, it is usually more effective to ask students to explain this themselves. Overall, then, questioning will take up much of the direct instruction lesson, and will be one of the main teaching activities for the teacher.

Eliciting a student response

Saying that interaction is crucial obviously begs the question of how to get students to answer the questions posed. This can be a problem, especially with older and shyer students. The first thing to note here is that this problem will be attenuated if students are used to interactive lessons, which will be the case if there is a school- or at least subject-wide teaching strategy that is based on interactive teaching. A non-evaluative, positive atmosphere is important as well. Students are more likely to get involved if they feel that a wrong response will not elicit criticism or ridicule from the teacher (or fellow students). A strategy that can be used to get all students to answer a question can be to make students write down their answers before the teacher shows the correct answer on the board, or to get them to find the answer using answer cards (such as number cards in mathematics) which they show to the teacher after first hiding their answer from the teacher and other students (e.g. by holding the cards to their chest).

The cognitive level of questions

The cognitive level of questions refers to the difficulty of the questions, in particular whether they require relatively sophisticated thinking skills from students ('higher' level) or more basic application of rules or retention of facts ('lower' level). Lower-level questions should be relatively easy to answer, and should in most cases elicit a correct response.

As higher-level questions require more thinking from students they will be more difficult to answer. Research has shown that effective teachers use more higher-level questions than less effective teachers, although the majority of questions used are still lower level. Obviously, the exact balance of the two must depend on the content taught. A topic requiring factual recall, such as multiplication facts in mathematics, would require lower-level questions than one which probes for higher level content, such as asking students to design an experiment in science. It is, however, important to ask higher level questions whenever possible, to help develop students' thinking skills.

Open and closed questions

A related distinction is that between open and closed questions. Closed questions have one clear answer (e.g. 'how much is 4 times 8'), while open questions have open ended answers (e.g. 'what do you think makes a country democratic'). Again, effective teachers have been found to ask more open questions than less effective teachers, although a large proportion of questions used by effective teachers are still closed questions. However, as with cognitive level, the right mix of open and closed questions will depend on the topic and goals of the lesson. Not using any open questions, however, may be ineffective as it may result in the teacher providing insufficient cognitive challenges to students.

Process and product questions

Another distinction is that between process and product questions. Product questions are designed to find the answer to a particular problem, while process questions are meant to elicit procedures, processes and rules used to get to the answer. The importance of product and process is a subject that has been debated in education recently, and in a lot of countries there is a move towards emphasizing process more strongly, as obtaining generic skills (such as 'problem-solving') is seen as more important in a rapidly changing world than accumulating factual knowledge. Research bears out that it is important not to limit questioning to product questions; effective teachers having been found to ask more process questions than ineffective teachers, within a mix that contains product questions as well. Once again the exact mix should depend on the topic and goals of the lesson, and more generally the overall mix will depend to an extent on the emphasis of the curriculum used on process or product. Generally speaking, product questions are closed, and often lower level questions, while process questions are often open, higher level questions.

Process and product questions can often be combined in one teaching moment. Thus, the teacher can ask a student a product question (e.g. 'what is the area of this room') and then ask the student to explain how she worked out that answer.

What to do when a student answers a question correctly

When a student makes what Rosenshine (1983) referred to as a correct, quick and firm response the correctness of this response must be acknowledged in all cases, and this must be done in a businesslike way. Effusive praise is usually unnecessary, and slows down the lesson. Often, depending on the student's self-confidence, age and background, a nod or gesture will be sufficient (although young students lacking in self-confidence and lower ability students may need more praise and positive reinforcement). According to research, it is a good idea to ask another question to the student who has just answered correctly, which will permit further feedback.

What to do when a student answers a question correctly but hesitantly

When a student answers a question correctly but hesitantly, something that can occur frequently when a topic has just been introduced, it is essential that the student receives positive feedback. Feedback in this case needs to be more explicit than when the answer is firm and unhesitant to help the student remember that the response was indeed correct. When a similar question next comes up she or he will hopefully be able to answer it less hesitantly as a result. If many students seem hesitant, it may be worth finding out the reasons for this hesitancy and if necessary reteach the material.

What to do when a student answers a question incorrectly

Two types of incorrect answers can be identified: incorrect answers due to carelessness or lack of effort, and incorrect answers due to lack of understanding. In both cases teachers need to acknowledge that the answer is incorrect in a businesslike way without resorting to personal criticism of the student. In the case of incorrect answers due to carelessness this may be difficult at times, but research has clearly shown that personal criticism is ineffective and may be harmful rather than helpful, turning the student against the teacher and leading to less subsequent effort. Once the teacher has pointed out that the answer is incorrect, she or he must move swiftly on to the next student. The denial of possible praise is the best response to this problem.

A different strategy needs to be followed when the answer is incorrect due to lack of understanding or knowledge. When this occurs it is best to prompt the student, simplify the question (e.g. by breaking it down into a series of small steps) or provide hints so she or he can find the answer and think things through. If this fails to elicit the correct response, one can go to the next student, and ask her or him to correct it. If possible, it is always better for the teacher to try to get another student to correct the answer rather than for the teacher to do it her or himself.

What to do though, if many students seem to be having problems with answering the question, even after prompting? A number of strategies have been proposed, such as reviewing the key facts or rules needed to get to the right answer, explaining the steps used to reach the solution, prompting with clues or hints representing a partially correct answer, or using a similar but different problem to guide a student to the correct answer (Borich, 1996). Doing this will not only help the student who has been asked to answer the question, but will help students more generally.

What to do when a student answers a question partially correctly

When a student answers a question partially correctly it is necessary first of all to acknowledge that part of the answer that was correct, making it very clear which part was and which was not, so as not to create confusion among either the responding student or the other students. Then the teacher should prompt the student who answered the question towards correcting that part of the answer that she or he answered incorrectly. If prompting in this way still does not elicit the correct response, one may need to ask another student to correct the part-answer. However, in all cases the teacher should first try to get the student who first answered the question partially to find the right answer.

Prompting

On a couple of occasions above we have referred to giving prompts in order to help students answer questions. There are three types of prompts which teachers can use for this purpose. The most obvious of these are *verbal prompts*. These can take the form of cues, reminders, instructions, tips, references to previous lessons or giving a part sentence for students to complete. Examples of this are 'what was the first step for solving this type of problem?' 'can you remember what we did yesterday during the experiment?' 'don't forget to add the comma' and so on. *Gestural prompts* are also used very frequently in lessons, allowing the teacher to model the behaviour of students early before they actually make the mistake. This can be done by pointing to the object one wants a student to use, such as a number line or microscope, or by modelling a behaviour such as holding a pen correctly. Among young learners, *physical prompts* may be necessary. This can be the case when the student does not yet grasp the motor skills needed to for example hold a crayon or form letters or numbers. One can then take the student's hand and guide her or him explicitly *hand over hand*. This method is also used during physical education.

Cooper, Heron and Heward (1987) recommend using the least intrusive prompts first. They consider the least intrusive to be verbal prompts, followed by gestural prompts and physical prompts. The reason for this is to stop the learner becoming overly dependent on the teacher's guidance as, according to these researchers, verbal prompts will fade from memory faster than (especially) physical prompts, and will therefore be more effective 'scaffolds' to students' learning leading to students being able to perform the behaviour independently.

Gender, shyness and interactive teaching

A criticism of direct instruction, and particularly the interactive part of the whole-class lesson, has been that it may advantage boys and be disadvantageous to girls and to shyer students.

The reason for this is seen to lie in the more assertive nature of boys, and the (obviously) less assertive nature of shy students in the classroom. This means that boys will be far more likely to volunteer to answer questions and to dominate lessons, and that shyer students will avoid doing so. In this way the more assertive boys may start to dominate the lesson at the expense of other students. A further potential problem in whole-class interactive teaching is deliberate non-involvement by certain students, the so-called 'free-rider effect'. This refers to the fact that certain students may choose to avoid actively taking part in the lesson and let others do all the work, because they are either unsure or unwilling.

These problems can easily be avoided by judicious teacher action, however. Thus, when questioning, teachers need to make sure that all students get to answer questions, not just the students who volunteer or are the most persistent. A way to make sure this is done is to go round the class in a certain (varying) order, or to have a list of students on the teacher's desk on which names can quickly be ticked off. When going round the class in order, the teacher needs to make sure the order is not obvious to the students, however, otherwise some students may go off task until they know their turn to answer is about to come. Teachers also need to make sure that girls get as much chance to answer questions as boys. Among younger students it is important to stop students shouting out answers, as it will usually be the most assertive students who will do this.

Another thing the teacher must avoid is the temptation to target mainly those students who she or he thinks are most likely to answer the question correctly. In order to avoid weaker students getting answers wrong too often, which will not help them to attain a feeling of mastery, it may be necessary to vary the difficulty of questions according to the student they are directed at. It is important to involve all students in the lesson.

What is the correct wait-time?

How long should one wait for a student to answer the question? This is an important matter, as one needs to ensure the smooth flow of the lesson and avoid embarrassing silences but also allow students enough time to think through their answers. Therefore wait-time has to depend on the type of question asked. If the question is a closed, lower level factual recall question, 3 seconds or slightly longer is the optimal wait-time. However, for open-ended, higher-level questions a longer wait-time (up to 15 seconds) is required. Waiting much longer than this may lead to the other students becoming restless. Prompting the student after the acceptable wait-time has been passed is therefore necessary. When asking a complex question requiring a lot of thought it can be a good idea to allow the students some time to work the answer out on their own (on paper for example) before asking them to provide the answer. Research has found that among beginning teachers leaving insufficient wait-time is more common than allowing too much wait-time (Rowe, 1986).

What percentage of questions should be answered correctly

At the end of a topic, the majority of questions asked should elicit a correct, firm and quick response. If 95 per cent of students are able to answer the question correctly the content has been well mastered. For lower-level content (such as mastering of facts) it is suggested that 60–80 per cent of questions following a presentation (in small steps) should be answered correctly before moving on to the next step. Obviously, for some types of open questions the concept of 'right' or 'wrong' answers may be less appropriate (e.g. when asking students for their opinion), and understanding must then be probed by means of the logical and consistent use of arguments by the student for which she or he needs to be prompted if necessary. Many questions have more than one correct answer (process questions such as how a student has worked out an answer in mathematics, for example), and all correct answers must be acknowledged even if the teacher was looking for another answer or a faster method. The student can then be prompted for the answer or method the teacher was looking for (e.g. 'That's correct. Do you know any other ways of doing that?').

Summary

In this chapter we have learnt about the importance of interaction between teacher and student, which is one of the most important aspects of direct instruction. Questioning can be used to check students' understanding, to 'scaffold' students' learning, to help them clarify and verbalize their thinking and to help them develop a sense of mastery.

Effective questioning is also one of the most widely studied aspects of teaching and, therefore, a solid body of knowledge exists on which strategies are most effective.

In direct-instruction lessons questions need to be asked at the beginning of the lesson when the topic of the last lesson in that subject is being reviewed, after every short presentation and during the summary at the end of the lesson. Teachers need to mix both higher- and lower-level questions, product and process questions, and open and closed questions. The exact mix depends upon the lesson topic, but teachers need to ensure that enough open, higher-level process questions are used.

Correct answers need to be acknowledged in a positive but businesslike fashion. When a student answers a question partially correctly the teacher needs to prompt that student to find the remaining part of the

Classroom discussion and its relationship to questioning

While questioning is the most widely used form of teacher–student interaction, it is not the only form of interaction possible, and indeed in some cases is not the most desirable form. Questioning is inevitably teacher-led, which in some cases may not be appropriate to the goal of the lesson.

Discussion can occur in the classroom in two settings: between students in small groups during co-operative small group work, or with the teacher and other students in a whole-class setting. Small group work will be discussed in the next chapter, in this section we will limit ourselves to whole-class discussion.

Classroom discussion can help fulfil three major learning goals: promoting students' involvement and engagement in the lesson by allowing students to voice their own ideas; helping them develop better understanding by allowing them to think things through and verbalize their thinking; and, finally, helping students obtain communication skills (not least the self-confidence to voice their own opinions in public and the ability to do so in a clear and concise way).

Discussion needs to be carefully prepared and usually needs to follow on from some prior activity such as a previous lesson on a certain topic. Alternatively the teacher can get students to read up on a particular topic before the lesson. Discussions can also follow brief presentations on a topic by the teacher or other students.

In order for a discussion to be effective it is important to keep it focused and to the point. As with direct instruction, teachers need to clearly set out the purpose of the discussion from the start. It can be useful to provide students with a couple of 'pointer' questions in order to focus the discussion, and to link the discussion to students' prior knowledge. During the discussion the teacher needs to keep students firmly on task, and avoid them wandering off to different subjects. Writing down the main points to emerge from the discussion on the board or a flipchart can help focus students and also emphasize the fact that the discussion is a learning activity and not a just a way of filling time.

During the discussion, the teacher needs to respond to student ideas in such a way as to encourage them to clarify and be more conscious of their thought processes. This can be done by seeking clarification (Could you clarify that for me . . .), by reflecting on student ideas (That's a novel idea, what I think you're trying to say is . . .), and by getting students to consider other points of view.

At the end of the discussion, it is once again useful for the teacher to briefly summarize the main points to have come out of the discussion, followed by a debriefing focusing on the process and how well the discussion did or did not proceed. Both can be done by the teacher or (often more appropriately) by asking for the students' comments.

Whether or not to use class discussion once again depends on the subject of the lesson, and also on the maturity of the students as well as their communication skills. A classroom climate in which mutual respect exists and in which the views of all students are valued is essential. All these factors will also determine the amount of teacher direction and structure given to the discussion.

One of the tensions that has been found to exist in lessons is that between questioning and discussion. Research (Askew *et al.*, 1997) has found that in some cases teachers' questions can function in such a way that they abort classroom discussion, by imposing the teacher's views on the students.

answer before moving on to the next student. When a student answers a question incorrectly, the teacher needs to point out swiftly that the answer was wrong. If the student has answered incorrectly due to inattention or carelessness, the teacher must quickly move on to the next student. If the answer is incorrect due to lack of knowledge the teacher needs to try and prompt the student to answer correctly.

Teachers need to make sure that girls and shy students, who may be less assertive, get the chance to answer questions.

Another form of interaction that may be effective in certain lessons is classroom discussion. In order for discussion to be effective it needs to be carefully prepared. The teacher needs to give students clear guidelines on what the discussion is about. During the discussion students need to be kept on task, and the teacher needs to write down the main points emerging from the discussion. After the discussion, these main points (the product of the discussion) can be summarized, and students can be debriefed by asking them to comment on how well the discussion went (the process of the discussion).

Self-study questions

1. Why is interactive teaching such an important part of the lesson?
2. What should the teacher do if a student answers a question incorrectly?
3. What is the role of the teacher during classroom discussion?
4. Is whole-class interactive teaching disadvantageous for girls?
5. When teaching basic skills, should the teacher refrain from using open-ended or process questions?
6. How long should the teacher wait for a student to answer a question?
7. When should a teacher reteach a particular topic?

3

Review and Practice

Advance organizers

In this chapter you will learn:

- Why review and practice are important to learning.
- The main elements needed to effectively implement individual practice.
- The main advantages and disadvantages of small group work.
- The main elements needed to effectively use small group work.

Introduction

The third part of the direct instruction lesson is individual (*seatwork*) or group practice. As we have seen in Chapter 2 the fact that a large part of the lesson needs to be spent on whole-class interactive teaching does not mean that individual and group work are unnecessary. On the contrary, they form an indispensable part of the lesson, whether undertaken in one block as in the 'three part lesson' structure suggested by the English National Numeracy Strategy (see Figure 1.2) or at various points during the lesson after short whole-class sessions. In this chapter we will discuss the best ways of managing this part of the lesson.

First, we will discuss the research evidence on effective seatwork, which is the way most practice has traditionally taken place in direct instruction lessons. It has to be remembered here that, although seatwork is an effective part of the lesson and is essential for practising previously taught material or as a preparation for the next lesson, it is not an effective way of learning new material. This can more effectively be done through presentation followed by guided practice (Brophy and Good, 1986).

While this part of the lesson has been the subject of less research than the direct teaching and interactive components, research does provide a number of guidelines on how this part of the lesson can be managed effectively.

Elements of individual practice

Preparing seatwork

A first essential element to bear in mind when preparing seatwork is to make sure that there is enough material available for students to use

27

during individual practice. If worksheets are used it is imperative not only to prepare enough worksheets so each child has one, but also to have some work in 'back-up' in case some or all students finish the task faster than expected. If the task requires use of manipulatives or materials, such as number lines or scissors, the teacher must make sure that enough of these are available as well.

The seatwork task needs to tie in with the objectives of the lesson and previously learnt material, and needs to be tailored to students' ability levels. Seatwork needs to take place as soon as possible after the questioning (guided practice) part of the lesson. In this way students will make fewer mistakes, enhancing their feelings of mastery over the content of the lesson.

Use of workbooks/textbooks

Frequently, seatwork will consist of exercises from workbooks or worksheets. Both can be effective and have advantages and disadvantages. Using published schemes, textbooks and workbooks makes preparation for seatwork less time-consuming, and attractively illustrated books can motivate (especially younger) students. However, teachers need to ensure that the exercises in the workbook are suitable for their students and tie in with the goals of the lesson and the content taught. If using a direct instruction approach it is also advisable to use a scheme that has been designed with such an approach in mind rather than one that has been designed to accommodate an individual learning approach. Worksheets are usually less attractively presented and can be a lot of work, especially if the teacher has to devise the exercises him or herself. The major advantage of worksheets is that they can be tailored accurately to reflect the goals of the lesson, and allow the teacher to lift content from a variety of sources. Generally speaking, slavishly following a particular scheme of work is not to be recommended as this may not suit the students or the content of the lesson, and also because the use of a variety of schemes and workbooks gives access to a wider range of good ideas for teachers to use.

Organizing seatwork

As with the lesson as a whole teachers need to clearly state the goals of the seatwork assignment. It can be necessary to make clear exactly what the (cognitive) reasons are for doing seatwork so students do not perceive it as merely filling time. The process goals need to be explained as well, as students can easily see the goal of seatwork as merely giving the right answers to specific questions (Arends, 1998).

The task needs to be clearly explained and needs to be unambiguous. If during seatwork monitoring it appears that the task has not been well understood by many students, the teacher may need to stop the work and explain it again. To ensure that students understand what they need to do it is useful to go through the first task with the whole class. The teacher needs to make clear to students that the task is one they can succeed at.

During seatwork students need to be continually monitored by the teacher. He or she has to go round checking students' work, both to ensure that students remain on task and to check for students' understanding. If students seem to be having difficulties with the task the teacher needs to intervene to help them. If a substantial part of the class seems to be having a particular problem, the teacher may need to stop seatwork and go over the problem with the whole class before letting the students return to the assignment. The teacher needs to be approachable; students must feel they can ask the teacher for help. A problem that can occur during seatwork is that the teacher ends up spending quite a bit of time helping a particular student or group of students and as a result fails to monitor the rest of the class. To avoid this becoming a problem it is necessary when helping a student to occasionally stop to monitor the rest of the class, to check whether other students are having problems or getting off task. Emmer *et al.* (1997) recommend giving roughly an equal amount of time to all students, and not spending too much time with one or a group of students. During some lessons it can be useful for teachers to mark students' work as they go round the class. Seatwork requires active teacher involvement that cannot be limited to sitting behind the desk waiting for students to come to him or her with problems.

The teacher also needs to be clear on whether and when talking is allowed during seatwork. Obviously if seatwork is meant to be collaborative talking will be allowed but if the task is not supposed to be collaborative it may be necessary to restrict talking or, in some cases, to prohibit it altogether. Seating arrangements can either facilitate or hinder student talk, i.e. seating students in groups around tables will encourage talk, while seating students in rows will make this more difficult (Johnson and Johnson, 1994; Arends, 1998).

Feedback on seatwork

In order for seatwork not to be perceived as a time-filler, students need to receive feedback on the tasks they have been doing. Feedback can be provided in a number of ways. During seatwork, the teacher can go round marking students' work and giving some verbal feedback to students while they are working. During seatwork the teacher can also get students to check on each other's work. The teacher can also collect in workbooks or worksheets and mark them outside of teaching time. A useful approach can be to go over seatwork during the final whole-class section of the lesson. Students can be asked for their answers or, if seatwork was differentiated, students can be asked to tell the class what their group has been doing. The teacher should aim for a high success rate in seatwork with most learners getting at least 60–80 per cent of problems right.

Differentiating seatwork?

A further decision that needs to be made before assigning seatwork is whether or not to differentiate tasks. There can be two different reasons for doing this. First, the teacher can decide to tailor the task to different ability levels in the classroom. Whether or not to do this will depend on the spread of ability in the classroom. This ability spread may be particularly large in mixed ability (as opposed to set) classrooms, and can be more pronounced in deprived areas, where the spread of ability appears to be greater than in more advantaged areas as, although due to social disadvantage the average levels are lower in these areas, there are usually some highly able students in these schools anyway (Muijs and Reynolds, 1999). If the ability range is large, it is recommended to differentiate tasks to ensure high rates of success among all students. Another reason to differentiate seatwork can be to let students do different parts of a task which can then be brought together during a whole class session. This can help illustrate to students the advantages of collaboration and interdependence and help maintain interest during the whole-class review as what other students have done will be directly relevant to their own work. If seatwork is differentiated, the teacher needs to make sure that seating arrangements reflect this, in particular if students are allowed to discuss their work with each other. Seating students working on the same task together is to be recommended.

An alternative to individual practice: collaborative small group work

An alternative approach to individual practice is the use of co-operative small group work during the review and practice part of the lesson. This method has gained in popularity in recent years, and has attracted a lot of research interest in a number of countries, such as the USA (Slavin, 1996). In other countries such as the UK this method is still underused, however. In a recent study in primary schools we found that less than 10 per cent of lesson time was spent doing group work (Muijs and Reynolds, 1999).

Benefits of small group work

The use of small group work is posited to have a number of advantages over individual practice. The main benefit of small group work seems to lie in the co-operative aspects it can help foster. One advantage of this lies in the contribution this method can make to the development of students' social skills. Working with other students may help them to develop their empathic abilities, by allowing them to see others' viewpoints, which can help them to realize that everyone has strengths and weaknesses. Trying to find a solution to a problem in a group also develops skills such as the need to accommodate others' views.

Why individual/group practice is important for student learning

The main learning goals of independent practice are *automaticity* and *unitization.*

Automaticity refers to processes becoming so well embedded in students' long-term memory that they no longer require conscious attention. For example, when first learning handwriting, the formation of every word requires careful and thorough attention. However, once it has been thoroughly learned the process becomes *automatic.* It is important that processes like that become automatic in order to free space in the short-term memory for the execution of more complex tasks. Some subjects may even require what is known as *overlearning.* If students practise just long enough to learn something, they are likely to forget a large part of what they have learned. If they continue to practise beyond this point, however, learning will increase. This phenomenon is known as *overlearning.* An example of a subject in which overlearning is important is multiplication facts in mathematics. Individual practice can help both automaticity and overlearning to develop (Woolfolk, 1997).

Unitization is a different process, and refers to the bringing together of facts and procedures into sequences that can be used for actual problem-solving. Independent seatwork allows students to do this under the teacher's guidance in a controlled environment. To ensure that unitization occurs the teacher must ensure that students have to consider all these disparate facts and procedures to be able to solve the problem, and to make sure they connect them into one fluent sequence of action.

Students can also provide each other with scaffolding in the same way the teacher can during questioning. The total knowledge available in a group is likely to be larger than that available to individual students, which can enable more powerful problem-solving and can therefore allow the teacher to give students more difficult problems than he or she could give to individual students.

One of the main advantages of co-operative small group work lies in the help students give one another. Not all kinds of help are necessarily useful, however. Just giving the right answer is not associated with enhanced understanding or achievement. In his review of research, Webb (1991) reports a positive relationship between giving content-related help and achievement. Giving non-content related help did not seem to improve student achievement, though. Receiving explanations was found to be positive in some studies, and non-significant in others, this presumably because the receiver has to understand the help given and be able to use it. This may well require training the students to give clear help. Receiving non-explanatory help (e.g. being told the answer without being told how to work it out) was negatively or non-significantly related to achievement in the studies reviewed, while being engaged in off-task activities (e.g. socializing) was negative. In a more recent study of grades 3 to 5 students Nattiv (1994) found that giving and receiving explanations was positively related to achievement, giving and receiving other help was slightly positively related to achievement, while receiving no help after requesting it was negatively related to achievement. Webb and Moore Kendersky (1984) report similar findings among high school students.

Effective small group work does require a significant amount of preparation, and a number of preconditions have to be met beforehand in order for it to be effective. First, students must be able to co-operate with one another, and to provide each other with help in a constructive way. A number of studies have found that while small group work is positively related to achievement when group interaction is respectful and inclusive, use of group work is actually negatively related to achievement if group interaction is disrespectful or unequal (Battistich, Solomon and Delucchi, 1993; Linn and Burbules, 1993). This is by no means a given, as many (especially young students and students from highly disadvantaged backgrounds) have been found to lack the social skills necessary to interact positively with peers.

Thus, students often lack *sharing skills*, which means that they have difficulty sharing time and materials and may try to domineer the group. This problem can be alleviated by teaching sharing skills, for example by using the Round Robin technique in which the teacher asks a question and introduces an idea that has many possible answers. During Round Robin questioning a first student is asked to give an answer, and then pass his turn to the next student. This goes on until all students have had a chance to contribute.

Other students may lack *participation skills*. This means that they find it difficult to participate in group work because they are shy or uncooperative. This can be alleviated by structuring the task so that these students have to play a particular role in the group (see below) or by giving all students 'time tokens', worth a specified amount of 'talk time'. Students have to give up a token to a monitor whenever they have used up their talk time, after which they are not allowed to say anything any more. In this way all students get a chance to contribute.

Students may also lack *communication skills*. This means that they are not able to effectively communicate their ideas to others, obviously making it difficult for them to function in a co-operative group. Communicative skills, such as paraphrasing, may need to be explicitly taught to students before small group work can be used.

Finally, some students may lack *listening skills*. This can frequently be a problem with younger students who will sit waiting their turn to contribute without listening to other students. This can be counteracted by making students paraphrase what the student who has contributed before them has said before allowing them to contribute (Borich, 1996; Arends, 1998).

Necessary elements for effective small group work

For small group work to be effective, one needs to take a number of elements into account in the structuring of the task. Before commencing the task, the goals of the activity need to be clearly stated and the activity needs to be explained in such a way that no ambiguity can exist over the desired outcomes of the task. The teacher needs to make clear that co-operation between students in the group is desired. According to Slavin (1993) these goals need to be group goals, in order to facilitate co-operation, which need to be accompanied by individual accountability for work done in order to avoid free-rider effects. Some form of competition with other groups can help students work together, as can using a shared manipulative or a tool such as a computer.

Avoiding free-rider effects can be aided by structuring the group task in such a way that every group member is assigned a particular task. One way of doing this is by making completion of one part of the task dependent on completion of a previous stage, so students will pressure each other to put the effort in to complete the stage before them. Johnson and Johnson (1994) suggest a number of roles that can be assigned to students in small groups, such as:

- The *summariser*, who will prepare the group's presentation to the class and summarise conclusions reached to see if the rest of the group agrees.
- The *researcher*, who collects background information and looks up any additional information that is needed to complete the task.
- The *checker*, who checks that the facts that the group will use are indeed correct and will stand up to scrutiny from the teacher or other groups.
- The *runner*, who tries to find the resources needed to complete the task, such as equipment and dictionaries.
- The *observer/troubleshooter*, who takes notes and records group processes. These may be used during the debriefing following the group work.
- The *recorder*, who writes down the major output of the group, and synthesizes the work of the other group members.

These roles should be given to different students for different tasks. Giving both individual grades (for the student's work in reaching the group goal) and collective grades (for the group as a whole) is an effective strategy for ensuring both group goals and individual accountability. (Slavin, 1993)

After finishing the group task the results need to be presented to the whole class and a debriefing focusing on the process of the group work (the effectiveness of the collaborative effort) should be held. A useful way of starting a debriefing session is by asking students what they thought has gone particularly well or badly during group work (the observers mentioned above should be able to do this). The teacher can then give feedback on which elements he or she thought went well or less well, and ask students how the process could be improved.

Research has shown that co-operative groups should be somewhat, but not too, heterogeneous with respect to student ability. Groups composed of high- and medium- or medium- and low-ability students gave and received more explanations than students in high-, medium- or low-ability groups or totally mixed-ability groups. Less heterogeneous group-ings were especially advantageous for medium-ability students. When students of the same ability are grouped together, it has been found that high-ability students thought it unnecessary to help one another while low-ability students were less well able to do so (Webb, 1991; Askew and William, 1995).

It is clear that collaborative small group work requires a lot of thought and preparation, and is far removed from merely seating students around a table and hoping effective collaboration will follow.

In this chapter we have treated collaborative small group work as a potentially powerful part of a direct instruction lesson. However, many educators consider small group work to be so advantageous that they have advocated structuring the whole lesson around co-operative small group work (e.g. Slavin, 1996). Within the approach discussed here col-laborative group work can take up a large part of the lesson (around 30 minutes out of a 1-hour lesson would seem to be a minimum), with the whole class session being limited in time if the teacher thinks that would help improve the effectiveness of teaching that particular topic.

Disadvantages of co-operative small group work

While co-operative group work can be a powerful teaching and learning strat-egy, it does have a number of disadvantages which mean that it needs to be used in conjunction with, and not as a replacement for, individual practice.

One of these disadvantages lies precisely in the co-operative nature of group work. A problem with this is that it does not naturally promote independent learning and can foster dependency on certain dominant members of the group. If this happens the student will not easily be able to develop the skills he or she needs to use independently in other situations. Furthermore, small group work can easily lead to 'free-rider effects' whereby certain members of the group do not effectively contribute and rely on the work of others.

A further problem can be the fact that misconceptions can be reinforced if they are shared by several students in the group.

The complexity of small group work can also make it harder to manage for the teacher. Collaborative group work requires a significant amount of preparation as teachers need to have a sufficient amount of tasks ready and need to prepare tasks that make for effective interaction in the group. Some research has also found that small group work can result in more time spent on lesson transitions.

Overall, while small group work can be a powerful method for teaching higher-level cognitive tasks, it can be less useful when teaching basic skills where automaticity and overlearning are paramount.

Summary

In this chapter we have learnt about the third component of the direct instruction lesson: review and practice.

Individual practice is important to foster automaticity (being able to do something without having to consciously think about it) and unitization (being able to integrate and apply a number of skills or procedures).

Seatwork needs to be well prepared and needs to tie in clearly with the objectives and goals of the lesson. Seatwork will often take the form of doing exercises in a workbook or on worksheets. It is important not to slavishly follow a publisher's scheme, however, but to tailor seatwork to the objectives of the lesson and the students taught.

Teachers need to monitor the whole class during seatwork to ensure all students stay on task. They need to go round the class helping students experiencing problems without staying with one or a group of students for too long.

Students need to receive feedback on their work either during the seatwork or afterwards during the review session at the end of the lesson. Differentiated seatwork for students of different ability can be necessary in heterogeneous classrooms.

An addition to seatwork is collaborative small group work. This is particularly suited to higher-order problem-solving but less suited to acquiring basic skills for which automaticity is desired.

Collaborative small group work requires that students possess the social skills necessary to collaborate in group.

Collaborative small group work requires a lot of preparation and organization by the teacher, and requires group goals to encourage co-operation alongside individual accountability to discourage free-rider effects.

After completing the collaborative task, the results need to be presented to the whole class and a debriefing, going through the process of group work, is advisable.

Self-study questions

1. When should teachers use collaborative small group work?
2. What are the main learning goals of individual seatwork?
3. What are the main differences between individual seatwork and small group work?
4. What are the main organizational issues in individual seatwork?
5. How can the teacher help avoid free-rider effects in collaborative small group work?
6. When can seatwork usefully be differentiated?
7. What are the main social skills students need to be able to effectively participate in small group tasks?

4

Classroom Management

Advance organizers

In this chapter you will learn about:

- The main studies on classroom management.
- How to avoid disruption during lesson transitions.
- Why and how to establish clear rules and procedures.
- What seating arrangements are most effective for different teaching situations.

Introduction

One of the main features to emerge from teacher effectiveness research as a correlate of student achievement and attainment is *opportunity to learn*. This refers to whether or not the content tested for (using whatever test is used to measure students' achievement) has actually been seen by the students during the course of the year. The main factors to influence opportunity to learn are curriculum coverage (the extent to which the content covered by the teacher actually matches the content covered by the test) and the related factor of how many hours are actually planned to study the subject tested. However, another major factor influencing opportunity to learn within the lesson is *time on task,* that is the amount of time within a lesson that students spend engaging with the curriculum rather than on other activities such as socializing, moving around the classroom and being disciplined (Brophy and Good, 1986; Reynolds and Muijs, 1999b).

Time on task in turn is crucially dependent on the quality of both classroom and behaviour management, in that ensuring a smooth flow of the lesson is important to both. Classroom management has consistently been found to distinguish more from less effective teachers (e.g. Pressley *et al.*, 1988; Muijs and Reynolds, 1999) and has also been found to distinguish expert teachers, who appear able to manage classrooms very smoothly by ensuring that activities blend into each other seemingly without effort from novice teachers, for whom classroom management appears to present significant difficulties. A major study of classroom management was undertaken in the 1970s at the Research and Development Center for Teacher Education at the University of Texas, by a team led by Edmund Emmer and Carolyn Evertson. Coming from a teacher effectiveness research perspective, they looked at differences between teachers in their students' on- and off-task behaviour and related these to the teachers' classroom management strategies (Emmer *et al.*, 1997; Evertson, 1997). A different perspective is that of 'classroom ecology' research, initiated by Kounin in the late 1960s and continued in the research undertaken by Doyle and Carter from the 1980s onwards. Kounin was one of the first to realize, after extensive studies, that students' behaviour was not just, and indeed not primarily, influenced by teachers' disciplining techniques, but by their classroom management (Kounin, 1970). In the UK the work of Wragg stands out in providing us with useful insights into classroom management (e.g. Wragg, 1995). Classroom management is closely connected to, and often discussed in conjunction with, dealing with student misbehaviour. In this book we will discuss the two separately, viewing classroom management as creating conditions under which student misbehaviour is less likely to occur. How to deal with misbehaviour when it does occur will form the subject of Chapter 5.

Elements of effective classroom management

Starting the lesson

An obvious but often neglected element of effective classroom management is starting the lesson on time. Reasons for lessons starting late are various, among others prior lessons running late, break time going on for too long, chaotic transitions from break time to lessons, and ineffective management of students coming into the classroom. While the teacher can her or himself help to alleviate these problems as we will see below, a whole-school policy aimed at maximizing lesson time is essential as well (Creemers, 1994).

The start of the lesson can involve several classroom management difficulties that the teacher needs to take into account. The main problem is that students will often be coming from the playground or lunch where different, more lax rules apply and therefore the transition to appropriate classroom behaviour may cause difficulties. The teacher can keep disruption to a minimum by instituting a number of set procedures for dealing with lesson starts. The teacher can, for example, write instructions on the board before the students come in so they can get started with the lesson immediately, train students to take the register and read instructions or have certain set activities that students can start doing as soon as they come into the classroom, such as chanting times tables.

Appropriate seating arrangements

Another important aspect of classroom management is providing appropriate seating arrangements in the class. One general principle is that students should have sufficient space to work comfortably. If movement in the class is desired or necessary students should be able to do this easily and without too much pushing and shoving. There should be enough room between seats for the teacher to be able to move around the classroom without bumping into or disturbing students. How exactly to arrange students and desks depends on the space and resources available.

There is also a pedagogic aspect to this in that choice of the exact seating arrangements will need to match the formats and goals of the lesson, as the way students are positioned can influence the effectiveness of different types of delivery (see Figures 4.1, 4.2 and 4.3). If a direct instruction style lesson is to be used in which the teacher will spend a substantial amount of time delivering content to and interacting with the whole class, it is essential that students are all able to see the teacher and the tools she or he is using (black/whiteboard, overhead projector [OHP] screen, number line) without straining. Students should not be sitting with their backs to the teacher. This still leaves a number of seating arrangements open to the teacher, such as seating students in rows facing the teacher, seating them in a semicircle or horseshoe shape or, with younger students, letting them sit around the teacher on the carpet or rug. Other lesson plans may require different seating arrangements, however. For co-operative small group work, for example, it is recommended to place the groups around tables to allow them to interact easily with one another. If individual work is required where students are not supposed to interact with each other too much, this seating arrangement should be avoided. Whole-class discussion can be facilitated by seating students around a big table or seating them in a circle or semicircle, while seating them in rows will impede discussion. A possible compromise (for young students) involves students sitting round the teacher on the carpet or rug during the whole-class part of the lesson and then moving them to sit around tables for small group work afterwards.

Dealing with external disruptions

Another factor that can take up valuable teaching time is disruptions from outside the classroom. These can take several forms such as the head coming in to make announcements, teachers from other classrooms coming in with questions and students coming in with various requests. While a whole-school strategy to limit this kind of interruption is desirable, some interruptions are inevitable. The teacher needs to make sure that interruptions cause minimum disruption to the lesson by having clear rules for students' behaviour during such disruptions (such as sitting quietly or getting on with seatwork) and by dealing with them quickly, if necessary telling the teacher or student who has come in to leave and come back later.

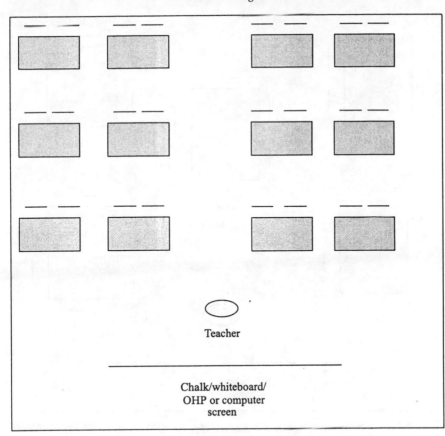

Figure 4.1 Seating in rows – this seating arrangement is effective for whole-class teaching but not for small group work or classroom discussion

Establishing clear rules and procedures

One of the main factors for ensuring smoothly run lessons is to establish clear rules and procedures from the start. *Rules* are formal, usually written, statements that specify what students are allowed to do or expected not to do. *Procedures* are informal arrangements that specify how things are to be done in a particular classroom. Rules are often specified school-wide, and have been identified in school effectiveness research as distinguishing more effective from less effective schools. Procedures can in many cases also be school-wide, but are often specified by the teacher for her or his class. Effective teachers have been found to spend a considerable amount of time and effort on specifying and clarifying procedures at the beginning of the school year. While this may seem to be at odds with the principle of maximizing opportunity to learn and time on task (spending as much time as possible on academic teaching), the additional time spent on this at the beginning of the year is more than made up for by the

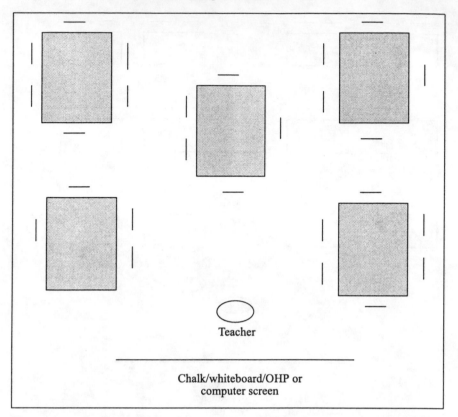

Figure 4.2 Seating arrangement suitable for small group work but less suitable for whole-class teaching and class discussion

time won through less time-wasting during the rest of the year. Below we will discuss a number of elements for which clear rules and procedures need to be established.

For rules and procedures to work they need to be actively taught to students. As in the school as a whole, it is better to stick to a small number of clearly understood and consistently enforced rules rather than a large number of (therefore) more difficult to enforce regulations. The rules taught need to become a routine and automatic part of student behaviour. This requires a good deal of reinforcement at the beginning of the school year. It is important that the teacher not only tells students what the rules are, but also explains the reason why they exist. Thus, when telling young students not to shout out answers the teacher should explain that the reason they should not do this is to give all students a chance of answering the question. Likewise, when telling them to be quiet while another student is answering the teacher needs to explain the reasons for this, such as showing respect to other students and being able to learn from their answers. Reasons for being careful with laboratory equipment need

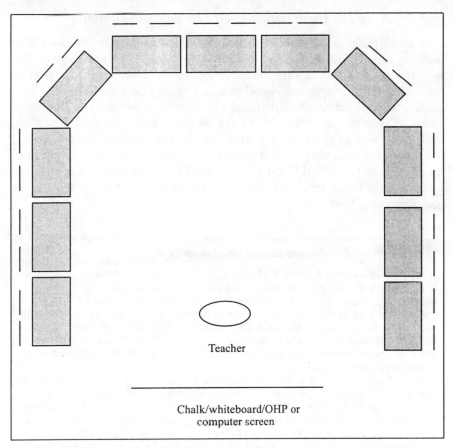

Teacher

Chalk/whiteboard/OHP or
computer screen

Figure 4.3 Seating suitable for class discussion and whole-class teaching but
not suitable for small group work

to be explained as being a matter of student safety (and not merely the
school's insurance policy!).

Many rules have to do with movement around the class, such as sitting
in a circle in an orderly way. These situations obviously need to be practised a number of times before they will run smoothly and like other
motor skills they need to be automatized as much as possible.

One of the main factors to take into account when setting up classroom
rules and procedures is to ensure they are consistently implemented. If
consistency is not enforced rules will soon break down. For example, if
the teacher has decided to prevent students shouting out answers to
questions this rule must be constantly enforced and as soon as a student
shouts out an answer she or he must be told off. If this does not happen
and one student is allowed to shout out an answer, soon more students
will start doing this and the teacher will have to take strong action to
restore the rule.

Smooth transitions between lesson segments

One of the main ways to ensure maximum time on task is to ensure that not too much time is wasted during transitions from one part of the lesson, such as teaching a new topic to the whole class, to the next part of the lesson, for example individual practice of the new topic. This can be a particular problem if students need to move from one part of the class-room to another like when they have to move from the carpet to their tables or need to get materials such as workbooks and pencils. If not managed appropriately such transitions can easily lead to time-wasting and can take up a significant part of the lesson (in recent research we found this to be up to 15 per cent of lesson time in some lessons) (Muijs and Reynolds, 1999).

Whole-school behaviour policies

School effectiveness research has long pointed to the importance of school-wide behaviour policies in creating the academically orientated, high-achieving school (e.g. Reynolds, 1992). Having a school-wide policy has an important advantage over teacher-made classroom rules in that it ensures consistency with students knowing what rules they have to follow in all lessons. For the teacher this clearly means less work spent teaching students the rules in her or his classroom. In order to reinforce these rules they can be displayed in all classrooms and in halls.

It can often be fruitful to involve students in the making of rules in order to encourage a sense of ownership and shared responsibility over them and to involve (especially older) students in policing rules and procedures as well. These rules can be more or less extensive but they should never be too numerous, otherwise students will start to perceive them as being petty. A limited number of well-understood and enforced rules will be more effective than a large number of detailed rules and procedures that are therefore more difficult to police.

An example of whole-school rules are:

- Use indoor voices at all times.
- Listen to others.
- Always do your best.
- Listen and respect other students.
- Do not run in the corridors.

Transitions need to be as short and smooth as possible. In order to make this easier effective teachers establish clear procedures for lesson transitions. These can include limiting how many students can move around at any one time (e.g. by letting one table move at a time) and assigning a particular child to clear away papers and pencils left on the table (it is a good idea to give this role to different students at different times). The best way to do this is to think of transitions as a set of steps that need to be executed by students. These can be displayed on a wall chart, and be taught to students. For example, the transition from whole-class work during which students sit in a circle around the teacher to seatwork at their desks could be as follows:

1. Students go to their tables in order, i.e. first table 1, then table 2, etc.
2. At their tables, they take a worksheet from the middle as well as their pencil.
3. Students write their name and the date at the top of the worksheet.
4. Students start working (Borich, 1996; Arends, 1998).

Another useful technique is cueing. This is a technique used to alert students to the fact that a lesson transition is about to occur. An example that is often used during seatwork is to tell students that they have 5 minutes left to work and to repeat this one minute before the end of seatwork. Cueing can help prevent the problem of students who continue to work on the preceding activity after they are supposed to have moved on to the following activity.

Student talk

Inappropriate student talk can disrupt lessons. Students talking during the lesson are off task themselves and can distract other students. Correcting this misbehaviour will slow down the lesson and make the classroom climate less pleasant. Therefore, clear rules on when and when not student talk is allowed are important. This does not mean that talking should be prohibited at all times. During small group work and some other types of seatwork low-level talk can be appropriate, but this is clearly not the case during whole-class presentations. Clear rules also need to be established for student behaviour during questioning. Students should not usually be allowed to shout out answers (except during quick-response games) and should be made to listen to each other's answers and ideas. A period when loud talk can occur is during lesson transitions. According to Borich (1996) it is best to institute a no-talking rule during transitions, as allowing low levels of talk is difficult and often unsuccessful.

Giving homework assignments

Giving (homework) assignments can be one of the more difficult parts of the lesson, not least because not all students will be keen to do them. In order to minimize these problems effective teachers give assignments immediately following related in-class activities. This ensures that the homework assignment often appears to be a natural part of the lesson and not something 'tacked on' afterwards. It is also important that the teacher makes it clear that homework is important and not just an obligatory time-filler. For example, the teacher saying 'It is important that you prac-tise this aspect, so you can use it well when we get to more difficult exercises, so I'll give you some homework on this', creates different expectations than the teacher saying something like: 'I have to assign you

homework, so do exercises 10 and 11 on page 32.' Homework should not
be used or presented as a punishment.

Maintaining momentum during the lesson

One of the most fruitful ways of preventing student misbehaviour during
lessons is to ensure the smooth flow of the lesson. Kounin (1970) described a number of ways in which teachers themselves can slow down
the momentum of lessons. Two of these refer to the teacher stopping an
activity already begun. A *dangle* occurs when the teacher starts to do a
particular activity, but then stops it halfway leaving it 'dangling in mid-
air'. This can happen for example when a teacher starts preparing a
seatwork activity and then suddenly decides she or he needs to teach
something else first. A variation of this is a *flip-flop*, in which a teacher
starts an activity but goes to another activity before finishing it after
which she or he goes back to the original activity once again. Both dangles
and flip-flops can cause confusion among some students, and can trigger
misbehaviour among the naughtier students. Both can be prevented by
good lesson planning on the part of the teacher.

   Another way in which teachers can impede lesson flow is through
overdwelling. This occurs when a teacher goes on explaining instructions
to students after they have totally grasped what they need to do. This will
lead to boredom and restlessness among students, and thus to a higher
chance of misbehaviour. *Fragmentation* occurs when the teacher breaks
down activities into too many different steps. An example would be the
teacher handing out papers in the following steps: 'Take the pile of handouts'; 'take one off the top and hand the pile to your neighbour'; 'now
take one off the top'. It has to be noted, however, that what constitutes
overdwelling or fragmentation may differ from group to group, depending among other things on the age and ability level of the class. As with
the dangle and the flip-flop, both these activities will slow momentum,
causing increased probability of disruption.

Downtime

Downtime refers to those parts of the lesson during which one or more
students (or the whole class) have time to fill because they have finished
seatwork early, because the lesson has finished early and there is no point
starting a new topic, or because students have to wait for materials to be
fetched, the computer to load and so on. These situations can easily lead
to disruption if clear procedures do not exist to deal with them. Effective
teachers have clear rules, such as 'if you finish early, go into the reading
corner and silently read a book' or 'if you've finished your work, come
and ask me for the answer sheet and mark your answers'.

   The best way to avoid downtime problems is to limit the amount of it
that occurs. This can be done by, for example, making sure that there are

enough additional worksheets and tasks available for students who finish quickly and ensuring that all materials to be used are in class before the start of the lesson. It is better to have more exercises available than everyone will be able to do during the allotted time than to be left with unproductive time which has to be 'filled'.

Ending the lesson

A final moment during which management problems are likely to occur is at the end of the lesson. Problems that can occur at this point include not leaving enough time for finishing the planned activities (research has shown that the end-of-lesson summary – see Chapter 3 – is especially likely to get shortened or even completely cut out, e.g. Muijs and Reynolds, 2000c), lessons running over time and instructions for homework getting lost as students rush to collect their belongings and go off for lunch or break time. Effective teachers experience fewer problems with ending the lesson than less effective teachers, through methods such as planning and pacing the lesson to leave sufficient time for activities at the end, giving out homework early so that no confusion occurs, establishing a set of rules for leaving the classroom (letting students go out one by one after answering a final question can be effective) and cueing so students know how long the lesson still has to go.

Summary

In this chapter we have learnt about what research has found to be effective classroom management techniques.

Research on classroom management started in the late 1960s, and identified a number of actions teachers can take to avoid student misbehaviour.

Student misbehaviour is most likely to occur during the start of the lesson, at the end of the lesson, during downtime (which should be limited as much as possible) and during transitions. In all four cases it is important to establish clear procedures for student behaviour. More generally, spending some time on establishing clear rules and procedures at the beginning of the year can save teachers a lot of time later in the year.

The teacher should limit the number of rules and procedures used, however, and rules must be rigorously enforced otherwise they will soon be ignored by students. The reasons for enforcing particular rules need to be explained to students, and it can be helpful to engage students in the process of making rules.

The teacher needs to maintain momentum during the lesson and has to avoid actions that can impede momentum such as 'dangling', 'flip-flops', 'overdwelling' and 'fragmentation'. Teachers will often need to limit or prohibit student talk.

When giving out homework assignments teachers need to make the educational value of the assignment clear and avoid giving the impression that it is a punishment.

Self-study questions

1. You are planning a lesson using whole-class teaching and individual student practice. What seating arrangements could you use?
2. How can you avoid disruption during lesson transitions?
3. Why is it best not to instigate too many rules?
4. During which periods of the lesson are disruptions most likely to occur?
5. How can the teacher her or himself impede lesson momentum?
6. Is it better for a school to instigate a whole school behaviour policy, or to leave this to individual teachers? Why?
7. What should teachers avoid doing when giving out homework assignments?

5

Behaviour Management

Advance organizers

In this chapter you will learn about:

- The main causes of student misbehaviour.
- When to deal most effectively with student misbehaviour.
- Some models for dealing with student misbehaviour.
- Effective and ineffective uses of praise, rewards and punishment.
- Assertive discipline.
- What behaviourist psychology has taught us about reinforcers and punishers.

Introduction

In the previous chapter a number of techniques were discussed which should contribute to the orderly and smooth conduct of the lesson. Applying these techniques should help avoid student misbehaviour occurring. However, as every teacher will tell you, even the best classroom management in the most effectively taught lesson will not avoid misbehaviour occurring at all times. The issue of discipline and what to do when students misbehave is therefore one of the main issues for beginning teachers and has received plenty of attention from researchers, often in conjunction with research on classroom management more generally (as discussed in the previous chapter).

Dealing with inappropriate behaviour

While dealing with the causes of misbehaviour such as those outlined below is important, in actual classroom situations it is often better to focus on the misbehaviour itself in order to allow the lesson to proceed smoothly and not impede student learning. It can be a good idea to ask the student to see the teacher after the lesson to discuss what problems she or he may be having that could be causing her or him to misbehave. In most cases it is crucial for teachers to spot the misbehaviour as quickly as possible and deal with it immediately (Borich, 1996; Arends, 1998).

A first rule for correcting misbehaviour is *not to overreact*. Minor off-task and attention-seeking behaviour should be dealt with quickly and

---

Causes of student misbehaviour

Student misbehaviour can result from a variety of causes, some of which are external to the classroom situation and some of which may be caused, or at least reinforced, by the classroom situation.

Home circumstances can predispose students to misbehaviour. Students who have just experienced or are experiencing parental divorce can often become withdrawn or, conversely, disruptive in school. Students from unstable backgrounds tend to be more disruptive in school, especially as some children may experience a lack of authority or caring at home. Schools in areas likely to suffer from these problems therefore need to provide a disciplined, structured and caring environment, in order to help compensate for what students are missing at home. A further problem may be that the values students are exposed to in the home may not be the same as those that are encouraged at school. Some parents have themselves found schooling to be a negative experience from which they have not benefited, and are therefore unlikely to take a strong interest in their children's performance at school. It is important that the school tries to develop a more positive relationship with these parents.

Developmentally, students at certain ages (particularly early adolescence) will feel the need to rebel and seek attention in the classroom.

Schools and teachers themselves can precipitate misbehaviour, however. Lessons which are perceived as boring or irrelevant by students may provoke misbehaviour more easily, while schools and teachers that are either too authoritarian or too lax on discipline are more likely to encounter disruptive behaviour.

Finally, there is a clear relationship between students' school achievement and their behaviour in school, low achievement often leading to misbehaviour as students become disenchanted with school. Therefore, misbehaviour can be limited by providing a relevant curriculum that allows all students to experience success.

---

with a minimum of fuss. After all, it would be counterproductive if dealing with the misbehaviour disrupted lesson flow more than the actual misbehaviour itself. One way to do this is through what is known as *overlappingness*, a term that refers to teachers' ability to nip misbehaviour in the bud in an unobtrusive way. Invading a student's physical space by moving close to the student or lightly touching him or her can quickly stop off-task behaviour, while allowing the teacher to continue teaching. One way to do this more effectively is by *scanning* the classroom, looking backwards and forwards through the class to try and spot any (emerging) problems.

An important skill that comes to some extent with experience is what Kounin (1970) referred to as *with-itness*. This is the ability to spot all misbehaviour quickly and accurately and to identify the right student as the culprit. This skill is quite difficult to learn for beginning teachers but once picked up it will significantly help the smooth flow of the lesson as trouble will be snuffed out before it can grow into anything more serious. Targeting the right student will stop possible resentment from students wrongly singled out.

In some cases it might be better to ignore minor misbehaviour altogether, as correcting every single occurrence of misbehaviour will disrupt lesson flow and may worsen classroom climate as students could perceive the teacher as being overly authoritarian. However, it is important to maintain a large degree of *consistency* in deciding which minor misbehaviours not to correct. If this is not the case, students will see the teacher's interventions as arbitrary, and may start to become more resistant.

However, the teacher will often have to deal with misbehaviour in order to stop it from escalating and causing increasing problems. Kounin (1970) refers to this as *desist incidents*. Evertson and Emmer (1982) suggest the following sequence for dealing with this type of behaviour:

1. The teacher should ask the student to stop the inappropriate behaviour. The teacher should maintain contact with the student until the behaviour has ceased.
2. The teacher should make eye contact with the student until appropriate behaviour returns.
3. The teacher needs to remind the student of what the appropriate behaviour is.
4. The teacher may need to ask the student to explain the correct behaviour to her or himself. If the student does not understand, she or he should be provided with feedback.
5. The teacher needs to impose the penalty for breaking the rule. This will usually consist of performing the procedure until it is done correctly. However, when the student understands what she or he needs to do but is doing it incorrectly on purpose the teacher can use some mild form of punishment, such as withholding privileges.
6. Often, off-task behaviour occurs when students are doing repetitive, boring tasks which they have already mastered. Varying activities, for example by going from seatwork to interactive teaching or by going on to another type of exercise or another topic can refocus students on the lesson.

Another model for dealing with misbehaviour is the LEAST model, which suggests five steps for dealing with desist behaviours:

1. Leave it alone. If the behaviour is not going to become troublesome, leave it alone.
2. End the action indirectly. This can be done by distracting the student from her or his misbehaviour through giving him or her something else to do.
3. Attend more fully. Teachers should try to get to know students, so they can get to the heart of the problem. Has she or he got problems at home? Is she or he being bullied? Does she or he have learning difficulties etc. This will help the teacher decide what to do.
4. Spell out directions. Remind the student of what she or he should be doing, and if necessary warn her or him of the consequences of not complying.

5. **Track** the behaviour. If there appears to be a recurring problem with misbehaviour of one or more students it is useful to keep systematic records of the behaviour, by using student tracking records for example. These can then be connected to a reward system: students who do not appear on the tracking sheet for a certain length of time receiving a reward, those that are marked for a certain number of times receiving some form of punishment (Arends, 1998).

In general, both approaches suggest three main phases once the decision has been made to correct a certain misbehaviour. Initially one can try to divert the misbehaviour by, for example, distracting the student by asking a question, picking up the pace, boosting interest by starting a new activity or removing certain tempting materials with which students can fiddle. If that does not help, more explicit correction may be needed, by moving close to the disruptive student, making eye contact with the student, using verbal cues such as naming the student (e.g. 'and, Daniel, the next topic is . . .'), pointing out in general that the class should be engaged with the lesson, or praising a particularly well-behaved student. If this still does not succeed in preventing misbehaviour, the teacher needs to go on to more severe warnings or, if necessary, punishment.

Using rewards and punishment

Behavioural psychological theory and classroom practice point to the importance of using rewards and punishments in classroom management. Using a reward may help to reinforce certain (desired) behaviours, whereas using punishment may deter certain behaviours. The basic principle in using rewards is to first identify what behaviours you want to reinforce, then decide what rewards would be appropriate to reinforce these behaviours and, finally, to use these rewards in such a way that they can most effectively reinforce the desired behaviour.

There are a number of rewards that can be used to reinforce desired student behaviours. The first is using *praise* in the classroom. This is probably one of the most frequently used behaviour management tools in classrooms and can be highly effective, although it should not be overused. However, a number of guidelines need to be taken into account to ensure the effectiveness of praise. Some further findings, largely from Brophy's (1981) research summary, are summarized in the 'Effective use of praise' box see p.54.

Teachers can also use specific *rewards, incentives and privileges* to reinforce desired behaviours. Rewards can take various forms such as house points resulting in a letter of praise to parents or entry into a prize draw, badges or symbols such as happy faces which children can wear and which can be used in conjunction with house points, honour rolls (listing 'students of the month' for example), sweets and so on. Privileges can include being excused from some forms of work or being given special responsibilities in class or in the school (which can range from being

---

Behaviourism and punishment/rewards

Behaviourist learning theory was initiated by researchers like Pavlov, Skinner and Thorndike before the Second World War. Initially, experiments with dogs and rats convinced these psychologists of the importance of the use of rewards and punishments to elicit certain desired behaviours, such as pushing a lever, in these animals. Over ensuing decades these findings were further tested and refined with human subjects, and became highly influential in education.

Skinner's theories, based on experiments with rats, are particularly relevant here. According to Skinner, who built on the work of Pavlov and Thorndike, a prime element of behavioural theory is the emphasis on consequences. Pleasurable consequences, or *reinforcers*, strengthen behaviour, while unpleasant consequences, or *punishers*, weaken behaviour. Behaviour is thus influenced by its consequences, but it is influenced by its antecedents as well, thus creating the A(ntecedents)–B(ehaviour)–C(onsequences) chain. Skinner's work concentrated mainly on the relationship between the latter two parts of the chain, and we will look more closely at these.

First it is important to know that no consequences are of necessity fixed to be reinforcers or punishers. Thus while sending a child to see the headteacher will be a punisher for most children, for some it may enhance their desired status as rebels and therefore, on the contrary, be a reinforcer of unwanted behaviour. What constitutes a reinforcer is an empirical question, not a given.

There are two broad types of reinforcement: *positive reinforcement* and *negative reinforcement*. Positive reinforcement occurs when a (positive) stimulus is given following a particular behaviour. In school, such stimuli include giving stars and praise. Negative reinforcement occurs when an aversive (unpleasant) stimulus is removed or averted. In the classroom this can refer to releasing a student from having to perform an unpleasant task. Thus, good behaviour and a good workrate can result in students not having to do additional homework. Negative reinforcement is thus not the same as *punishment*. Negative, like positive, reinforcement strengthens a behaviour, while punishment (e.g. sending a child to the headteacher) weakens a behaviour.

Like reinforcement, punishment comes in two forms, *presentation* and *removal* punishment. Presentation punishment is the use of unpleasant consequences, e.g. a student has to write 'I will not misbehave in class' 50 times. Removal punishment refers to the removal of reinforcers, such as when a student must stay in class at break. Use of punishment is controversial among behaviourist researchers, some researchers claiming that it has only temporary effects. The majority of behaviourists claim that punishment is less effective than reinforcement.

If people are learning a new behaviour, they will learn it faster if they are reinforced for every correct response. This is called a *continuous reinforcement schedule*. However, once the behaviour has been mastered, it is better only to reinforce it *intermittently*. The main reason for this is that this helps the student not to expect reinforcement of behaviour every time and, of course, it is also rather time-consuming for the teacher to reinforce each and every behaviour (Muijs and Reynolds, 2000c).

---

allowed to wipe the chalkboard to becoming form captain). It is often useful to involve students themselves in deciding what rewards to use, as in that way the teacher can ensure that rewards given are indeed valued by the students themselves. It is important to remember that what is valued by students can differ according to such factors as age and gender.

However, one needs to be careful of overusing external rewards as these can interfere with the student's own intrinsic motivation to learn. For this reason an increasing amount of research has turned to the use of so-called *natural reinforcers*. These are reinforcers which are naturally present in the classroom. While for some students these may lie in their motivation to learn, for others these can be elicited by using reinforcement. The way one can do this, once the behaviour one wishes to reinforce has been selected, is to think about what natural consequences result from that behaviour. For example, writing an essay has consequences such as writing sentences, being able to express one's ideas, filling up a page, etc. The teacher then needs to choose which behaviour she or he wants to reinforce. In the case of essay writing, a desirable consequence may be enhancing the ability of the student to express his or her ideas. In order to be effective, this consequence should be obvious to the student. The teacher then needs to design the lesson in such a way that these desirable outcomes are made conspicuous. Focusing on how the task is done, as well as on outcomes, may help. The teacher also has to select a *back-up reinforcer*. These are extrinsic, but, in contrast to many rewards they must be there in the classroom and have educational value. Then, once the students have started doing the task, the teacher should give feedback pointing out the natural consequences which should (hopefully) become natural reinforcers. The back-up reinforcers should be given initially but, over the course of time, should be removed. The natural reinforcers should be pointed out for a longer time, but it should hopefully become less and less necessary to do this explicitly as they become internalized (Horcones, 1991; 1992).

While using rewards is one of the most effective behaviour management tools, in some cases it will be necessary to use *punishment* as well. Punishment is designed to create an avoidance response, in that students should avoid behaviours which result in punishment in future. Such punishments usually include taking house points away for misbehaviour, making students stay in after school or during break time, removing privileges, expelling the student from class (or, in the worst instances, from school) or giving verbal warnings in the classroom. Usually, the teacher should start by giving a verbal warning for non-major misbehaviour, before going on to more serious punishments. However, after giving two or three warning some punishment should follow to avoid damaging the teacher's credibility in the eyes of students, who could otherwise start to believe that the teacher is not really serious about preventing this misbehaviour.

In general, though, research has found that punishment is less effective than praise in most cases. There are a number of reasons for this:

1. The effects of punishment are usually specific to a particular context and teacher. They are less likely to be carried over to other teachers or classrooms, or to other types of misbehaviour; e.g. if a student is

punished for talking during the lesson of teacher A, this may stop her or him from talking in that teacher's lesson again, but not from talking in other teachers' lessons or from engaging in other misbehaviour during the lessons of teacher A.

2. Punishment does not always guarantee that the desired response will occur. Because punishment is seen by students as specific to a particular context, it may keep the student from engaging in behaviour that gets her or him punished while not necessarily getting the student to engage in the desired behaviour instead. For example, in the above situation, the student may refrain from further talk during the lesson, but that does not mean that she or he will instead engage in on-task behaviour. Instead, she or he may daydream or fiddle as long as this does not get her or him punished.

3. The punishment may also become associated with the punisher rather than with the behaviour of the punished student. Teachers who use punishment too often may find that the punishment becomes associated with themselves rather than with the behaviours they are trying to avoid.

4. Likewise, punishment that is designed to stop an undesired behaviour, but that is not associated with a desired behaviour, seldom has long-lasting effects. Students may not understand what the desired behaviour is and, therefore, will not start behaving in the way desired.

5. Punishment can also sometimes have negative side effects. For example, in the above case, the student may decide not to risk talking at all any more, and may become less willing to make substantive contributions during lessons.

6. Occasionally, punishment can lead to aggressive or violent reactions from students (Borich, 1996; Arends, 1998).

Therefore, while punishment is sometimes necessary, it should be used as a last resort and not as an automatic reaction to student misbehaviour.

An important aspect of effective use of rewards and punishment is consistency, both within the practices of one teacher and across the school. If the use of rewards and punishment is inconsistent, it will be perceived by students as unjust and arbitrary, and will lead to a resentment that may ultimately lead to more rather than less misbehaviour. This is the case at school level as well as at teacher level, and research in school effectiveness has clearly shown the importance of consistent school-wide behaviour management policies (Creemers and Reezigt, 1999).

Summary

In this chapter we looked at behaviour management, defined as what to do when students misbehave.

Effective use of praise

Brophy (1981) developed the following guidelines for the effective use of praise, based on extensive research:

Effective praise	*Ineffective praise*
• Is delivered contingently.	• Is delivered randomly or unsystematically.
• Praises the particular behaviour it wants to reinforce.	• Is non-specific and global.
• Is perceived as credible by students, through signs that it is non-routine and spontaneous.	• Is blandly uniform, suggesting that it is an automatic reaction made with minimal thought.
• Rewards attainment of specific performance criteria (which can include effort).	• Rewards mere participation, without consideration of processes or outcomes.
• Provides the students with specific information about their accomplishments.	• Provides no information to students, or information about their status.
• Orientates students towards better appreciation of their own task-related behaviour and thinking about problem-solving.	• Orientates students towards comparing themselves with each other and thinking about competing.
• Uses students' own prior accomplishments as the basis for comparison.	• Uses the accomplishments of peers as the basis for comparison.
• Is given in recognition of noteworthy effort or success at difficult tasks (for this student).	• Is given without regard to the effort expended or the meaning of the accomplishment.
• Attributes success to effort and ability, implying that similar success can be expected in future.	• Attributes success to ability alone or to external factors such as luck.
• Encourages internal attributions (gets students to believe they expend effort on the task because they enjoy it and/or want to develop task-relevant skills).	• Encourages external attributions (gets students to believe they expend effort on a task for external reasons, such as to please the teacher, to get a reward, etc.).
• Focuses students' attention on their own task-relevant behaviour.	• Focuses students' attention on the teacher as an external authority figure who is manipulating them.
• Fosters appreciation of, and desirable attributions about, task-relevant behaviour after the process is completed.	• Intrudes into the ongoing process, distracting attention from task-relevant behaviour.

Assertive discipline

A classroom and behaviour management programme that has received a lot of interest is the 'assertive discipline' programme developed by Lee and Marlene Canter (1976; 1989). This is based around the principle that teachers should react assertively towards student misbehaviour.

To adopt an assertive discipline approach, teachers and students (who need to be involved for this approach to be more effective through students feeling ownership of the rules) need to design at the outset a set of rules for school and classroom, along with clear procedures for dealing with infringements of these rules. Rules and consequences need to be communicated to parents, and stringently followed through by teachers.

Teachers should react assertively to misbehaviour, according to the procedures agreed, and should not accept any excuses from students. Teachers should not react in a hostile, angry or guilt-inducing way (e.g. 'You'll be sorry . . .') or in a passive way.

While popular, this approach has not been well-researched for effectiveness, may put too much emphasis on punishment and may disrupt lesson flow if procedures to deal with misbehaviour are too complicated or take too much time to administer.

The main elements that may predispose students to misbehave are situations outside school such as students' psychological development, school and classroom factors such as boring, irrelevant lessons and curriculum, or overly lax or authoritarian rules.

When misbehaviour occurs, the teacher should not overreact to minor misbehaviour but try to deter it in the most inobtrusive way possible. Constantly scanning the classroom and overlapping can help stop problems at an early stage.

If the behaviour is serious enough to warrant intervention there are a number of models that have been proposed to deal with misbehaviour, such as the Evertson and Emmer model and the LEAST model.

One of the main ways of correcting behaviour is the use of rewards and punishment. One of the most frequently used forms of rewards is teacher praise. However, not all praise is effective. In order for praise to work it should not be an automatic reflex. Praise needs to be specific, credible and orientated towards both effort and ability, encapsulating the expectation that similar performance can be attained in future. Rewards can further take the form of house points, stars, badges and privileges such as responsible roles in the school. Although effective, these rewards can lead to students becoming externally orientated rather than valuing learning for its own sake. To counter this, some researchers advocate the use of 'natural reinforcers', which are educational and available in the classroom.

Punishment is sometimes inevitable, but should not be overused, as it has been found to be less effective in engendering desired behaviours than the use of rewards.

Self-study questions

1. Does the teacher need to correct every occurrence of misbehaviour?
2. In what ways can the school and the teacher contribute to the occurrence of student misbehaviour?
3. What are the disadvantages of relying too strongly on punishment in behaviour management?
4. Why, according to behaviourist learning theory, are rewards and punishment effective?
5. How can the teacher make the most effective use of praise?
6. What are natural reinforcers?
7. Explain why assertive discipline could be an effective behaviour management system, and what disadvantages it could have.

6

Classroom Climate

Advance organizers

In this chapter you will learn:

- How to create a pleasant and productive classroom climate, through the use of attractive displays, enthusiastic teaching, and a caring relationship with students.
- The uses, advantages and disadvantages of three types of classroom climate: competitive, co-operative and individual.
- The importance of teacher expectations and how to avoid negative expectations of students.
- The importance of taking into account cultural differences in the classroom.

What is classroom climate?

Classroom climate as defined here is quite a wide-ranging concept encompassing the mood or atmosphere that is created in the teacher's classroom through the rules set out, the way the teacher interacts with students, and the way the physical environment is set out (Freiberg and Stein, 1999; Creemers and Reezigt, 1999).

The climate of the classroom has been widely studied since the 1960s, using a variety of instruments developed for that purpose, such as the Classroom Climate Inventory (Furtwengler, 1987). Most of these studies have identified classroom climate as an important concomitant of student achievement, both in Europe (Muijs and Reynolds, 1999; Mortimore *et al.*, 1988) and in the USA (Brophy and Good, 1986; Rosenshine, 1979). A large-scale meta-analysis conducted by Wang, Haertel and Walberg (1997) found classroom climate to be one of the most important factors to affect student achievement. Learning environment was also found to be related to achievement in Fraser's (1994) review of 40 studies on the effects of classroom climate. Apart from this relationship with student achievement on tests, a warm, supportive classroom climate has also been linked to a number of other factors, such as students' self-esteem (Fraser, 1994), students' participation in the classroom, and even students' democratic values (Cotton, 1997). Creating a positive climate was identified as a prime characteristic of quality teachers in a study of teaching in 11 countries (OECD, 1994).

School climate and classroom climate

While in this book we are focusing on classroom teaching, it is clear that certainly with respect to classroom climate teachers do not operate within a vacuum. School climate will strongly influence classroom climate, and in order to be effective the two need to be complementary. A teacher going against the prevailing school climate will find it difficult to change students' established habits. If, for example, students are not used to contributing ideas in other lessons they will find it hard to change their habits for one particular teacher.

The school can do a number of things to help create a warm, supportive atmosphere. As in the classroom, the use of pleasant, bright displays will help, with students' work put up in hallways and dining areas. Schools should have strong and strictly enforced anti-bullying policies and should be open and receptive to problems students are having outside school. Good support services can help all students reach their potential. Minimizing noise and clean and pleasant communal spaces (hallways, dining room) will make a difference as well (Freiberg, 1999).

Creating a pleasant classroom environment

The most important aspect of classroom climate is the *relationship between teacher and students*. This relationship can range along a continuum from formal to informal, and from warm to cool. A warm, supportive environment has been found to be important to teacher effectiveness, especially in encouraging students to contribute constructively to the lesson. Teachers who are perceived as being understanding, helpful and friendly and show leadership without being too strict have been found to enhance students' achievement and their affective outcomes, while teachers who come across as uncertain, dissatisfied with their students and admonishing produce lower cognitive and affective outcomes (Wubbels, Brekelmans and Hooymayers, 1991).

Teachers should create an unthreatening environment, in which students' opinions are valued, respected and solicited. Wrong answers should not provoke negative reactions on the part of the teacher, but need to be perceived as part of students' learning processes. This can be done by reacting positively to wrong answers and by trying to emphasize what was right about the student's thinking process.

Teachers who are concerned with students' emotional and social, as well as academic, needs have been found to engender more student involvement in lessons. Research has also pointed to the role of classroom climate in encouraging students with problems to request help. Often it can be the case that it is precisely those students who need help most who are most reluctant to request it, the most able students having been found to be the most likely to request help. However, this gap can be reduced if not closed by teachers who value the emotional needs of their students and create a warm and not overly competitive environment.

Measuring school and classroom climate

In order to be able to improve school and classroom climate it is necessary first of all to find out what the climate in school is like, and where possible problems may lie. A number of direct and indirect measures have been proposed, which can involve teachers, students, parents and other members of the community. Getting information from students as well as teachers is important, as they can often have a somewhat different perspective on school and classroom climate. Thus, Fraser (1999) has found that teachers have a more positive perception of the climate in their classrooms than their students. Involving students by getting them to give feedback on classroom climate has the further advantage of making them feel valued and important, and can therefore contribute to school and classroom climate in and of itself.

A number of checklist and rating scales have been proposed that can be used with either teachers, students, school management or parents, such as that proposed for Dutch primary schools by Creemers and Reezigt (1999) or Fraser's (1999) Learning Environment Questionnaires. Fraser (1999) proposes measuring both students' and teachers' perceptions of school climate and measuring both actual and preferred climate among students. This can allow teachers and heads to see where the main discrepancies between actual and preferred climate lie and to target interventions specifically at those areas. Questionnaires aimed at parents and other members of the community have also been designed (Stevens and Sanchez, 1999). A useful suggestion is the use of entrance and exit questionnaires. Students entering secondary school could be asked questions such as: (1) What do you like about your current school? (2) What is one concern you have about going to secondary school? (3) What is something you will do to improve your success in secondary school? and (4) What is one message you would like to give your teachers? Students leaving the school could be asked: (1) What did you like about this school? (2) What was your most memorable experience in this school? (3) What area would you like to have improved in this school? and (4) What is one message you would like to give your teachers (Freiberg, 1999)?

With very young students the use of questionnaires is inappropriate. A way of collecting classroom climate measures from these students can be to ask them to draw a picture of their classroom. This can provide valuable insights into how much distance they perceive from their teacher, how formally or informally the classroom is run and what parts of the classroom (such as the blackboard or the reading area) are perceived to be important (Freiberg and Stein, 1999).

Data such as the number of referrals of students to the head by a particular teacher or the number of absences in the school as a whole are also useful indicators of school and classroom climate. In order for these measures to be of practical use, however, the results they generate need to be used to improve the school climate. As many of the measures mentioned above are quite fine grained and look into various areas in some detail, specific points can be targeted. Feedback on the results can be discussed, on the basis of which an improvement plan can be drawn up. Some time after the reform has been implemented the same form can be used to measure school/classroom climate again to see whether the reform has had any effect (Fraser, 1994).

A basic but often overlooked element in creating good classroom relations is the *use by the teacher of student names*. This can appear trivial, but not knowing students' names can create the impression that the teacher does not care about her or his students as people. Therefore the teacher should address students by name as often as possible. In the beginning of the year when faced with a new class (and, especially in secondary school, with one of several new classes) this can be more difficult than it sounds. These are a number of ways of making this more easy, such as the following:

1. Have students give their name each time before they speak, until the teacher feels she or he knows everyone.
2. Have students make name tags they can put on their table, so every time the teacher looks at the student she or he can associate the face with the name. It can be helpful to ask students to write down some memorable characteristic or hobby, which the teacher can associate with the student and which will help her or him get to know the students better.
3. Have a list of names with the students' photographs on the teacher's desk.
4. Try and memorize one row of students a day.
5. Ask students to introduce themselves to the class, giving their names, likes and dislikes, and other personal informtion.

An important component of classroom climate is the *enthusiasm* shown by the teacher. If the teacher her or himself is unenthusiastic about the subject or lesson being taught, this attitude is likely to rub off on students. Teachers who enjoy teaching and their subject and can put their enthusiasm across are more likely to motivate their students, and research (e.g. Mortimore *et al.*, 1988) has found a positive association between teacher enthusiasm and student involvement during lessons. It is no coincidence that most people, when they are asked to describe their favourite school teacher, will tend to pick out a teacher who managed to inspire them through their enthusiasm about the subject. Of course, no teacher can be equally enthusiastic about all subjects or on all days. It is, however, important to avoid expressing overt dislike of the subject or topic through comments such as, 'I know this is boring, but we have to do it because it is in the curriculum'.

An aspect of a pleasant classroom that the teacher has a large amount of control over is creating attractive and pleasant *displays*. Colourful and bright displays can cheer up the classroom and make it a more pleasant environment, while also giving the teacher the opportunity to allow peripheral learning to occur. This can be done by displaying learning materials on classroom walls which can aid learning in an almost subliminal way by drawing students' attention to the displayed educational materials. Classroom climate can also be improved by displaying students' own work on the wall, as this can encourage students to take pride in their work and can motivate them. It is, however, important to give all students the chance to have their work displayed and not just to display the 'best' work if this means constantly displaying work from the same students.

Other aspects of the physical environment of classrooms and schools can also impact on school climate. Clean and tidy classrooms, hallways and toilets can create a better atmosphere across the school. Small things matter. High noise levels in, for example, the dining room or the hallways can have a strong negative effect on school climate and student behaviour but can often be quite easily reduced (Freiberg, 1999).

Some of what has been said in this chapter about the need for classrooms to be warm, relaxed environments may appear to contradict what was said in earlier chapters about the need for the classroom to be a disciplined, work-centred environment. If one veers to the extremes of either position this can indeed be the case. The best teachers, however, are able to create a classroom that is all these things, rather than either being either overly authoritarian or undisciplined. In our own research (Muijs and Reynolds, 1999) we found that good classroom discipline and a positive classroom climate were strongly related to each other, which suggests that in practice effective teachers are able to strike the right balance between the two.

Sometimes it can be necessary to put in place a strategy to improve school and classroom climate. The best way to do this is to do something that can be quickly implemented and is highly visible, for example greeting all students when they come to school in the morning (Freiberg and Stein, 1999). Students should be involved in the improvement effort as much as is possible as this will mean the climate is improved in ways that are important to them and because it will help them feel involved and valued, which in itself can improve school climate. Giving students authority in the classroom can improve classroom climate and encourage students to take responsibility for their environment. This has been identified as one of the differences in favour of Japanese schools when compared with American schools (Linn *et al.*, 2000).

Three types of classroom climate

Borich (1996) defines three types of classroom climate that the teacher may wish to use in different lessons: competitive, co-operative and individualistic. These three types are arranged along a continuum where the authority ceded to the students by the teacher ranges from none to quite extensive, and where teaching and learning move from being very teacher led to being very student centred.

In a *competitive* classroom students will compete among themselves to give the right answer or to attain a standard set by the teacher. The teacher is the sole arbiter of the correctness of the response, and no authority is given to students. The teacher leads the class, presents and organizes the material and evaluates the correctness of the students' responses. In whole-class lessons this can take the form of students competing by having the turn to give the right answer. In group work groups can compete against each other, for example through group games. During individual work the teacher can get students to compete by giving a prize to the student who has correctly completed answers on a worksheet most quickly or for having the largest number of correct answers. A competitive climate can motivate students, especially boys, and can thus enhance student achievement. This type of classroom also allows for a large amount of teacher guidance, which can be important to student learning. Structured, whole-class teaching has been found to be effective in raising students' achievement. The possible negative effects are damaging the self-confidence of less able students through the constant comparison involved, which may lead to them becoming disengaged from the lesson and possibly school and learning in general, and the fact that this method will not inculcate co-operative skills in students.

In a *co-operative* classroom students engage in dialogue that is monitored by the teacher. They are allowed to discuss and bring up their own ideas, but the teacher intervenes to help them sharpen up and clarify their ideas and to encourage higher-order and creative thinking. In this type of classroom students have more authority than in the competitive classroom, in that they are allowed to present their own opinions and ideas, and discuss these freely with one another. The teacher's role is to stimulate discussion, arbitrate the discussion and make sure disagreements between students do not get out of hand. At the end of discussions the teacher will summarize and organize the ideas presented by students. In whole-class lessons this can take the form of students being allowed to call out hints or clues when another student is having difficulties. During individual work students can be made to co-operate with their neighbour by exchanging papers, checking each other's work or sharing ideas. This climate type lends itself particularly well to group work, in which students can co-operate by discussing a topic or working out problems with all students being allowed to contribute. A major advantage of this type of classroom is that it will help develop students' social and co-operative skills, which are becoming more and more important in the workplace. Students often enjoy working with one another, which means that co-operative work can be highly motivating. Being able to articulate their own ideas can help develop students' thinking skills. Disadvantages are that exchanges can easily become dominated by one or two highly self-confident individuals, with others allowing them to do all the work, the so-called 'free-rider effect'. Also, students can strengthen each other's misconceptions, and there is a risk of classrooms getting out of hand with students shouting out answers if not managed well.

The final type of classroom climate identified by Borich is the *individualistic type*. In that type of classroom the emphasis will be on students getting through work independently and testing themselves. Students will complete assignments monitored by the teacher, and are encouraged to give those answers that they think are best, rather than answers that are considered to be 'right' or 'wrong'. The students' role will then be to complete the assignment with the best possible responses, while the teacher's role will be to assign the work and make sure that orderly progress is made towards completing it. In a whole-class setting (not the most natural one for this type of classroom) this can take the form of the entire class chanting out answers in unison. When group work is used in the individualistic classroom, subgroups will complete their own as-signed topic which will be independent of topics undertaken by other groups. Results are not shared with the class. During individual work, students will complete seatwork on their own without direct teacher intervention. Advantages of this type of classroom are the freedom it allows for students to work at their own level and develop their own answers to questions. This will encourage students' individual problem-solving and independent learning skills. Negative effects can be that par-ticularly less able and averagely able students will suffer from lack of teacher guidance and make insufficient progress when left to learn in this way. Students will also not have the opportunity to develop co-operative skills, and for most students using too much individualized instruction has been found to be ineffective.

Teacher expectations

One of the most important factors both in classroom climate and in school and teacher effectiveness generally are the teacher's expectations of her or his students. From the late 1960s onwards (see 'Pygmalion in the class-room' box) research has found that teachers' expectations of their stu-dents can become a self-fulfilling prophecy. Students that teachers expect to do well tend to achieve better, while students who are expected to do badly, usually tend to fulfil their teachers' expectations as well. Similarly, school effectiveness research has paid a lot of attention to this factor, which has been found to be one of the most consistently important factors in this type of research (Rutter *et al.*, 1979; Mortimore *et el.*, 1988; Reynolds *et al.*, 1996).

Of course, one could argue that the relationship between teachers' expectations of their students' achievement and students' actual out-comes is merely the result of teachers having accurate perceptions of their students' ability. However, research has shown that, although this is obviously the case to a large extent, there is more going on. The initial research came about as a result of finding that teachers form expectations of students even before they have any evidence for their performance. These expectations have been found to be related to student ethnic, gen-der and background characteristics. Thus, teachers tend to have lower expectations of working-class students than of middle-class students, they tend to have lower expectations of students from ethnic minorities and, in the past, they tended to have lower expectations of girls, although there is some evidence that this has changed to the extent that gender expectations in many cases may have become reversed (Rosenthal and Jacobson, 1968; Covington and Beery, 1976).

Pygmalion in the Classroom

The first major study on the teacher expectancy effect was undertaken by Rosenthal and Jacobson (1968) in the 1960s. At the start of the school year teachers were provided with a list of students who were said to be expected to bloom intellectually in the coming years on the basis of a test, but who in fact did not differ from their peers in this respect. Students were retested on three occasions during that school year and during the following year. Results indicated that 'bloomers' gained more in IQ than did control group children, although the effect wore off among the younger subjects, while growing in strength among older students. Grades in reading ability also improved significantly among the experimental group children, who were also rated more positively by their teachers on factors such as intellectual curiosity. Since then, the effect has received considerable empirical support (Covington and Beery, 1976; Burns, 1979). Harris, Rosenthal and Snodgrass (1986) failed to find an expectancy effect in their study of kindergarten and 2nd grade learning, but this is probably due to the short teaching span (10-minute sessions) and the unnatural learning situation.

These expectations can affect students in a variety of (often subtle) ways. Teachers communicate their expectancy of certain students to them through verbalizations (which according to Burns [1979] are fraught with evaluatory statements), by paying closer attention to high expectancy students and spending more time with them, by failing to give feedback to responses from low expectancy students, by criticizing low expectancy students more often and praising them less often, by not waiting as long for the answer of low expectancy students, by calling on them less to answer questions, by asking them only lower-order questions, giving them more seatwork and low-level academic tasks, and by leaving them out of some learning activities (Brophy and Good, 1986). These expectations are then internalized by the students and the peer group, who start to behave in the way expected of them by the teacher. Sometimes these expectations can be communicated more directly than this as well, though. In our own research we observed a teacher say to her class with an air of resignation: 'I know this topic is too difficult for you, but it is in the National Curriculum, so we have got to do it.'

Negative teacher expectations can be a particular problem in schools in disadvantaged areas, where an ethos of negative expectations can take over the whole school, creating an atmosphere in which teachers will say things like 'well, what can you expect with students like ours'. This will often lead to less effort being made to help these students achieve and can lead to a negative spiral in which teacher expectations and student expectations feed on each other.

Even where teacher expectations are unbiased and accurately reflect a student's ability in a particular subject, a form of expectation effect can occur, in that when a student's achievement suddenly improves (or goes backwards), the teacher's expectations remain unchanged. For example, a student who usually gets high marks for a subject, may continue to receive high marks on a bad essay she or he has written. Another example occurred with a student in our university who had not achieved well in French classes when at school. At one point this student returned to his old school for a former-student evening. When asked what he was doing, he (truthfully) told his former French teacher that he had just obtained a first at university. The teacher furiously accused him of being a liar.

The question then is how best to avoid these negative expectation effects. The first thing is for teachers to be aware of their own (often unwanted) biases. Students from a different ethnic group and social class may look and act somewhat differently from the teacher's norms. Teachers should be aware of this, and not treat this as a sign of lesser ability. Changing unconscious beliefs is no easy task. There are, however, a number of things teachers can do to help overcome this problem:

- Remember that all students can learn, and communicate that belief to students.
- Teachers should make sure all students get the chance to answer questions, contribute to discussions and so on. To ensure that this is the case it can be a good idea to make a list of students that can be systematically checked to make sure that no students are forgotten.
- Teachers should try and be aware of how often they call on girls and boys and students from different ethnic groups. It can be useful to have a colleague to observe the lesson to point out if there are problems there. One needs to take account of both verbal and non-verbal interactions in this respect.
- Teachers should try to use objective criteria when marking students' work. To check whether this is the case one can occasionally have students' work double-marked by a colleague who does not know the students.
- Teachers should monitor how they distribute rewards and punishments. It is important to remember that expectancy effects can manifest themselves through allowing students of whom the teacher has low expectations to behave worse and be off task and disengaged from the lesson more often than high expectancy students, as well as through giving them more punishments and fewer rewards than high expectancy students.

Summary

Classroom climate can be defined as the mood or atmosphere created by a teacher in her or his classroom, the way the teacher interacts with students, and the way the physical environment is set out.

Research has shown the importance of classroom climate, not only to student achievement, but to their self-esteem and lesson participation as well.

One of the main elements in developing a positive classroom climate is creating a warm, supportive environment in which students feel unthreatened and are therefore willing to make a positive contribution to the lesson. The enthusiasm of the teacher has likewise been found to be an important factor. Therefore, even if the teacher is not feeling that enthusiastic on a particular day, she or he should avoid communicating negative feelings about the subject, lesson or curriculum to students. Creating a bright and pleasant classroom with displays of student work and educational materials can not only motivate students, but can create peripheral learning as well.

Borich (1996) identified three types of classroom climate. In competitive classrooms students are encouraged to compete with one another. These classrooms are very teacher led, with little autonomy for students. Competition can be motivating to students, while teacher-led classrooms have been found to enhance achievement.

In co-operative classrooms the emphasis is on students co-operating, with the teacher intervening to steer students towards learning goals. These classrooms are effective at developing important co-operative learning skills, which can enhance student achievement.

In individual classrooms the emphasis is on individual work with a minimum of teacher intervention. These classrooms can help develop independent learning skills, although too much individualized instruction has not been found to be effective.

Teacher expectation effects occur when teachers attribute certain characteristics to students (usually ability) based on factors such as class, gender and ethnicity. These expectations can easily turn into self-fulfilling prophecies, and must therefore be avoided as they can damage the achievement of students from these groups. While this is difficult, being aware of the problem is a first important step. Teachers should also carefully monitor their own behaviour, or have a colleague observe them, to see whether they are, for example, giving more attention to boys than girls.

Self-study questions

1. How can teachers communicate low expectations to students?
2. What can teachers do to encourage low-ability students to request more help?
3. What are the advantages and disadvantages of the three types of classroom climate?
4. What is culture shock and what can teachers do to overcome its negative consequences?

5. What can teachers do to counter the effects of low expectations of students?
6. What display elements can help create a positive classroom climate?
7. Can classrooms be both businesslike and warm environments at the same time?

7

Effective Use of Homework

Advance organizers

In this chapter you will learn about:

- The main types of homework in use, and its main goals.
- What research has to tell us about the effectiveness of homework as a learning tool.
- How to use homework effectively.
- The importance of establishing a school-wide homework policy.
- The role of parents and what the school can do to help them.

Introduction

Homework is one of the most widely used but also one of the more controversial aspects of teaching. Unpopular with students, and often with teachers and parents as well, it remains a central part of school life. In this chapter we will review research that has looked at whether or not homework is an effective learning tool and research that has looked at how to use it most effectively.

Homework can be defined as out-of-class activity that is an extension of classroom work. It can be either individualized or assigned to the whole class. LaConte (1981) classified the three main types of homework as:

- Practice assignments, which reinforce newly acquired skills or knowledge. An example of this can be when students have learnt about different types of leaves, and are asked to look for examples in their environment.
- Preparation assignments, which are intended to provide background to particular topics. For example, students can prepare for a lesson by reading texts or by collecting material in advance.
- Extension assignments, which are designed to practise learnt material or extend the students by encouraging them to do more research on the subject after the topic has been studied in class.

Homework is designed to meet a variety of purposes, such as

- increase student achievement;
- reinforce and strengthen topics taught in class;

- complete unfinished work;
- develop independent study skills;
- develop self-discipline;
- develop time management skills;
- involve parents in helping their children's learning;
- allow preparation for future lessons and topics;
- develop students' research skills;
- review and practise topics taught in school; and
- extend the school day.

The precise form that homework will take will depend on the goals that the teacher is trying to accomplish. However, the bottom line of all these goals is aiding students' learning, which leads us to the question of whether homework is an effective learning tool.

Is homework effective?

There is quite a bit of research that has attempted to answer this question, often with ambiguous results, however. The main reason for this ambiguity is that it is very difficulty to isolate the effects of homework from a variety of other factors affecting students' achievement.

A major recent overview of research was published by Cooper (1989; 1994) who looked at 120 studies categorized into three subsets based on whether or not the study had been designed to compare homework versus no homework, homework versus in-school supervised work or were non-experimental, looking at the statistical relationship between the amount of homework done and achievement as found through questionnaires of students and teachers (*correlational studies*). Looking at 17 studies that have compared homework with no homework, Cooper found that homework can strongly benefit student achievement. Seventy per cent of the studies he looked at found that students who did homework made more progress than students who did not. Furthermore, students who did more assignments per week achieved better than those who did fewer assignments per week, as measured by how both groups differed from students who did no homework. However, if a homework assignment spanned a long period of time, such as several weeks, the impact was less strong. Studies comparing homework with in-school supervised study also found homework to be more beneficial, although the difference was not as large as for students who did no homework.

According to Cooper the following positive effects for homework have been put forward: in the short-term, homework can lead to better retention of facts and knowledge, increased understanding, better critical thinking, better information processing and the possibility of extending the curriculum. Long-term effects include the development of better study habits, the development of more positive attitudes towards school and studying, and the encouragement of learning outside school hours.

Non-academic long-term effects include the development of greater self-direction, greater self-discipline, more independent learning and problem-solving, better time organization and more inquisitiveness. Finally, homework can be used to complete tasks that students were not able to complete in class.

Negative effects posited include satiation, as students become tired of studying, which can lead to a loss of motivation and loss of interest in academic work; cheating, copying either from fellow students or from published work; and lack of time for out-of-school leisure activities.

Cooper's review also suggests that while homework can significantly benefit student achievement the extent of these benefits differs by grade and subject. Homework appeared to have the largest positive effect for science and social studies, and the smallest effect for mathematics. Reading and English were in the middle.

Grade differences were even stronger. Homework had the largest effect in high school (higher secondary), where students who received homework outperformed those who did not by 69 per cent. In junior high school (lower secondary) they outperformed no-homework students by 35 per cent, while in primary school students who received homework did not outperform their peers who did not receive homework. According to Cooper, homework at this level does have a positive impact, however, as it helps develop good study habits and attitudes towards school and learning.

Other American reviews have also provided support for the view that setting homework can improve students' achievement. (e.g. Keith 1987; Foyle and Bailey, 1988; Faulkner and Blyth, 1995). Keith found that homework was particularly effective for students from disadvantaged backgrounds.

Rutter *et al.* (1979), studying British secondary schools, found a strong positive relationship between the number of minutes of homework assigned and students' achievement, attitudes towards school and attendance.

A study in Israel likewise found a positive effect for homework, students who were said by their teachers to complete more homework receiving higher teacher grades (Chen and Ehrenberg, 1993). However, it is clear that this could be as much the result of higher-achieving students having more positive attitudes to school and therefore completing more homework than the other way round.

Some studies do not find positive effects, however. Thus, in a British secondary school study, Cassidy (1999) reported no positive effects on achievement in classrooms in which more homework was assigned. Some research has also pointed to negative effects of too much homework

Overall, then, homework does seem to be an effective learning tool, especially for students in the higher grades. However, this conclusion leaves many questions unanswered, such as how homework should be most effectively employed. These will be looked at now.

Effective use of homework

In order for homework to be an effective learning tool, it needs to adhere to a number of principles.

The first principle, which goes against a lot of present classroom practice, is *not to use homework as a punishment*. Doing so will lead to students resenting homework, and to homework not being seen as a learning activity. Students will get the impression that the teacher does not value homework as a learning tool, and will attempt to complete it as quickly and perfunctorily as possible. As a way of motivating students or extending learning outside the classroom, this practice can be very harmful (Cooper, 1989).

That the teacher is taking homework seriously is also indicated by the way she or he does or does not provide *feedback* on homework. Homework should be marked and returned as soon as possible. It should always be properly corrected, as uncorrected homework gives students the impression that all that matters is completing the task, no matter how. This will obviously not encourage them to make an effort to produce correct or quality work, and will thus not aid student learning. One way to do this that saves marking time is to let students correct each other's homework. As students are usually asked to complete homework within a set time frame, marking and returning homework speedily will set the right example and not give students the impression that different rules apply to student and teacher. One of the findings of Cooper's (1989) overview was that homework that is checked contributes more to student achievement than homework that is assigned but not checked. Ornstein (1994) suggests that it is better to give less homework but correct it, rather than give more homework which remains uncorrected. Cooper (1989) suggests that feedback on homework should be instructional rather than graded. This because grading homework might lead to students losing intrinsic motivation to do homework and lead to them completing it out of fear of bad grades instead.

Corrected homework can also provide helpful feedback to teachers on students' progress in the subject. One way of increasing the usefulness of homework as a feedback tool for teachers is to log beforehand how long she or he expects the homework to take. Students can then be asked to write on the homework sheet how long it has actually taken them to complete it. If this period is particularly long, this could be an indication that the student is having problems understanding that particular topic.

Homework should also be integrated into the lesson or topic studied. One way to do this is to review homework at the start of the lesson. When routinely done, this will ensure that homework is seen as an integral part of the lesson and may also be a good way to link previous and current lessons. While practice of skills during homework can be necessary, research does suggest that homework is most effective when it reinforces major curriculum ideas (Black, 1997). Homework should be challenging, but students should be able to complete it successfully. It should not be confusing or frustrating for students. According to Cooper, almost all students should be able to successfully complete homework, which should therefore not be used as a way of testing students. One way to help achieve this, which can also help overcome some of the problems involved with teaching a heterogeneous set of students, is to individualize homework, so that it is tailored to students' levels in the subject.

A way of making homework more relevant to students is to connect what they have learnt in the classroom to their *everyday life*, for example by using television guides to help them learn the time by looking at when their favourite programmes are on, by measuring their room and estimating how much paint would be needed to paint it and how much that would cost, or by interviewing relatives to learn something about local history or media use habits. Preparing new topics by asking students to bring in material they have collected, such as leaves of different types for a biology lesson, can also help achieve this aim. Researching something on the Internet can likewise be both useful and enjoyable, though in-school provisions need to be available for those students who do not have a computer or Internet link at home. Apart from heightening the relevance of homework, using real-life experience and materials in homework can help students to more easily remember what they have learnt in school (Boers and Caspary, 1995).

Homework planners can help students develop independent learning and organizational skills. Homework planners can, for example, take the form of a small calendar, in which students have to note what homework they need to be doing and when they have to complete it. Students will need to be taught how to use homework planners initially, but will find them very useful once taught. Using homework planners can help students develop good study habits, and use of planners is recommended practice for other forms of independent study as well.

If homework is not completed, consequences need to be attached to this, such as making students complete homework during breaks, giving them a negative mark in a behaviour log, withdrawing privileges, etc. If no negative consequences follow non-completion of homework, students will soon start to take it less seriously leading to non-completion becoming an endemic problem.

Homework does not have to be a solitary activity as it is possible to set co-operative homework tasks. These can take the form of co-operative research assignments or tasks which require two or more students to work together to complete it. As with co-operative work in general it is necessary to ascertain that students have the necessary social skills to work co-operatively and, if this is not the case, to teach them these skills first (see Chapter 9). Both joint goals and individual accountability are likewise necessary for co-operative homework to be successful.

As was remarked in the overview of research above, the effectiveness of homework seems to differ according to grade level. Also, it is a well-known fact that as they get older students' concentration levels and independent learning abilities increase. This leads to the question of how much homework to assign at the different grade levels.

School-wide homework policies

In order for homework to be most effective, a school-wide approach is recommended. Research in school effectiveness has found homework to be important (e.g. Rutter *et al.*, 1979), and more generally school-wide policies that support classroom practice are considered to contribute to school effectiveness (Creemers, 1994).

One of the benefits of school-wide policies is that they can create an ethos in which all students feel they are treated the same, as all teachers apply the same rules. Also, school-wide co-ordination can help avoid the problems that can occur when different teachers give large amounts of homework to be completed during the same period. Furthermore, school-wide policies on homework, as on other aspects of school life, help create equity within the school with all students benefiting from the same level of homework whoever is their teacher.

School-wide policies can take a variety of forms. A set amount of homework per week in different subjects can be helpful, as can establishing set nights to do homework in different subjects (e.g. Monday is mathematics homework day). Developing some form of standardization for such things as homework headings can save time and effort, as can the use of standardized school-wide homework planners. Homework policies should also contain guidelines for teachers on systematically correcting and returning homework within a specified time frame. The policy should also set out what is expected from parents.

Use of homework clubs and opening the school library after hours can help students who have difficulty completing homework at home. School-wide co-ordination of such activities is necessary, though, so that facilities do not become too full and a sufficient number of support staff are available.

For the youngest children too much homework can be harmful as they are already tired when they come home from school and homework can put extra pressure on them. Thus, in primary school, some researchers advocate not assigning homework, not least in the light of the fact that no effects on achievement were found. There are a number of reasons to assign at least some homework to primary age students, though. One is to help students develop their independent learning skills and help attain the attitude that learning can take place outside of school as well as in school. However, it is clear that young children should not be overburdened by homework. It is generally recommended that children from nursery to the first three or four years of primary school should spend at most 20 minutes a day doing homework, and no more than 30–40 minutes a day in the upper primary years.

As children move to secondary school, the evidence on the positive effects of homework becomes stronger, and there is clear support for setting homework at this level. The development of young people allows for more time to be spent on homework and, as the student becomes older, the development of independent learning skills becomes ever more important in the light of the move to higher education and the workforce. Therefore, daily homework is recommended for secondary school students, which can take up to 90 minutes a day (Cooper, 1989).

Apart from differences in the amount of time to be spent doing homework, homework at different grades will also serve different purposes and may therefore take different forms. As students grow up more complex tasks can be assigned, which can be increasingly long term, including writing papers based on some kind of extended research.

Parental involvement with homework

The attitude of parents to homework is often ambiguous. On the one hand they believe it may aid their children's school achievement, and may see homework as a good way of finding out more about what their children are actually doing at school, on the other hand they may feel that it takes time away from other worthwhile activities, and some parents may be at a loss as to how best to help their children to do their homework successfully.

One of the main ways in which parents can help their children is to provide a quiet and private space where the child can do her or his homework. This does not necessarily mean that parents should make sure that children turn the radio off or do not listen to music. On the contrary, according to some research listening to music can aid concentration (Hallam and Cowan, 1999). Probably this will differ from child to child and children should be allowed to listen to music while studying or completing homework if they feel comfortable doing so.

Parents should encourage their children to complete their homework and should support their children when they ask for help without actually doing the homework for them. Showing an interest in homework will help give children the feeling that homework is important and valued. Parents can also help by establishing a routine in which a certain time of the day is set aside for homework completion. If possible, parents can help students develop their time management and organizational skills, although some guidance from the school can be necessary to help parents do this. This is particularly important with younger children, who need more parental help to successfully complete their homework assignments. Secondary school children should largely be able to complete homework independently.

The school can help parents by giving them the information they need and regularly communicating with them on homework. If there is a school-wide homework policy this should be communicated to parents. Teachers should let parents know how much homework they plan to assign and approximately how long assignments should take. The homework planner, mentioned above, can be used to communicate to parents what homework has been assigned, and it might be useful to ask parents to sign the planner as well. If there are consistent problems with a child not completing assignments or completing them to a standard that is well below what one would expect or what the child seems able to do in class, teachers should discuss this with parents to ascertain whether there are circumstances at home, such as lack of a quiet working space, that may hinder the child completing homework satisfactorily. If possible, teachers should involve parents in developing a strategy to solve the problem. It is important to remember, though, that parents may not be aware of what is happening while students do their homework due to them returning late from work, for example (Hoover Dempsey, Bassler and Burow, 1995). It is also important to provide support to parents on how to help students because confusion can result from students receiving different advice or methods from parents than they do from teachers at school.

Especially with younger children, parents should be encouraged to do some homework activities with their children, such as reading aloud to them or playing games with them. Explaining to parents at the beginning of the school year how they can help in this way will be helpful to them, as will designing certain homework assignments for students to work on with parents. One method that can help involve parents in their children's homework is to give homework in the form of games that can be played with parents and siblings while reinforcing principles that needed to be learnt (Bryan and Sullivan-Burstein, 1997).

For some parents, especially if they suffer socio-economic deprivation, it may be impossible to provide the calm, supportive space needed for children to be able to successfully complete homework. A small minority of parents may not even be willing to do so. Here the school can help out by providing students with the space they need by setting up in-school homework clubs where students can come to study and complete homework outside school hours, as has successfully been done in schools in a wide number of countries, including the UK.

A further problem may be the differential access that children have to material in the home that they can use for research purposes, for example. This can be a particular problem with homework assignments that do not provide merely practice of the day's lesson, but ask students to do research on a topic or find out something to prepare for coming topics. Here again the school can help out by providing library facilities that students can access outside school hours.

Summary

Homework can fulfil a number of different goals, such as increasing student achievement, reinforcing and strengthening topics taught in class, completing unfinished work, developing independent study skills and involving parents in helping students' learning.

Most studies have found homework to be an effective way of improving students' achievement. However, this positive effect is not uniform across grades, being strongest in the latter years of secondary school and weakest in primary school where no significant effect was found. Homework can still be useful for primary age students, however, as it helps develop independent learning skills, helps foster the attitude that learning can occur outside as well as in school, and helps develop students' organizational skills.

In order for homework to be effective, a number of elements have to be taken into account, though. It is imperative that homework should not be used as a form of punishment. Students should receive feedback on homework as soon as possible so they will realize homework is valued and important. For this reason homework should also be an integral part of the lesson. One goal of homework can be to allow students to connect school work to life outside school. This can be done by making sure that assignments use real-life experience and materials collected in the students' environment as much as possible. Use of homework planners can help students develop their organizational skills and can provide useful practice for other forms of independent learning. The amount of time students should spend doing homework increases as students get older, from no more than 20 minutes per day in the early primary years up to 90 minutes a day in the higher secondary grades.

Parents can help their children by providing them with a quiet space to complete their homework, by encouraging them to complete their assignments and, especially for younger students, by helping them if necessary. Teachers can help parents by regularly communicating with them on what homework has been assigned and what is expected from students. If there are problems with a student's homework completion, teachers should discuss with parents what can be done to alleviate these problems.

Some parents may not be able to help their children or provide them with a quiet study environment. Homework clubs, where students can come to school to do homework after school hours and teachers are available to help them, can help solve this problem.

Self-study questions

1. Is homework an effective learning tool for primary school students?
2. Why should homework not be used as a punishment?
3. What benefits could a school-wide homework policy have?
4. What can parents do to help their students complete their homework assignments successfully?
5. Should homework be graded?
6. What are the possible disadvantages of homework?
7. How much and what kind of homework should be given to students of different ages?
8. How can teachers help ensure that students value homework?

8

Problem-Solving and Higher-Order Thinking Skills

Advance organizers

In this chapter you will learn:

- Why there is an increasing focus on thinking skills in education.
- What learning theories underlie research into thinking skills and problem-solving.
- The main elements of the heuristic approach to problem-solving.
- The main aspects of the metacognitive approach to thinking skills.
- The main aspects of the formal operations based approach to thinking skills.

Introduction

In recent years, there has been an increased emphasis on teaching thinking skills and problem-solving in school. This has been caused in part by research that has pointed to the link between students' generic thinking skills and their achievement in school subjects such as mathematics, but also by changes in society especially the move towards a society in which knowledge and information are becoming ever more complex and ever more quickly redundant. This means that increasingly possessing a large amount of knowledge is insufficient. Children and adults will need to possess the skills to make choices and to solve problems using logical reasoning (Resnick, 1987).

For this reason an increasing number of programmes have been developed that aim to improve students' thinking skills. These are usually based on one of three main learning theories (see 'Piaget, Vygotsky and the cognitive model' box), and can be classified into three main areas (e.g. Nickerson *et al*, 1985; Hamers and Csapo, 1999):

1. Based on Piagetian theories, the *formal thinking* approach aims to help students to more easily make the transition between the various stages they are supposed to pass through according to Piaget's theories. Thinking-skills programmes taking this approach will tend to integrate their programme in regular classroom teaching.

2. Another approach is to teach students a number of problem-solving skills, the so-called *heuristic* approach. The task will first be analysed so that it can be broken down into manageable subsets. These can then be tackled using problem-solving strategies that have been taught previously. Programmes based on this approach will often be content-free.

3. Finally the *metacognitive* approach starts from the premise that performance can be improved through a better understanding and awareness of one's own thought processes. Teaching students this self-awareness is the mainstay of this approach.

These three approaches have all generated programmes aimed at improving students' thinking skills. We will discuss approaches based on these three theories in the following sections.

Heuristic problem-solving strategies

In the heuristic approach, the aim is to learn specific problem-solving skills, which students can use when they have to take on any particular problem. To do this more easily, the problem-solving process needs to be deconstructed into its composite parts. A lot of research in this paradigm has been done on solving word problems, for example mathematical questions in context (e.g. a bus, travelling from Antwerp to Brussels (40 km) sets out at the same time as a car travelling in the other direction. The bus travels at 90 km per hour, the car at 120 km per hour. After how many kilometres will they cross one another?) The following sequence has been proposed: (1) understanding and representing the problem; (2) selecting or planning the solution; (3) executing the plan; and (4) evaluating the results (Polya, cited in Orton, 1992).

Understanding and representing the problem

The first step in problem-solving is finding out exactly what the problem means. This entails finding the relevant information in the problem and disentangling what is relevant to solving the problem from those elements that are not. This is typically a situation that is created in mathematical word problems, in which students have to find the relevant mathematical problem from within the contextual information that surrounds it. As well as identifying the problem, it is necessary to develop an accurate representation of the problem. This requires two main elements. The first is *linguistic understanding*, which means that the student needs to understand the full meaning of all sentences in the problem. This entails more than just understanding the words, as it also means that students need to understand the logical structure of the sentences. Students usually have more problems with relational propositions (e.g. bus A goes 10 miles per hour faster than bus B) than with assignment propositions (e.g. a

Piaget, Vygotsky and the cognitive model: learning theories that have influenced thinking skills research

Piaget's stages of development
A number of learning theories have strongly influenced research on thinking skills and the development of thinking skills programmes. The first of these is Piaget's theory of the development of thinking in children and adults. The Swiss psychologist Jean Piaget (1896–1980) argued that in order to understand how children think one has to look at the qualitative development of their ability to solve problems. Cognitive development, in his view, is much more than the addition of new facts and ideas to an existing fund of information. Rather, children's thinking changes qualitatively; the tools which children use to think change, leading children and adults, and indeed children at different stages of development, to possess a different view of the world. A child's reality is not the same as that of an adult.

According to Piaget, one of the main influences on children's cognitive development is what he termed *maturation*, the unfolding of biological changes that are genetically programmed into us at birth. A second factor is *activity*. Increasing maturation leads to an increase in children's ability to act on their environment, and to learn from their actions. This learning in turn leads to an alteration of children's thought processes. A third factor in development is *social transmission*, learning from others. As children act on their environment, they also interact with others and can therefore learn from them to a differing degree depending on their developmental stage.

According to Piaget, learning occurs in four stages:

1. *The sensori-motor stage (0–2 years)*
The baby knows about the world through actions and sensory information. She or he learns to differentiate her or himself from the environment. The child begins to understand causality in time and space. The capacity to form internal mental representations emerges.

2. *The pre-operational stage (2–7 years)*
In this stage children take the first steps from action to thinking, by internalising action. In the previous stage children's schemes were still completely tied to actions, which means that they are of no use in recalling the past or in prediction. To accomplish these one needs to make these schemes symbolic, and that is one of the main developments during the pre-operational stage. The ability to think in symbols remains limited in this stage, however, as the child can only think in one direction. Thinking backwards or reversing the steps of a task are difficult.

Another innovation that starts to take place during this phase is the ability to understand conservation. This means that the child can now realize that the amount or number of something remains the same even if the arrangement or appearance of it is changed. This remains difficult for children in this phase. Children in this phase still have great difficulty freeing themselves from their own perception of how the world appears. Children at this age are also very egocentric. They tend to see the world and the experiences of others from their own standpoint.

3. *The concrete operational stage (7–12 years)*
The basic characteristics of this stage are: (a) the recognition of the logical stability of the physical world, (b) the realization that elements can be changed or transformed and still retain their original characteristics, and (c) the understanding that these changes can be reversed.

Another important operation that is mastered at this stage is classification. Classification depends on a student's ability to focus on a single characteristic of objects and then to group the objects according to that single characteristic (e.g. if one gives a student a set of differently coloured and differently shaped pens, they will able to pick out the round ones). Students can now also understand seriation, allowing them to construct a logical series in which A is less than B is less than C and so on. Thus at this stage the child has developed a logical and systematic way of thinking which is, however, still tied to physical reality. Overcoming this is the task of the next phase.

4. *The formal operational stage (12+)*
In this stage, which is not reached by all students, all that is learned in previous stages remains in force but students are now able to see that a real actually experienced situation is only one of several possible situations. In order for this to occur students must be able to generate different possibilities for any given situation in a systematic way. This includes scientific reasoning. Students are now able to imagine ideal, non-existing worlds. Another characteristic of this stage is adolescent egocentrism. Adolescents tend to incessantly analyse their own beliefs and attitudes, and often assume that everyone else shares their concerns and is in turn analysing them. A goal of many thinking-skills programmes, such as CASE (see below), is to help students get to the formal operational stage.

Vygotsky's social constructivism
Alongside the influence of Piaget, another major influence on constructivist thought has been the work of his contemporary, the Soviet psychologist Lev Vygotsky.

Vygotsky's main interest was the study of language development, which he believed initially develops separately from thought, but starts to overlap with thought more and more as the child grows up. According to Vygotsky, a non-overlapping part still remains later in life, some non-verbal thought and some non-conceptual speech remaining even in adults.

A major disagreement between Piaget and Vygotsky was that Vygotsky did not think that maturation in itself could make children achieve advanced thinking skills. Vygotsky, while seeing a role for maturation, believed that it was children's interaction with others through language that most strongly influenced the level of conceptual understanding they could reach.

Vygotsky thus believed that we can learn from others, both of the same age and of a higher age and developmental level. One of the main ways this operates is through *scaffolding* in the *zone of proximal development*. This latter concept, one of Vygotsky's main contributions to learning theory, refers to the gap between what a person is able to do alone and what she or he can do with the help of someone more knowledgeable or skilled than her or himself. It is here that the role of teachers, adults and peers comes to the fore in children's learning, in that they can help bring the child's knowledge to a higher level by intervening in the zone of proximal development by providing children's thoughts with so-called scaffolds, which once the learning process is complete are no longer needed by the child. Not all children are as *educable* in this respect, some being able to learn more in the zone of proximal development than others.

Thus, for Vygotsky, it is *co-operation* that lies at the basis of learning. It is – formal and informal – *instruction* performed by more knowledgeable others, such as parents, peers, grandparents or teachers that is the main means of transition of the knowledge of a particular culture. Knowledge for Vygotsky, as for Piaget, is embodied in actions and interactions with the environment (or culture), but unlIke Piaget, Vygotsky stresses the importance of *interaction* with a living representative of the culture.

Information processing theory
While a number of researchers have continued to develop Piaget's developmental theories, others have gone in a different direction and have constructed the *information processing model* of human development.

The basic assumptions of information processing theory are based on the analogy of people-as-computers. Humans are, according to this view, information processors who construct symbolic representations of the world. Especially important in this theory is the role of memory in learning processes. The memory consists of three parts: the sensory buffer, the working memory and the long-term memory. (Figure 8.1)

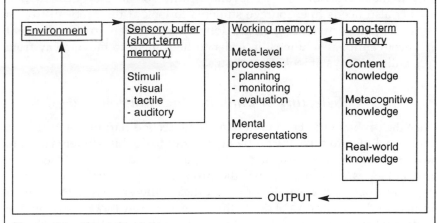

Figure 8.1   Structure of memory

The memory works as follows: one's experiences (tactile, visual or auditory) are registered in the sensory buffer, and then converted into the form in which they are employed in the working and long-term memories. The sensory buffer can register a lot of information but can only hold it briefly. Some parts of the information in it will be lost, other parts will be transmitted to the working memory. The working memory is where 'thinking gets done'. It receives its content from the sensory buffer and the long-term memory but has a limited capacity for storing information, a fact that limits human mental processes. The working memory contains the information that is actively being used at any one time.

The long-term memory has a nodal structure, and consists of neural network representations whose nodes represent chunks in memory and whose links represent connections between those chunks. As such, nodes can be equated with concepts and links with meaningful associations between concepts. Together these form schemata, or clusters of information. Activating one item of the cluster is likely to activate all of them.

bus ticket costs 35 pence). Once all sentences have been understood students have to assemble them into a whole, and have to be able to understand the whole problem. Many students tend to decide too quickly what the problem is, based on observable cues. It is therefore important that they are taught to unravel problems thoughtfully, reading the whole problem before deciding what the question is (Woolfolk, 1997).

One way of helping students do this is by letting them see many different kinds of examples worked out for them. This has been found to be more effective than just giving a few examples and then having students solve problems on their own. One can also help students by teaching them to recognize and categorize different problem types and to select relevant and irrelevant information contained in the problem. The teacher needs to make sure that students understand the problem by asking them to explain it to other students, by asking them to verbalize the assumptions they are working under, and by asking them to make clear what they think is relevant and irrelevant information in the question. The teacher also needs to encourage students to look at the problem from a variety of perspectives. This can be done by asking them to offer different or unconventional solutions, in order to help them to move away from conventional ways of looking at things.

Selecting or planning the solution

Once the problem has been understood, the second part of the process is to design a plan to solve the problem. In order to do this, students need to have a general problem-solving strategy, a so-called *heuristic*. One of the best strategies is to break down the problem into a number of smaller steps and then find a way to work out these different steps. There are a number of different ways of doing this. One is *working backwards*, from the goal to the unsolved initial problem. Solving mathematical proofs can often usefully be tackled in this way. Another strategy is to use *analogical thinking*. This means limiting the search for solutions to strategies the student has already used to solve problems that resemble the problem faced at present. Explaining strategies selected can help as well, as it can lead to students more clearly understanding the problem-solving sequence. Research has shown that students who were asked to explain each step in their problem solving were more successful than students who were not asked to do this (Gagne, 1965).

Having done this, students should be able to choose a right *algorithm* for each part of the problem. An algorithm is a step-by-step procedure to achieve something, which is usually subject (or topic) specific (e.g. computations in maths). A problem that occurs when students have not carefully selected a heuristic is that they will tend to randomly apply algorithms, based not on understanding the problem but on the understanding that, for example, certain algorithms have been used in mathematics lessons before so they think might as well try them here. Students will then go through a number of standard algorithms in a random way. In some cases this may even lead to the right result eventually, but obviously no real understanding will have been achieved. This is another reason to make students explain their answers.

Teaching heuristics can be aided by asking students to explain the steps they are taking as they are solving the problem. The different types of heuristics mentioned above can be explicitly taught.

Executing the plan

The third part of the process involves finding the actual solution to the problem. If the heuristic chosen in the previous step has led to the right plan with respect to which algorithm to use this step is usually straightforward, entailing merely the application of the chosen algorithm. However, many students do make algorithmic mistakes, so a good knowledge of the basic algorithms is necessary for effective problem-solving.

Evaluating the results

The final step is checking the answer. A common-sense, but often forgotten, check is simply to consider whether the answer makes sense. For example, an answer of 7,000 miles per hour when calculating the speed of a car clearly indicates a mistake in either calculation, choice of algorithm or heuristic. Estimation can help here, for example, if the answer involves calculating 101×31, it can easily be estimated that the answer will be somewhat over 3,000. Also, students need to check for all evidence and data that could contradict (or confirm) their answer.

To be effective in developing higher-order thinking skills problems need to follow a number of rules. Problems should be new activities, which are meaningful to the students and which must be sufficiently close to their current level of knowledge to be assimilated, and yet sufficiently different to force them to transform their methods of thinking and working and develop their understanding. This means that such problems are by definition 'difficult', though not too difficult (Sosniak and Etherington, 1994; Grugnett and Jaquet, 1996). Problems can be made easier for students by using familiar, real life contexts and by the use of pictures (Hembree, 1992).

That heuristic training can be effective was shown in a meta-analysis of problem-solving studies conducted by Hembree (1992), who reports that children who had received instruction in problem-solving skills performed significantly better than children who had not.

The metacognitive approach

An important element in problem-solving is metacognition. This term basically encompasses knowledge about one's own thought processes, self-regulation and monitoring what one is doing, why one is doing it and how what one is doing helps to solve the problem (or not). This allows one to ascertain whether the strategies one is using are effective, and thus to change strategies if necessary (Schoenfeld, 1992). It is clear that these kinds of skills are of great importance to children not only to develop their problem-solving skills but to develop thinking skills more generally. Developed metacognition will also lead students to be more aware of their own strengths and weaknesses (Schoenfeld, 1987; Lester, 1994). Lack of metacognition leads to children using ineffective (correct but slow or inefficient) problem-solving strategies. In order to learn more effectively, therefore, metacognitive processes must be brought out into the open and self-regulation needs to become a conscious process.

Schoenfeld (1987) suggests a number of techniques to teach children metacognitive strategies:

1. Develop awareness of thinking processes among students. To do this it is important to explain why problem-solving strategies are important. Schoenfeld suggests activities such as showing a video of other students engaged in co-operative problem-solving, so that students can see others using ineffective problem-solving strategies. This can impress upon them the importance of awareness of what one is doing.
2. Work problems through on the wallboard by presenting the whole problem resolution rather than just the neat solution. Both this technique and the one previously presented are useful because they bring certain behaviours to centre stage and highlight the importance of metacognitive skills. They must be used sparingly, though.
3. Let the class as a whole work on a problem, with the teacher taking the role of moderator of student discussion. The students will choose to do certain things which may or may not be right. If their strategy does not turn out well new solutions should be tried until the right solution has been found. This should be followed by a debriefing conducted by the teacher. This activity has been found to help self-regulation.

Developing metacognitive skills can also be aided through specific activities. Co-operative group work can be used to this effect, not least because of the scaffolding that it makes possible. It has been suggested that students working in small groups can be given cards containing a number of basic questions that should help them to think about their own thinking. These include: 'What am I doing now?', 'Is it getting me anywhere?' and 'What else could I be doing instead?' (Salomon and Perkins, 1989). This will help them reflect on their problem-solving, until in due course this 'scaffold' (the cards) can be removed once students have internalized metacognitive thinking.

A major criticism of thinking-skills programmes like those discussed above is that they are content-free. Some research has suggested that it is better to teach heuristics and problem-solving in a highly contextualized way, connecting the techniques to students' existing knowledge (Perkins and Salomon, 1989). Teaching heuristics or thinking skills in a decontextualized, stand-alone fashion has shown rather mixed effects in teaching thinking skills.

Heuristics intervention programmes

Apart from applying the general guidelines given here, a number of researchers have put into place specific intervention programmes aimed at improving students' thinking skills.

One of the best known is De Bono's CoRT programme. This is a content-free thinking-skills programme for secondary school students (and adults). This approach sets out to teach a number of heuristics such as looking for the plus points, minus points and interesting points in any situation (PMI), considering all factors in a situation (CAF), exploring the consequences of decisions (consequence and sequel, C&S), and looking at goals, orders and objectives (AGO). In total CoRt consist of 60 lessons. The effectiveness of the programme has been evaluated in a number of studies, but results have been inconclusive (Edwards, 1991).

Feuerstein's instrumental enrichment (IE) programme tries to address a range of thinking skills, such as seriation, classification, verbal reasoning, numerical ability and spatial relations. While this programme, like CoRT, is not subject specific and is taught in specific IE lessons, it differs from the former in that rather than directly teaching heuristics, it attempts to teach strategies designed to help students find their own heuristics when they are confronted with a particular problem. Students will, for example, learn strategies to gather information, use information gathered, and express the solution to a programme.

Evaluations carried out in Israel, where the programme was developed, showed positive effects on school achievement and general intelligence (Feuerstein *et al.*, 1980; Rand *et al.*, 1981). However, an American study showed no effect (possibly due to weaknesses in study design). Two different studies were carried out in the UK, one showing positive effects, the other no effects (Shayer and Beasley, 1989)

Improving formal thinking: cognitive acceleration in science and mathematics

In the light of the problems involved in teaching students heuristics and thinking skills out of context, a number of intervention programmes have been designed that have aimed to teach thinking skills within a particular subject.

One of the first such programmes that tried to use the principles of instrumental enrichment within specific subject contexts rather than in separate lessons was the Somerset Thinking Skills programme in the UK (Blagg, Ballinger and Gardner, 1988).

One of the most effectively worked out cognitive intervention programmes is the CASE (Cognitive Acceleration in Science Education) project, designed by Adey and Shayer (1994) in the UK. This project is based on Piagetian and Vygotskian thinking in that the aim is to bring students up to the formal operational thinking stage (see 'Piaget, Vygotsky and the cognitive model' box), in part through making them work as much as possible in their zone of proximal development. The programme is subject-specific, developed for science and containing specific science topics in each lesson. More recently, a related Cognitive Acceleration in Mathematics (CAME) project has been developed as well.

The project, containing 52 lessons, has five main elements:

1. Concrete preparation to introduce the necessary vocabulary and clarify the terms in which the problem is to be set. This means that the teacher needs to set the problem in context, and explain the meaning of the vocabulary that the student will need. An example given by Adey and Shayer (1994) is that of introducing the concept of relationships. First, the students must be introduced to the concept in a simple way, not least by giving examples in which no relationship exists.
2. The teacher needs to introduce 'cognitive conflict'. This occurs when students are introduced to an experience which they find puzzling or which contradicts their prior knowledge or understanding. This can lead to students moving towards their zone of proximal development, but only if the activity is well managed by the teacher. Otherwise the danger exists that the discordant information will simply be dismissed or distorted to fit students' existing schemata.
3. Students then need to move on to a *construction zone* activity. This is an activity which ensures that students go beyond their current levels of understanding and competencies. This has been facilitated by the cognitive conflict, which has forced students to challenge their own preconceived notions and thought processes. Teachers can help students do this by helping them to build up step by step the higher-level reasoning patterns they need to access.
4. Students need to reflect consciously on their problem-solving (metacognition) in ways similar to those described above.
5. Students then need to 'bridge' their new skills or knowledge, i.e. be able to apply them in different contexts. A number of the methods proposed above can be used to facilitate this.

CASE lessons typically involve a lot of student–teacher and student–student interaction, and often collaborative group work as well. The teacher's role is obviously an important one, and a lot of what has been described here may sound somewhat daunting to beginning teachers. While this method does indeed require good classroom management and interactive teaching skills and the self-confidence to allow a lot of student direction in the lesson, the programme developers provide worked-out material for each lesson as well as professional development training activities.

Some highly positive effects of this method have been reported, in that students involved in the project performed significantly better on the age-16 national science examination in the UK (GCSE exams) than a matched control group, not just in science but in other subjects as well. This would suggest that the thinking skills obtained do transfer to other subjects as well. Interestingly, no effects were found on a post-test given to students following the intervention, suggesting that the effects may lag and be long term rather than having strong short-term effects.

Transfer of thinking skills

One of the problems with both the heuristic and the metacognitive methods is transfer of the skills learned in the 'real' world, outside the classroom. A problem can be that the techniques and heuristics learnt can be applied easily to classroom problems that are very similar to the problems that first demonstrated the heuristic, but that when they are confronted with new problems in or outside of the classroom students will revert to inefficient random application of algorithms or guessing. While it is difficult to totally counter these problems, there are a number of strategies teachers can follow to make transfer more likely.

Actively involving students in their learning is one such strategy. Students who have been actively involved in learning, through discussion, interactive teaching, independent research or experiments, have been found to be more likely to transfer their knowledge to other situations.

When teaching new concepts it is important that they are practised in a wide range of different problems. Simply repeating similar problems is likely to lead to the student only transferring the skills learned to the same type of problem. Practice should include some unstructured, complex problems of the type the student may encounter in real life.

Forms of simulation in which the learning takes place in an environment similar to that in which it will be applied also aids transfer. An example of this is driving lessons, which usually take place at least partly along the routes to be followed during the driving test.

Overlearning, practising a skill until it becomes automatic, has also been found to aid transfer. For example, most people taught times tables at school can still use them in later life when confronted with multiplication problems.

Finally, teachers can draw students' attention to the thinking skills learnt in previous lessons when during a lesson a situation occurs in which use of these skills will be useful.

A number of methods that can encourage students' thinking skills were discussed in Chapters 1, 2 and 3 on direct instruction. These include asking students higher-order and open questions and making sure they verbalize their answers and explain their thought processes, and allowing student discussion and input into the lesson. Teachers can also make sure that lessons (and tests) focus on processes as well as, or more than, on outcomes. This can be aided by giving marks for incorrect solutions if the processes used are good.

However, not all the recommendations given in the chapters on direct instruction are in accordance with those recommended by thinking-skills researchers. One of these is pace. If students are to develop problem-solving and thinking skills by doing demanding problems they need to have the time to solve the problem. This may necessitate giving over a large part of the lesson to individual or group work. When presenting a problem the teacher must not give too many clues as students need to be encouraged to think over the problem for themselves. Therefore, while the effective teaching methods discussed under direct instruction are the best way to teach basic skills or topics which necessitate transfer of content, an exclusive reliance on this technique could lead to neglect of another important and basic part of teaching, developing students' higher order cognitive skills.

Summary

In this chapter we looked at ways of enhancing students' thinking skills and problem-solving, something which has received increasing attention in education in response to societal developments.

Three main learning theories underlie thinking-skills research and practice. Piaget's learning theory posits that students go through a number of developmental phases: the sensori-motor phase, the pre-operational phase, the concrete operational phase and the formal operational phase, that entail qualitative changes in their thinking. Programmes based on this theory will try to get students to reach a higher phase, eventually culminating in the formal operational phase, which is not reached by all adults.

Vygotsky emphasizes the role of social interaction in learning. Learning, according to him, occurs in the 'zone of proximal development'. This is the zone in which students surpass their present level of skills and knowledge and move to a higher level without being so far advanced from their present level that they cannot understand it. In order to achieve learning at this level they need 'scaffolding', in which another student or adult assists them to attain this higher level of learning.

Finally, information processing theory focuses on the role of memory. According to this theory, memory consists of three parts. The sensory buffer can register a lot of information, but can only hold it briefly. Some parts of the information in it will be lost, other parts will be transmitted to the working memory. The working memory is where 'thinking gets done'. It receives its content from the sensory buffer and the long-term memory but has a limited capacity for storing information, a fact that limits human mental processes. The working memory contains the information that is actively being used at any one time. The long-term memory has a nodal structure, and consists of neural network representations whose nodes represent chunks in memory and whose links represent connections between those chunks.

Heuristic thinking skills programmes like CoRT aim to teach specific problem-solving skills which students can use when they have to take on any particular problem. To do this more easily, the problem-solving process needs to be deconstructed into its composite parts. Polya proposed the following sequence: (1) understanding and representing the problem; (2) selecting or planning the solution; (3) executing the plan; and (4) evaluating the results (Polya, cited in Orton, 1992).

Metacognitive strategies aim to improve students' conscious self-regulation. The term refers to knowledge about one's own thought processes and monitoring what one is doing, why one is doing it and how what one is doing helps to solve the problem (or not). This allows one to ascertain whether the strategies one is using are effective, and thus to change strategies if necessary. A number of strategies have been proposed to enhance students' metacognitive strategies, by for example making them work in small groups and providing them with cards telling them to reflect on 'What am I doing now?', 'Is it getting me anywhere?' and 'What else could I be doing instead?'.

Finally, strategies based on Piagetian and Vygotskian thinking include the successful CASE programme, which is a subject-specific programme built around 52 science lessons.

A number of methods that can help easier transfer of knowledge to different contexts include practising problem-solving in different contexts, using complex real-life examples, reminding students of learnt thinking skills during relevant parts of other lessons and actively involving students in learning, and overlearning.

Self-study questions

1. Why can we say CASE has been influenced by Piagetian and Vygotskian thinking?
2. How can transfer of thinking skills be facilitated?
3. What is metacognition?
4. How can students be taught to find effective heuristics for problem solving?
5. What do you think teachers can do to help develop students' thinking skills during regular lessons?
6. Describe Piaget's four developmental stages.
7. What is information processing theory?
8. Shoenfeld suggested some methods to improve metacognitive skills. Can you describe them?

PART 2

TEACHING SPECIFIC SKILLS AND STUDENTS

9

Developing Students' Social Skills

Advance organizers

In this chapter you will learn:

- The importance of peer relations to children's development.
- Characteristics that may lead to children being unpopular with peers.
- How social skills can be taught or enhanced.
- What parents can do to help develop their children's social skills.
- How to help children suffering from persistent shyness.

Introduction

Peer relations are highly important to children's development. Friends provide companionship and support, allow children to take part in social recreational activities they cannot do on their own, and are important to students' social skill development. By interacting with peers, children will learn to join a group, make new friends, manage conflict and learn to co-operate. Therefore, there is a vicious circle for some children, in that lack of social skills makes it difficult for them to join a peer group, which in turn hinders the development of their social skills.

A great deal of research has been done into students' peer relations and social skills in recent decades, often using so-called socio-metric methods. Socio-metric research involves asking children to nominate peers whom they like or dislike. Children can then be categorized as either popular or unpopular based on the number of positive or negative choices they have received, and the characteristics of the popular and unpopular children can then be compared on a number of factors, such as school achievement. Another fruitful research method in this area is ethnographic research, in which the researcher spends a long period of time in the child's social setting, for example the school, and directly observes what social group-ings exist and which children participate in which ways in those groups.

Research has shown that children tend to fall into one of four categories with respect to their popularity in school (Kupersmidt and Coie, 1990):

- Popular children who have successfully established relationships with a variety of peers and social groups. They are well known and well liked in school and other social settings.

- Controversial students are well liked by a group of peers with whom they have successfully established social relations, but may be unpopular with other groups of children.
- Isolated children are not openly unpopular, but are often ignored by their classmates, and are not always a part of existing social groups.
- Rejected students are actively disliked and are often subjected to bullying or harassment from peers.

Children who experience rejection by peers are likely to be lonely and exhibit low self-esteem, as well as being more likely to drop out of school, to be involved in delinquent activities and to have lower school achievement (Parker and Asher, 1987). Isolation from peers is associated with a number of social and psychological adjustment problems such as low self-esteem and perceived competence (Moran and Eckenrode, 1991; Newcomb and Bagwell, 1996), and unpopular children are at risk of academic failure, mental health problems and later delinquency (De-Rosier, Kupersmidt and Patterson, 1994). Thus, Goodenow (1993) found identification with school belonging to be one of the main predictors of school motivation, while in Rotheram's (1987) study academic performance was highly related to the possession of social skills in elementary school children. Once a child is rejected by peers, she or he tends to stay rejected across settings. Early rejection also has a continuing impact on anti-social behaviour, DeRosier, Kupersmidt and Patterson (1994) reporting that aggression among their subjects was stronger the more times they had been rejected by peers in the past and the more proximal the last rejection. Furthermore, one rejection at an early age was still significantly associated with later aggression.

In a study of 881 5th graders, Parker and Asher (1993) report children who are not accepted by peers to have fewer best friends than average or highly accepted children, low-accepted children's friendships to be qualitatively less satisfying than high-accepted children's friendships, and low-accepted children to be more lonely than high or averagely accepted children. Roe (1983) found isolated adolescents to be very high television viewers, a result probably of both lack of peer-related leisure time activities and of the use of television as a companion. Van Schie *et al.* (1996) similarly report a significant relationship between computer-game playing and self-reported loneliness among primary school girls. Muijs (1997) likewise found unpopular children to be higher users of most electronic media, including television, computer games and music.

A question then is what causes friendships to develop, and what causes some children to become isolated from their peers. An important aspect is a child's social skills. Children are looking for friends who are fun to be with, make them feel good and are perceived as trustworthy. Similarity is also important, children with similar interests and backgrounds being more likely to form friendships. Which of these aspects is most important changes as children get older. Young children are largely concerned with whether or not their friends are fun to be with, while adolescents strongly value trust-worthiness and loyalty. Williams and Asher (1993) give the following list of characteristics for childhood and adolescent friendship choices:

Acceptance	Rejection
Is this child fun to be with?	
Sense of humour Resourceful/skilful Participatory/readily involved Co-operative	Aggressive/mean Disruptive Bossy/domineering Withdrawn/apprehensive Low cognitive skills
Is this child trustworthy?	
Reliable Honest Loyal	Aggressive/mean Dishonest Betrays confidence
Do we influence each other in ways I like?	
Co-operative Responsive	Aggressive/mean Bossy/domineering Resistant/rigid
Does this child facilitate and not undermine my goals?	
Co-operative Helpful	Disruptive Impulsive
Does this child make me feel good about myself?	
Supportive/kind Responsive Likes me	Insulting/demeaning Non-responsive Dislikes me
Is this child similar to me?	
Common values and interests Respect for peer conventions Same gender, race, age	Different values and interests Non-conformity to peer conventions Superior manner Handicapped

Of course, having one or two 'rejection characteristics' will not necessarily cause rejection. Rather, it is a collection of all these characteristics that is likely to be problematic. Research does show, however, that for a number of children many of these characteristics do indeed coalesce (Muijs, 2000).

Some ways of helping to develop children's social skills

It is important, when trying to improve the socials skills of unpopular children to focus not just on behaviours that seem to make them unpopular with other children (such as starting fights) but on developing their social skills more generally, as apart from these overt behaviours they may lack other social skills and find it difficult to know how to respond in social situations.

The first problem is how to find out what (less immediately obvious) skills the child may lack. In order to do this one needs to carefully observe the child in her or his interactions with peers and adults so one can ascertain both what skills the child already has and what skills she or he may be lacking. The observer needs to take account of what situation is being observed (is the child trying to maintain a conversation, join a group, play a game) and make notes on what is going on in order to be able to intervene where necessary. These observations can then be grouped under one of the six categories mentioned in the acceptance/ rejection list (is the child fun to be with, sense of humour, resourceful/ skilful, participatory/readily involved, co-operative) so both the child's strengths and weaknesses can be listed and the weaknesses can be addressed (Williams and Asher, 1993). Looking at the behaviour of children during organized games can be a good guide to their social skills in general (Dodge *et al.*, 1986).

One way of improving students' social skills is through social skills coaching. The underlying principle of social skills coaching is that children's social skills problems are often caused by the fact that children do not know what to do in social situations, and that they can be taught to overcome these deficiencies. The coaching thus involves direct instruction in crucial social skills. Williams and Asher (1993) suggest a three-part coaching session. The first part involves the coach (a responsive adult, for example the child's teacher) talking to the child about how to interact better with peers. While doing this the coach needs to focus on what the child should do, rather than what she or he should not do. The second part of the coaching involves practising the activity with other children. Finally, the coach and the child can discuss the use of the social concept during that activity. Social skills instruction should not just consist of a description of the skill and why it is important, but also explain and demonstrate how to implement the skill and when and why to implement it. Practising the skill is vital (Brophy, 1996). Sometimes it can be useful to practise the skill in a role-play before applying it to real-life situations. Modelling the desired behaviour by the teacher or other professionals in the school can contribute to the child's understanding of prosocial behaviour.

According to Williams and Asher (1993) four basic concepts should be taught in social skills coaching: co-operation (e.g. taking turns, sharing materials and making suggestions during games), participation (e.g. getting involved, getting started and paying attention during a game), communication (e.g. talking with others, asking questions, talking about yourself, listening skills, making eye contact, using the other child's name) and validation (e.g. giving attention to others, saying nice things to other people, smiling, offering help or suggestions). Individual children may need additional coaching in specific areas as well. For example, some children may be excluded from games and activities because of their lack of basic games or sports skills. Some training in these skills can therefore help such children become better integrated into existing peer groups.

As well as specific social skills, there are a number of other things classroom teachers can do to help unpopular children. The first of these is to try and find out what hobbies, interests or talents the unpopular child has and to publicly 'advertise' them, by encouraging them to bring objects relating to their hobbies into the class or by letting them give a presentation on their hobby. This should help position the child as an expert on something, which can strengthen her or his prestige in the group.

Giving the child a responsible role in the class can also help to increase peer acceptance, but among adolescents in particular one must beware of positioning the child as a 'teacher's pet' (Lavoie, 1997).

Among pre-school children, visible acceptance of the child by the teacher may be helpful, in that this behaviour may be imitated by the students (Lavoie, 1997).

Collaborative group work, while requiring good social skills from students, can also help develop these skills. Making a rejected child work with a high-status peer in paired work can increase her or his acceptance, but the teacher has to ensure that the child is accepted by this peer first. Grouping less socially skilled students with their more skilled peers in both collaborative group work and games can help them learn through observing these more socially able peers (Kemple, 1992; Lavoie, 1997).

Some rejected children behave aggressively, because they do not possess any other conflict-resolution skills. These children need to learn different ways of dealing with conflict (such as taking their turn or sharing), which can be done either through direct instruction in these methods or through activities such as role-plays and discussions in which other solutions are presented. Once these have been learnt, the teacher may still need to initially give the child on-the-spot guidance when conflict does occur in class (Kemple, 1992).

In order to avoid the unpopular child always being 'picked last' for games, the teacher could assign children to teams her or himself, for example by random selection.

Some research suggests that unpopular and rejected children may be less well able to interpret others' emotions than popular peers, and may therefore respond to others' emotions in inappropriate ways. These children can be helped by giving them clues on other children's emotions, such as 'look at Jane, what do you think she is thinking? Do you think she is happy with what you have done?'

Parents

Parents and siblings have an important role to play in helping to develop children's social skills.

Children's social skills development has been linked to the parenting style used most often by the child's parents. Parenting styles can be defined along two continua: parental warmth or responsiveness and parental control or demandingness (Baumrind, 1991). This leads to four distinct parenting styles:

- Permissive parents are warm and accepting. They are non-traditional and lenient, and allow their children a lot of leeway. They avoid confrontation with their children.
- Authoritarian parents, on the other hand, are highly demanding and restrictive, and expect their orders to be obeyed without question or explanation. They score low on the warmth dimension.
- Authoritative parents are both warm and demanding. They expect discipline, but are supportive of their children as well.
- Uninvolved parents are low on both continua, being neither demanding nor accepting.

Children from both authoritative and permissive households have been found to have better social skills than children of unresponsive and authoritarian parents. Children of authoritative parents do better in school and are less likely to show problem behaviour than children of permissive parents. This means that though children of permissive parents tend to be friendly and sociable, they tend to lack knowledge of appropriate behaviour in different social situations and do not take responsibility for their own actions.

Lack of social skills can also partly be caused by more extreme family circumstances. Children whose parents have a disruptive relationship, in which antisocial and aggressive behaviour are common, or whose parents do not converse with them regularly will tend to develop antisocial behaviour.

There are a number of things parents can do to help their children's social skills development. One is providing children with opportunities to play with peers. Encouraging children to join out-of-school recreational groups or engage in hobbies that they can do with other children will help them develop their social skills as well as, hopefully, being fun.

Shy children can benefit from interaction in small groups, so encouraging children to invite other children over one at a time to do something may help them.

Parents playing with their young children can help their children to develop the skills they will need for play with peers. Research has shown that children whose parents have played with them in this way have more advanced social skills than children who have not had this experience, especially if the play was 'peer-like' and for the sake of having fun (Lindsey, Mize and Pettit, 1997). The parent must not try to dominate the play, or to correct the child, but should attempt to play as equals. In this way the child will learn a lot of the social skills needed to interact successfully with children his or her age.

Talking with children about peer relationships has also been found to enhance their social skills (Laird *et al.*, 1994). This usually takes the form of a conversation about daily activities the child has taken part in.

Parents must take children seriously when they come to them with peer-related problems and help them to consider various options and solutions to the problem, always encouraging friendly, prosocial solutions.

When children do get excluded from, for example, a play situation, as inevitably happens on some occasions even to children who are not unpopular, parents should avoid defeatist comments like 'maybe they don't like you', and instead say something more constructive like 'maybe they're just having a bad day, they might want to do something tomorrow'.

Shyness

A related but different problem to lack of social skills is shyness. Shyness is a feeling that all children have at some point, but if it becomes too prevalent shyness may hinder children's social development. Shyness in children can be recognized quite easily through such signs as an averted gaze and physical and verbal reticence. Shy children often speak softly and hesitantly. Young children sometimes suck their thumb or act coyly.

In normal doses, shyness is not a problem, and can even be a healthy form of social adaptation. Young children will usually be quite shy with strangers, but this shyness will diminish as they get older and get more used to interacting with different people. However, when shyness is not limited to new social situations or new encounters, or if it does not diminish over time, it can become problematic. Shy children can have problems making friends and fitting into peer groups, and often have low self-esteem. The fact that they do not integrate into peer groups can further hinder their social skills development.

Shy children can be helped in a number of ways. Frequent praise can build up their self-esteem. Being sensitive to the child and trying to get to know her or him slowly can help build up a relationship. Pushing them into new situations too rapidly is not a good idea, though, because this can exacerbate their social anxiety. Finally, some social skills training can be useful, such as teaching entry strategies, and how to use questions like 'Can I join your game', or role-playing entry techniques (Hyson and Van Trieste, 1987). Brophy (1996) found that effective teachers use a variety of strategies to help shy children, such as changing their environment by seating them with friendly children or assigning them to a sociable partner, encouraging increased responsiveness from them, minimizing their exposure to stress, engaging them in special activities and involving them in frequent private talks. Giving them roles that force them to communicate, such as being a messenger, is another strategy that has been found to be effective.

Shy children may perceive large groups as threatening, and can therefore benefit from initially interacting with peers in small groups.

When children are having problems expressing their feelings and thoughts, it can be necessary to explain what they want to the other children, for example 'John would like to join in'. However, one must be careful not to force other children to play with an unpopular child as this may cause resentment and make the child even more unpopular.

Helping students to get to know each other at the beginning of the year, for example by asking all students to tell the class something about themselves including hobbies and interests, can show children that they have some things in common with children who might otherwise be unpopular.

Throughout the year, primary students can learn about friendship and acceptance of different students through various activities. Children's literature, for example, provides many examples that can be fruitfully used to encourage students to interact with all other children. Many books treat the theme of making friends, and can be used as a starting point for discussions, role-play and lessons about making friends. Other books explicitly look at making friends with 'unusual' children or adults, or discuss themes such as handling rows.

It is important to start developing students' social skills early on. Hartup and Moore (1990) found that if children have not developed social skills by age 6 they are at risk of experiencing problems throughout their life.

Summary

Research into children's relationships with same-age peers is often done using socio-metric techniques, asking children to nominate peers they like or dislike. This research has led to the identification of four types of children: popular children, who have successfully established relationships with a variety of peers and social groups; controversial children who are well liked by a group of peers, but may be unpopular with other groups of children; isolated children who are not openly unpopular, but are often ignored by their classmates; and rejected students who are actively disliked and are often subjected to bullying or harassment by peers.

Being isolated or rejected can be harmful to children's development in a number of ways and has been linked to low school achievement, school drop out and mental health problems. One of the reasons students can become isolated from or rejected by peers is through a lack of social skills. In order to be accepted by peers, children must be perceived as being fun to be with, as having an influence that is perceived as positive, as facilitating the others' goals, as making peers feel good about themselves and as being similar to peers in a number of ways.

In order to determine where the problems of an unpopular child lie an adult can observe the child (in structured play settings, for example). The child can then be coached in the social skills she or he is missing. This coaching needs to start off with an explanation of the skill and why it is important, but must not stop there. Practising the skill in role-play and real-life situations, followed by discussion of the skill as practised are essential. The four basic skills that will most often need to be addressed are co-operation (taking turns, sharing materials and making suggestions during games), participation (getting involved, getting started and paying attention during a game), communication (talking with others, asking questions, talking about yourself, listening skills, making eye contact, using the other child's name) and validation (giving attention to others, saying nice things to other people, smiling, offering help or suggestions). Teachers can also help unpopular children by 'advertising' their interesting hobbies or specialist knowledge and structuring co-operative work with popular peers.

Parents can help by encouraging their children to participate in out-of-school group activities and hobbies, playing with them in a peer-like way when they are young, and discussing their social life with them.

Self-study questions

1. Why is developing healthy peer relations important?
2. What can be done to help shy children?
3. What is the relationship between parenting styles and children's social skills?
4. What would you do if you saw a child who seemed unpopular in your class?
5. Describe the four types of children identified by socio-metric research.
6. What are the main social skills that need to be coached according to Parker and Asher?
7. Can you name some factors that can cause a child to be rejected by peers?

10

Enhancing Students' Self-Esteem

Advance organizers

In this chapter you will learn:

- The meaning of the terms self-concept and self-esteem.
- What research has found on the relationship between these concepts and school achievement.
- Whether students' age and gender affect their self-concept.
- What some pioneering psychologists of the self had to say about the self-concept.
- What teachers can do to improve their students' self-concept and self-esteem.

Introduction

Self-concept and self-esteem are concepts that are often discussed not just in the context of schooling but in the context of solving various problems of young people's behaviour in society. Having low self-esteem (or a negative self-concept) has been posited as having a detrimental effect on students' achievement and life chances, and low self-esteem has been implicated as a cause of factors as diverse as eating disorders and juvenile delinquency. It is therefore not surprising that developing students' self-esteem and self-concept has been put forward as a goal that schools and teachers need to pursue.

In this chapter we will look at what research has to say about the effect of students' self-concept and self-esteem on achievement, and what schools and teachers could do to improve both. First, however, we need to clarify what is meant by these two often confused concepts.

Shavelson and Bolus (1982) and Shavelson, Hubner and Stanton (1976) define the self-concept as *a person's perceptions of him/herself, formed through experience with the environment, interactions with significant others and attributions of his or her own behaviour.* As such it is both evaluative and descriptive, referring to both what one thinks about oneself in a certain dimension, and how one feels about that.

Self-concept, according to this theory, which is well supported by research (e.g. Marsh, Relich and Smith, 1983; Muijs, 1997) is both *multidimensional* and *hierarchical*. The multidimensional aspect refers to the fact

102

that one can have a different self-concept about different aspects of one's life. In school, for example, one can feel that one is good at English, but not particularly good at mathematics. Likewise, one can feel that one has excellent social skills, but is not a good athlete. The number of aspects that one can have a self-concept about is virtually unlimited. However, Shavelson hypothesized that among children and adolescents seven dimensions were the most important: self-concept about school subjects, self-concept about English, self-concept about mathematics, self-concept about relations with peers (other children), self-concept about relations with parents, self-concept of appearance and self-concept of athletic ability. These factors are arranged in the mind in a hierarchical manner, meaning that the three school-related factors go together to form an *academic self-concept* (e.g. I'm generally a good student) while the other four factors go together to form a *non-academic self-concept*. These then form the overall or global self-concept, as depicted in Figure 10.1.

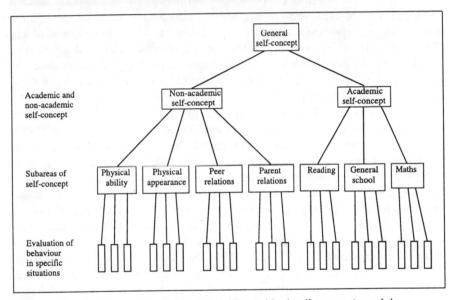

Figure 10.1 Shavelson's multifaceted, hierarchical self-concept model
Source: Byrne and Shavelson (1986, p. 476).

Self-esteem is usually used to refer to a person's view of him or herself in a similar way to Shavelson's global self-concept, and can be defined as *a personal judgement of worthiness that is expressed in the attitudes the individual holds towards him or herself* (Coopersmith, 1967). While in Shavelson's model it is formed out of the different self-concepts a person can hold on different aspects, different people can consider different aspects to be more or less important. Thus, for a professional footballer, self-concept of physical ability is likely to be particularly important to global self-esteem, while academic self-concept may be less important. For the authors of this work, self-concept of 'research ability' will strongly influence global self-esteem. There is also some evidence that shows that people tend to set more store on aspects of self-concept that they feel positive about when forming their global self-esteem. One can often see that students who are not doing well at school will try to diminish the importance of school achievement to their self-esteem by compensating by attaining expertise about music, for example. This does not mean that people are entirely free to choose what aspects they will value. Society imposes certain values such as physical attractiveness or, for school-age students, academic achievement, which are disseminated through parents, peers and media, and therefore self-concept problems in key areas like that will almost inevitably impact on self-esteem.

Is self-concept related to students' achievement?

The existence of a self-concept–school achievement relationship, and a stronger school achievement–academic self-concept association is supported by a large body of research. Purkey (1970) in his review of research up to 1970 concluded that a significant relationship existed between self-concept and school achievement, noting that the unsuccessful student as opposed to her or his successful peers was characterized by low self-concept. Burns (1979) in his review reports average correlations of 0.3 to 0.4 of school achievement with general self-concept and higher correlations with academic self-concept. West, Fish and Stevens (1980) cite correlations ranging from 0.18 to 0.5 between general self-concept and achievement, and correlations of 0.27 to 0.70 between academic self-concept and achievement. In a meta-analysis of 128 studies, Hansford and Hattie (1982) found a mean correlation coefficient of 0.21. While these reviews focused largely on American research, recent studies also support the existence of this relationship in a large number of other countries such as Flanders (Stas and De Wever, 1985; Muijs, 1998a), Sweden (Johnsson-Smaragdi and Jonsson, 1995), Norway (Skaalvik and Hagtvet, 1990), Israel (Orr and Dinur, 1995) Boputatswana (Maqsud and Rouhani, 1991), Australia (Marsh, Parker and Barnes, 1985), Germany (Pekrun, 1990) and Finland (Keltikangas and Jarvinen, 1990).

Most research finds a far stronger relationship between academic self-concept and school achievement than between global self-esteem and school achievement. The relationship becomes even stronger when one looks at specific subjects, such as the relationship between language self-concept and achievement in that language, correlations reaching 0.6 between Dutch language self-concept and achievement in reading and spelling in a recent Flemish study, for example (Muijs, 1997). Similar results are also reported in a number of studies in England, Australia and the USA with children and adolescents, in which subject achievement in English and mathematics was consistently found to be most highly correlated with self-concept in that area, less highly correlated with self-concept in other academic areas, and not (or very slightly) correlated with non-academic self-concept facets. (Marsh, Relich and Smith, 1983; Marsh, Parker and Barnes, 1985; Marsh, 1990).

The relationship has been found to differ by age in some studies. Hansford and Hattie (1982) found significant *age* differences in the mean relationship between general self-concept and achievement, the relationship being lowest in pre-school, then climbing in primary and in secondary school, to go down again in university students (possibly because students at university are likely to be higher achievers, and therefore students with a more positive self-concept than the population as a whole). This seems to be consistent with Chapman and Tunmer's (1995) finding that different subcomponents of reading self-concept were more strongly related to reading achievement each year between the first and fifth year of primary school among their school children in New Zealand. West, Fish and Stevens (1980), however, failed to discern age related patterns in their research overview. In Keltikangas and Jarvinen's (1992) study of 12- and 15-year-old Finns, self-esteem was a stronger predictor of achievement in junior high than in senior high school for girls, but there were no significant age differences for boys. Another age effect is that students' self-concept tends to start off by being very positive in the lower primary grades. It then tends to dip among many students, as they become better able to integrate feedback about their performance into their views of themselves, and drops again just after the transition to secondary school. Thereafter it usually tends to stabilize, and in some cases increases slightly.

Boys and girls have also been found to have different levels of self-concept in a number of studies. These differences are not particularly pronounced when looking at global self-esteem, for which different studies have reported different findings. But when we look at self-concept in different areas, clear patterns do emerge. Girls have a more positive self-concept in the area of peer relations, while boys have a more positive self-concept in the area of physical ability (Marsh, Parker and Barnes, 1985). Differences are also apparent in academic self-concept. From primary school onwards boys tend to develop a more positive self-concept in mathematics, while girls develop a more positive self-concept in English. This has been found to be the case in a number of different countries, and a number of studies have found that this occurs whether or not boys actually outperform girls in the subject or vice versa. Muijs (1997) found that among Flemish primary school children boys had a more positive mathematical self-concept, although their grades in mathematics were no better than those of girls. This points to the importance of not letting societal prejudices about 'male' and 'female' subjects influence teaching and the way teachers interact with students of different genders, as this may influence self-concept and ultimately achievement.

Finding a relationship does not tell us what causes what. Do students who start off with a negative self-concept then start to do worse in school, or do students who do worse in school start to get a more negative

---

The development of self-concept research in psychology

Interest in the self started early in the history of psychology, William James being the major contributor. He divided the global self into two parts, the Me, or the self as object, and the I, or the self as subject. The Me represented the contents of experience, which could be studied by empirical psychology, the I subjective experience which could only be the subject of philosophical thought. James saw the empirical Me as composed of four selves, the spiritual self, the social self, the material self and the bodily self (hierarchically ranked in order of importance for the individual) which are combined in unique ways to constitute a person's view of himself (Burns, 1979; Wylie, 1974).

Cooley was the first to stress the interaction of self and society, and the importance of subjective feedback in self-formation. The self-concept, he believed, arises out of symbolic interaction between an individual and his various primary groups (= a group characterized by face-to-face interaction, relative permanence and a high degree of intimacy). The self-concept is influenced by what you believe others think of you, the so-called looking-glass self (Burns, 1979). According to Mead (1934) the self arises in interaction as an outgrowth of the individual's concern about how others react to him or her. The process of communication has an important role in this theory, as communication means anticipating the others' reaction through language in order to elicit a reaction in those others. It is through the internalization of these others' expected reactions, necessary for effective communication, that the individual learns to see her or his environment as others see it. This is how society exerts its influence on the individual.

By the 1940s interest in the self in psychology started to rise again, as the limits of behaviourism became clear. The necessity of introducing intervening variables in behaviourist models was becoming obvious and the exclusion of many domains vital to human experience from psychology was becoming frustrating to a number of theorists and researchers. New theoretical schools, such as neo-Freudianism and phenomenology, reserved an important place for the self.

One of the main post-war theorist on the self was Carl Rogers. Behaviour, according to Rogers (1967), is not directly influenced by organic or cultural factors but by the individual's perception of them. Self-concept is developed and maintained through perceptions of the external world. Once it has been formed, it is difficult to alter, as maintenance of the self-concept is one of the most fundamental human motives. In this way the self-concept can act as a screen, blocking out perceptions which are in conflict with the established self-concept (= selective perception). The self-concept, being the way a person sees and feels about himself, can only be studied from the standpoint of the individual. It includes both real and ideal self (Rogers, 1967; Burns, 1979).

---

academic self-concept? A number of researchers have attempted to unravel this so-called 'causal chain', using path analysis and structural equation modelling.

While early results had been contradictory, most recent research using more sophisticated statistical methods is starting to present more uniform results. Hoge, Smit and Crist (1995) found paths from grades to specific and general academic self-concept to be stronger than those in the other direction, though none of the paths was strong. Studying general self-esteem rather than academic self-concept, Rosenberg, Schooler and Schoenbach (1989) similarly report the effect of grades on self-esteem to be more powerful than that of self-esteem on grades in their study of US high school panel data. Skaalvik and Hagtvet (1990) found achievement to be predominant over academic self-concept among 3rd- to 4th-year primary school students, while by the 6th year the relationship had become reciprocal, both influencing each other more or less equally. This was also the result of a model using data on 2000 grade 10 boys conducted by Rosenberg *et al.* (1995). Likewise Muijs (1998a), studying 1000 4th- and 5th-grade students in Flanders, found achievement and self-concept to both influence one another, but the effect of achievement on self-concept was stronger than the other way round. Overall, then, self-concept and achievement influence each other, but the effect of achievement on self-concept is the strongest. Thus it would seem that getting low grades causes students' self-concept to decline, which in turn leads them to achieve less well.

Self-concept affects school achievement, but schooling can in turn affect the self-concept and indirectly self-esteem, as academic self-concept will influence a child's global self-esteem. In the next section we will look at things that schools can do to try to improve their students' self-esteem and self-concept.

Enhancing students' self-esteem in school and classroom

As self-concept affects school achievement, and self-concept is in turn hierarchically related to global self-esteem, improving students' self-esteem could improve their school achievement. Low self-esteem is also related to depression and other mental problems, and enhancing self-esteem is therefore a positive psychological outcome in its own right. Many commentators also believe that improving students' self-esteem could strongly benefit society, as low self-esteem is posited to be related to such factors as juvenile delinquency. The evidence for this latter assertion is weak; delinquent youths are not necessarily found to suffer from low self-esteem (Muijs, 1997). There is, however, a relationship between low achievement at school and delinquency, which means the indirect effect of improving students' self-esteem may be significant. Many students come to school with negative self-esteem already developed, often due to the circumstances they have grown up in such as poverty.

A number of elements have been proposed to enhance students' self-esteem in school. The main element is to create a supportive and loving environment with clear boundaries, an environment that has been found most beneficial to improving self-concept not just in school, but in the home as well (Coopersmith, 1967). This means that while supportive and caring, schools that foster self-esteem should also be disciplined, orderly environments with clear, though not stifling, rules and procedures.

One of the main factors in improving self-concept is having high *expectations* of all students. This element was discussed in Chapter 6, but one way in which self-fulfilling prophecies can occur is through low expectations being expressed by teachers which will then negatively impact on students' self-concept for that subject and on their global self-esteem, which in turn may lead to lower achievement. This is therefore another reason to maintain high expectations of students. Teachers should beware of the hidden messages that they are sending out. Verbal and non-verbal cues can send out the message that the teacher is not interested in the student, does not trust her or him, or does not value the student. Examples are giving responsibility only to a small group of students, giving out the message that the others cannot be trusted, or saying something like 'you're now in secondary school, you should be able to do secondary work', which implies that the student is stupid.

Another element that has already been touched on is *correcting misbehaviour*. This should always be done in such a way that students' self-concept is not damaged. It is important in this respect to avoid personal criticism. The teacher should focus on the misbehaviour giving reasons why the behaviour is inappropriate and criticize the behaviour, not the person. As you can see, these recommendations follow those mentioned in Chapter 5, on behaviour management. Teachers should avoid name-calling (stupid . . .), belittling, put downs or deliberately embarrassing students in front of classmates. They should refrain from labelling students (e.g. you're irresponsible) and label the behaviour instead (Burns, 1979).

Giving students responsibilities helps build up a sense of personal power, which will enhance self-esteem. Students should be given the opportunity to make choices and should be allowed to make an active contribution to lessons. Younger students should be given responsibility over small tasks, such as keeping the classroom tidy, wiping the board etc., while older students should be actively involved in developing classroom rules. Teachers should be supportive of students and create a climate in which their contributions are valued. Praise is useful, but should not be overused, because otherwise it will be perceived to be insincere. Praise must also be realistic. Praising a student for something she or he has done wrong will not be taken seriously by the student and will lead to future praise being devalued (Purkey, 1970).

Teachers should emphasize students' successes rather than their failures. They should draw attention to those parts of a task that were done well, and emphasize that learning occurs through trial and error, and that making mistakes is a way of learning rather than something to be ashamed of. Teachers should let students know what they are doing right as well as correcting their mistakes. Students should be encouraged to strive for their own personal best, rather than competing with others or constantly comparing their results with those of classmates.

A number of specific activities to develop students' self-esteem have also been proposed. One such activity is the so-called 'magic circle'. This is an activity during which one child receives a badge, saying something like 'I'm great'. She or he will then be asked to leave the room, while the other students are asked to think of all the nice things they can say about her or him. These are then conveyed to the student when she or he comes back into class. All comments have to be preceded with the words 'I think . . .' or 'I believe . . .' in order to make it easier for the recipient to accept them as opinions which cannot be contradicted. At the end of the exercise the student is asked to say something positive about her or himself, something of which she or he is proud (Mosley, 1996). The effectiveness of this type of activity is unproven, however. Another activity that has been proposed is positive self-talk. Getting children to talk positively to themselves internally (saying things to themselves like 'I'm going to do well in maths today') is supposed to improve self-esteem. This is based on the psychological theory that what we repeat internally to ourselves can affect our moods and beliefs. Again, the effectiveness of this method, though strongly supported by some psychologists, remains unproven.

The research reviewed above has shown that the effect of achievement on self-concept is stronger than the effect of self-concept on achievement. Therefore the best way to improve self-concept is probably to improve students' achievement. Just improving achievement for all students across the board may not be sufficient, however, as research has shown that self-concept is developed by comparison. Therefore, even a well-performing student may have a negative academic self-concept if she or he is not performing as well as other students in the school. One way to overcome this would seem to be not to publish student grades. However, apart from the positive benefits of performance feedback on student achievement (see Chapter 18) an admittedly small scale study by Muijs (1997) showed that self-concept differences were as pronounced in two schools in which grades were not shown to students as in two matched schools in which they were. Students thus seem very well able to judge their own competence through classroom interaction. One must also beware of shielding students too much from reality, or of building up unrealistic expectations, as this will catch up with them in the long term and can potentially be harmful (Begley and Rogers, 1998). This is another argument for the use of formative feedback aimed at improving students' weak points rather than just publishing student grades (Black and William, 1998).

The most effective way of doing something about students' self-concepts thus seems to be to make sure that all students have the opportunity to experience success (Covington and Beery, 1976; Nunn and Parish, 1992). This can be done through teaching that ensures that students reach a high level of mastery in a given subtopic or skill before moving on to the next part of the lesson. Presenting information in small chunks and working towards mastery also ties in well with other research on effective teaching, as discussed in Chapter 1. Giving students the chance to participate in a wide range of extracurricular activities (not just sport!) can also help them experience success.

Summary

Self-concept is defined as a person's perceptions of him or herself, formed through experience with the environment, interactions with significant others and attributions of his or her own behaviour. People have self-concepts in a variety of areas, including their competence in various school subjects, and in school subjects in general. Self-esteem is a more global concept, referring to people's general view of their own worth.

Research has clearly established that there is a relationship between students' self-concept and self-esteem and their school achievement. This relationship is strongest with academic self-concept, and lower with global self-esteem. The relationship is reciprocal, meaning that self-concept affects achievement, but achievement affects self-concept as well. Thus, low achievement will lead to negative self-concept, which will in turn lead to lower achievement. The effect of achievement on self-concept is stronger than the effect of self-concept on achievement, however.

There are a number of things teachers can do in the classroom to improve their students' self-esteem. Most of these tie in with what was written in Part 1 about effective teaching. Having high expectations of students will improve their self-concept as well as their performance. When correcting misbehaviour it is important to correct the behaviour, rather than criticizing the student through name-calling for example. To build up students' self-worth they should be given some responsibilities in the classroom. With younger students this can take the form of being responsible for things like keeping the classroom tidy, older students should be involved in decision-making. Teachers should emphasize students' successes by telling them what they are doing right as well as correcting their mistakes, and should show that their contributions are valued.

The most important aspect, however, is to ensure that all students experience success. This can be achieved by teaching to high levels of mastery and by teaching content in small steps, and making sure that students have grasped a concept before moving on to the next part of the lesson. Providing them with range of extracurricular activities can help them experience success in other areas as well.

Self-study questions

1. Shavelson's model posits seven self-concept dimensions. Can you think of some others that are important to you?
2. What dimension of self-concept would you expect to be most strongly related to a student's performance on a history test?
3. Why can mastery of learning help students' self-esteem?
4. Why might using a magic circle help improve students' self-esteem, and why might it not?
5. How might non-verbal cues affect students' self-concept?
6. What could a teacher do to help students attain a positive self-concept?
7. Is there a relationship between students' self-concept and their gender?

11

Teaching Students with Special Educational Needs

Advance organizers

In this chapter we will learn

- The characteristics of a number of types of special needs teachers may encounter, such as learning disabilities, autism, hearing problems and behavioural difficulties.
- What research has to say about the effects of inclusion of students with special needs in ' mainstream' classrooms on their academic achievement.
- What teaching methods are most effective in teaching students with reading problems and other learning disabilities.
- How best to deal with students with attentional disorders.
- What methods are most effective in teaching students with other disabilities, such as hearing problems, Tourette's syndrome, autism and mental retardation.
- What parents can do to help children with learning disabilities.

What are special needs?

Special needs is a broad term, referring to very different students with a wide range of different needs and problems. The Department for Education and Employment in the UK defines special needs as follows:

> A child is defined as having special educational needs if he or she has a learning difficulty which needs special teaching. A learning difficulty means that the child has significantly greater difficulty in learning than most children of the same age. Or, it means a child has a disability which needs different educational facilities from those that schools generally provide for children of the same age in the area. The children who need special educational education are not only those with obvious learning difficulties, such as those who are physically disabled, deaf or blind. They include those whose learning difficulties are less apparent, such as slow learners and emotionally vulnerable children. It is estimated that up to 20% of school children may need special educational help at some stage in their school careers.

> (DfEE, 2000)

One group of students with special needs that we will discuss in the next chapter are *gifted students*. At the opposite end of the spectrum of academic achievement we find students with *learning disabilities*.

Learning disability, unlike a number of other disabilities such as blindness, is an invisible disability that is connected to problems with linking information in different parts of the brain. Learning disabilities take a number of different forms, which according to the American *Diagnostic and Statistical Manual of Mental Disorders* can be broadly categorized into three main subparts (APA, 1994):

1. Developmental speech and language disorders.
2. Academic skills disorders.
3. Co-ordination disorders and other learning handicaps.

People with *developmental speech and language disorders* will typically have difficulties producing speech sounds, speaking or understanding what other people say. These difficulties can take three forms. Children with *developmental articulation disorders* may have trouble controlling their rate of speech or may lag behind other children in learning to make speech sounds. This disorder affects about 10 per cent of young children, but can often be successfully treated through speech therapy. Children who have specific problems expressing themselves in speech suffer from *developmental expressive language disorder*. *Developmental receptive language disorders* occur when children or adults have trouble understanding certain parts of speech, notwithstanding the fact that they do not have hearing problems.

Students with *academic skills disorders* often lag behind their classmates in one, or more often more academic skills, such as reading, writing and maths. This lag may be measured in years rather than months. Once again this type of disorder can take three forms. *Developmental reading disorder* or *dyslexia* refers to problems involved in reading, often caused by problems distinguishing the sounds in spoken words, a skill that is crucial in learning to read (see Chapter 15). In the higher grades, when comprehension becomes more important, other reading disorders appear such as an inability to relate new ideas to those stored in memory. Other children can suffer from *developmental writing disorders*, which can result from problems in a number of areas such as vocabulary, grammar, hand movement and memory. Finally, *developmental arithmetic disorder* can arise from problems in memory, recognizing symbols and numbers, and understanding abstract concepts.

A number of other categories have also been identified, like *motor skills disorders* and 'other' disorders such as delays in acquiring language, co-ordination problems and *attention disorders*. Students with attention disorders tend to pay little attention to tasks, have short attention spans, do not listen when spoken to directly, do not follow instructions, have difficulty organizing tasks, avoid tasks that require sustained mental effort, are easily distracted, lose things and are forgetful in daily activities (APA, 1994). Attention disorders seem to have become increasingly prevalent, and include a tendency to daydream excessively in some children. In others this problem can take the form of *attention deficit hyperactivity disorder* (ADHD) in which attention problems are combined with hyper-activity. Children with ADHD will tend to act impulsively and cannot sit still. They will tend to run around or blurt out answers in the classroom, and are incapable of waiting their turn in games. In adolescence, these children tend towards fidgeting and restlessness. In adulthood this problem can take the form of inability to concentrate or organize tasks at work.

Learning disabilities are often related to and may be caused by social factors. Children from impoverished backgrounds more often manifest these problems, as do children with less intellectual ability, leading some researchers to propose that the concept of learning disabilities is erroneous and confounded with these two factors (Lyon, 1999).

Other disabilities include *hearing difficulties*, which can range from mild difficulties in hearing that can be easily remedied by the use of amplifiers, to deafness, which in some cases can be alleviated through the use of cochlear implants. There are three major types of hearing disorders. *Conductive loss* occurs when something goes wrong with the outer or middle ear which results in sound waves not being conducted to the inner ear. *Sensoneurinal loss* refers to damage to the inner ear or auditory nerve that stops the sound data from being sent to the brain. Finally, in some people the neural system involved in understanding what is heard is impaired. This is called *central auditory processing disorder* (Easterbrooks and Baker-Hawkins, 1994).

Autism is a neurological developmental disability that affects people's ability to communicate, understand language and interact with others. Autistic children will tend to isolate themselves from social situations. Intellectually some may be mentally retarded, but others can be intelligent and even gifted. As well as problems with social relations, autistic individuals often exhibit unusual and/or repetitive movements, strong resistance to change, over- or under-sensitivity to certain stimuli, tantrums and aggressive behaviour.

While most students misbehave at some points in time, some suffer from more or less severe *behavioural disorders*. These students consistently demonstrate behaviour that is different from the expected classroom and community norm and are in need of remediation (ERIC, 1993).

Mental retardation refers to people whose general intellectual functioning is significantly subaverage (an IQ score below 75), and who have problems with such areas as communication, self-care, home living, social skills, self-direction, health and safety and academic achievement. It manifests itself before age 18 (AAMR, 2000). The precise nature of the retardation can vary significantly from person to person. Students with mental retardation will learn with more difficulty and experience problems with memory, problem-solving, logical thinking and attention compared with their peers (Beirne-Smith, Patton and Ittenbach, 1994; Hawkins-Shepard, 1994).

Tourette's syndrome is a neurological disorder that is outwardly characterized by repeated, involuntary body movements such as twitching, leg jerking or other 'tics', and repetitive vocal sounds such as throat clearing. These tics will occur frequently throughout the day, often in bouts, but may disappear for periods of time. The specific tic of the Tourette sufferer may also change in type, number or severity over time. Tourette sufferers do not generally suffer low IQ, but may often suffer from attention and learning disorders (Bronzheim, 1994; Knoblauch, 1998).

Once a child has been diagnosed as possessing a learning or other disability (different procedures for this exist in different countries) schools need to provide the necessary support for these children. Several options exist, for example: placing children in 'special schools' explicitly designed to accommodate disabled children; placing them in regular so-called 'mainstream' schools, but in special separate classrooms; placing them in mainstream schools in regular classrooms, but have them taken out of class for special education; or 'full inclusion' in mainstream class-rooms (in this latter case the necessary adjustments to this classroom will have to be made to meet children's special educational needs). In recent years, there has been a clear shift towards inclusion and away from placement in special schools or classrooms, often for philosophical rea-sons pertaining to students' human rights, as well as because of argu-ments concerning students' social growth. One of the arguments goes that included students will have enhanced self-esteem as they are not being labelled and secluded from peers to the same extent as when placed in special schools or classrooms. Conversely, non-disabled students will get used to being around disabled peers, leading them to be less likely to discriminate against disabled people in adulthood. In this way it is hoped disabled students will be able to develop into active and respected mem-bers of the community.

The inclusion debate

One of the main questions argued over by supporters and opponents of the inclusion of students with special needs is whether integration into mainstream classrooms will benefit or harm students' academic progress. Supporters of placement in special schools/units usually argue that the smaller class sizes and specific attention given to special needs students by experts will aid their academic progress (Gartner and Lipsky, 1987). On the other hand, proponents of integration argue that students in special schools/units may suffer from a lack of academic press and may lack the benefits of interaction with higher-achieving peers. Furthermore, typical practices in special units/schools have often been found not to be in accordance with effective classroom practices, being characterized by lower cognitive demands, little use of higher-order cognitive skills, slower pacing, little time devoted to academic tasks and little direct in-struction (Gartner and Lipsky, 1987; Walberg, 1993; Zigmond and Baker, 1997). Proponents of programmes in which students spend most of their time in mainstream classrooms but are pulled out for 1 or 2 hours a day to follow lessons in a special unit generally see this as a good compromise between mainstreaming and segregation, while opponents claim that this process leads to them missing parts of the mainstream programme, making it more difficult for them to follow the curriculum, especially as there often seems to be scant co-ordination between regular classroom teachers and teachers in these so-called pull-out programmes (Zigmond and Baker, 1997).

In their review of studies up to the mid-1980s (described as small in number and often methodologically flawed), Slavin and Madden (1986) report that while some studies found students in full-time special placement did as well as students in mainstream settings, and others found they did worse (according to Slavin and Madden these latter tended to be the better designed studies), no studies reported that students in full-time placement did better academically than students in mainstream settings. Some evidence emerged that students who did not receive any support in mainstream classrooms did worse, however (Madden and Slaven, 1983; Slavin and Madden, 1986). No clear differences emerged between students in part-time placement and students in mainstream settings. A meta-analysis conducted by Wang and Baker (1986) (reviewing 11 studies conducted between 1975 and 1984) reports a slightly favourable effect of mainstreaming over full-time placement for academic outcomes. Sixty-five per cent of measured effects were positive, and mainstream students seemed to make more progress than segregated peers did. These results were consistent across grade levels and when controlling for contextual variables.

When full-time mainstreaming was compared with pull-out programmes the former was found to be non-significantly more effective. In an earlier meta-analysis, Carlberg and Kavale (1980) found 'educable mentally retarded' students did worse in special classes than in mainstream classes. A review of three meta-analyses by Gersten *et al.* (1999) found small positive effects for inclusion. Gartner and Lipsky (1987), reviewing a large number of studies, found that the mean academic performance of special needs students in mainstream settings was on average in the eightieth percentile compared with non-special needs students, while the performance of students in segregated settings was in the fiftieth percentile. In three studies using a reading test as the outcome measure Zigmond and Baker (1997) found inconclusive results; half the students with learning difficulties educated in mainstream settings made reliable gains, while 40 per cent made gains of less than half the magnitude of their peers. As these students were not compared with special needs students in segregated settings this does not tell us much about the relative effectiveness of mainstreaming.

A more recent review (Manset and Semmel, 1997) looked at the effects of a number of integration programs for students with special needs in the USA. Three out of the five reviewed programmes (Success for All, Adaptive Learning Environments Model, and an untitled programme by

Jenkins *et al.*, 1994) reported significantly higher achievement gains for students in the programme than for students in 'pull-out' programmes (students spend most of their time in mainstream classrooms, but are removed from class for 1 or 2 hours a day for teaching in a special unit). These programmes seemed to share the common feature of highly focused instruction with individual basic skills tuition. Deno *et al.* (1990) compared students in three integrated programmes (Adaptive Learning Environments Model, the Comparison Reading Programme and Data-Based Intervention) with students in resource room programmes, and found that low achievers and students with mild learning difficulties who participated in the programmes scored higher on the Basic Academic Skills Survey.

Lipsky and Gartner (1997) report few differences between special needs students in mainstream education and in pull-out programmes. They also report that the gap in achievement between students with mild learning difficulties and their mainstream peers did not widen as fast when these students were mainstreamed as when they were in pull-out programmes. In a study using the Metropolitan Achievement test to compare learning disabled students in two schools, Jenkins *et al.* (1994) found that students in the integrated schools showed significantly higher overall gains than students in a school using a pull-out resource room method. In a small-scale study Banerji and Dailey (1995) reported that 2nd- to 5th-grade students with specific learning difficulties achieved better in a mainstream classroom than in a pull-out programme. Schulte, Osborne and McKinney (1990) studied elementary school students with learning difficulties who spent (a) 1 hour per day in a resource room setting, (b) 2 hours per day in a resource room setting, (c) students permanently in mainstream classrooms in which a special education teacher provided some additional instruction to the child and (d) students in mainstream classrooms where special education teachers provided technical assistance to the mainstream teacher, but no instruction in class. It was found that students in the mainstream classroom with extra teaching did significantly better overall (though not in specific subjects) than students who spent 1 hour a day in the resource room. No other significant differences were found.

In a review of reviews focusing on students with moderate learning difficulties, Williams (1993) reported that studies seemed to slightly favour mainstreaming. However, the deficiencies of the studies led the author to state that a no-effects conclusion was safest. Galloway (1985) reaches a similar conclusion.

Generally, then, these studies seem to point to positive effects of mainstreaming over full-time and, to a lesser extent, part-time placement in special units. However, many studies were methodologically flawed and sample sizes were small. Conclusions must therefore be highly tentative, although there does seem to be some cumulative evidence for higher effectiveness of mainstreaming over full-time placement for special needs students in general. The picture with regards to pull-out programmes must be considered inconclusive, however. Also, it seems clear that whether inclusion or placement are preferable may also depend on the nature and seriousness of the disability.

In order for inclusion to work, a number of conditions need to be met. Teachers must believe the included student can succeed, and must prepare the other students in the class to accept the disabled student. The classroom and school need to be physically prepared if necessary, and all school staff need to understand the needs of the students with disabilities. Staff development needs to take place to prepare staff to support the student, and good working relationships need to be established with the special educators in the school.

Teaching students with learning disabilities

According to the extensive studies carried out by the National Institute for Child Health and Development in the USA, the main predictor of *reading difficulties* are problems with phonemic awareness, followed by vocabulary deficits and inadequate background knowledge of information presented in the text, lack of familiarity with semantic and syntactic structures that can be employed to predict and better understand word and grammatical relationships, and lack of knowledge about different strategies employed by the author to achieve different purposes, such as humour and dialogue. One of the most important aspects of treating reading disabilities therefore is teaching these students word–sound correspondences to decipher reading codes (the *phonics system*). This approach has been found to be effective in a number of studies (Lyon, 1994; McElgunn, 1996). This decoding skill needs to become automatic so memory capacity that should be used for strong comprehension of the text to occur is not wasted on the decoding process. Strong comprehension is also influenced by students' background knowledge and vocabulary. Thus, both direct structured instruction in phonics and a literature-rich environment can help students with reading difficulties (Lyon, 1999).

Another problem that students with reading difficulties seem to have is an inability to properly self-monitor while reading a text. They fail to understand that they must pay attention to how well they understand the text and that they should reread a paragraph or sentence if they do not understand it. Students with this problem can be taught a number of self-monitoring skills, such as asking themselves questions while they read and summarizing what they have read. However, once taught these students often experience difficulties in generalizing these skills to other situations (Gersten, 1999).

More generally, a meta-analysis of research on students with learning disabilities but of average intelligence looking at studies conducted over a 30-year period found that the most effective strategy for teaching learning disabled students combined elements of direct instruction (see Chapters

1–3) with components focusing on the teaching of learning and mnemonic strategies. The main components of this strategy include sequencing (breaking down the task, providing step-by-step prompts), a drill–repetition–practice sequence, segmentation (breaking down the task into small segments and then synthesizing them as a whole), directed questioning and response, use of technology, modelling and small group instruction. The most important factor was found to be control of task difficulty, proceeding from simple to more difficult aspects in small, teacher-directed steps. The effectiveness of this combined direct instruction-strategy approach was strongest in reading, and somewhat less strong in mathematics and social skills (Swanson, 1999). Use of small (three to ten students) teacher-directed groups rather than the whole class was found to be beneficial to learning disabled students in a meta-analysis including 20 studies conducted between 1975 and 1997. Peer tutoring was likewise found to be effective. Smaller groups (three to five students) appeared more effective than larger groups. These grouping procedures could most usefully be combined with whole class instruction according to these researchers (Erlbaum *et al.*, 1999).

A problem for many learning disabled students is a negative self-concept. As mentioned in Chapter 10 there are two possible approaches to dealing with this: a skills development approach, that aims to enhance students' academic achievement which should in turn enhance their self-concept; and a self-enhancement approach, which uses a therapeutic approach to change self-concept. A meta-analysis on the effectiveness of these two approaches among learning disabled students concluded that an approach that combined the two worked best. Collaborative work appeared to be a factor that enhanced self-concept in many interventions (Erlbaum and Vaughn, 1999).

Students with *attention disorders*, which some evidence suggests are becoming increasingly prevalent, can be particularly problematic in integrated settings as they can easily disrupt lessons and disturb other students.

There are a number of things a teacher can do to help maintain the attention of all and, in particular, attention disabled students. Employing a range of introductory attention grabbers and stressing the importance of the topic to students' daily lives could help, as could presenting material in small steps, explaining the relevance of each step along the way. Students should be encouraged to learn from their mistakes, and be actively involved in the lesson. Helping students to set short-term, not too hard to reach goals can also be beneficial. Using a variety of teaching methods and a quick succession of activities can help focus students' attention and keep them from becoming bored too quickly (Fulk, 2000). Students with attention disorders often seem to suffer from disorganization as well. They may have difficulty remembering dates and assignments, bringing required materials into class and may incorrectly record assignments, use time inefficiently, fail to properly structure essays and written work, fail to express themselves in an organized fashion and fail to plan. It is important to provide these students with a clear structure and routines, and specify exactly what they are expected to bring to class at each point in the day. The teacher needs to give students clear and simple directions, and have her or him repeat these. Assignments need to be clearly presented and written on the same place on the board each time. Students must be made to copy these assignments. Teachers should try to minimize clutter on handouts and assignments. Modelling problem-solving and essay-writing skills can help, especially when students are given large assignments, which they may find confusing. Various ways of storing material and being tidy need to be presented to them. They can be taught mnemonic techniques and use of memory aids, such as a note attached to the student's backpack or satchel. Furthermore, students should be praised and rewarded for improvements in their organization, but they should also receive the consequences of their disorganization in order to provide them with an incentive to do better (Shore, 1998).

Children suffering from ADHD have been found to have problems dealing with change. Consistency is therefore important. Most ADHD children should where possible, be placed at the front of the class, where they have the least chance of observing other children move as they write things down and answer questions. However, some hyperactive children can, when seated at the front, disturb their classmates through their constant movement and fidgeting. These students clearly are not best left at the front (Stevens, 1997). Students with ADHD should be surrounded by students who can act as positive behaviour models. They should not be placed near possibly distracting objects, such as heaters, windows and doors.

Teaching students with other disabilities

When students suffer from *behavioural disorders*, the first step is to identify exactly what it is that the student is doing that makes her or him cause problems in the classroom. Then one has to identify what it is that one wants the student to do instead, and what means could be used to get there. Teachers should try to avoid focusing on the undesired behaviours and try to focus on the desired behaviours instead. Opportunities should be provided for the student to practise the desired behaviours, such as interacting appropriately with peers and adults. There are two possible problems that may need to be addressed with students with behavioural disorders, skills deficits and performance deficits. Which of these two situations is present can be assessed by having the student role-play various situations or by asking her or him what she or he would do in a certain situation, such as if the teacher reprimanded her or him. If she or he can give the correct response to this type of question or can perform the appropriate behaviour in role-play but not display the appropriate behaviour in actual classroom situations, then the problem is one of performance deficit. If she or he is not able to give an appropriate response to the question, then the

---

Parents and children with learning disabilities

A number of tips for parents of students with learning disabilities have been suggested that can help children become more independent and better learners. The National Center for Learning Disabilities (2000) in the USA has suggested the following:

1. Let children help with household tasks, using activities that can help build children's self-concept and self-confidence, and show that this activity is meaningful and appreciated by the rest of the household.
2. Keep instructions clear and simple, providing verbal cues if necessary.
3. Set clear routines.
4. Minimize distractions when children are studying, i.e. turn off the television and radio and establish calm work spaces.
5. Be patient and offer helpful reminders when children forget things. Remember, they are not doing it on purpose.
6. Reward effort as well as outcomes and give the child a lot of praise. Feedback should be immediate and connected to the task done. It is better not to rely on gifts and monetary rewards, but use praise, smiles etc. instead.
7. Read to your child and let her or him read to you.
8. Help other family members and friends understand the nature of the learning disability your child is suffering from.
9. Be consistent. Establish rules that everyone in the family understands and be consistent with discipline and praise.
10. Do not be fooled by promises of quick cures or treatments, and do not believe all unsubstantiated reports that appear in the media. When in doubt, contact a professional.
11. Encourage your child to join with peers in social activities, and seek out parents with whom you can share experiences.

Providing children with oral language and literacy experiences from the start is crucial to avoiding reading problems. Reading to children, and engaging them in play with language through nursery rhymes and storybooks can also help develop children's language awareness (Lyon, 1999).

---

problem may be a skills deficit. In the latter case, direct instruction in the required skill will be necessary before proceeding to practise the skill. If the problem is one of performance, providing more situations to practice the appropriate response may be sufficient (ERIC, 1993).

Deaf or *hard of hearing* students can be educated in a number of ways. One of these is the *auditory–oral* approach. This method attempts to get hard of hearing children to acquire spoken language in an environment in which spoken language is used exclusively, including both the classroom and the school. The home environment is crucial in this process, as is the use of hearing amplifiers, such as hearing aids and cochlear implants, depending on the seriousness of the hearing problem. As well as listening skills, students are taught speech production skills starting at the phonetic level (individual syllables), and proceeding from there to the phonological level (whole words and sentences) immediately. If successful, this approach will allow hard of hearing children to communicate with a wide range of others. Some research (Geers and Moog,

1988) found that 16–17-year-olds who had been taught using this technique had a reading age of about 13–14 years, which is almost double that of US deaf students in general. A possible problem may be that the hearing loss is too serious to be overcome even with the use of cochlear implants (Stone, 1997). The *auditory–verbal* approach works from a similar idea. In this approach hearing problems are identified at the earliest possible stage and the best possible medical treatment or amplifier is then sought out. Then children are taught listening and speech skills. The idea is to identify the child's problems as soon as possible and to intervene by teaching the necessary strategies to the parents of young children (Goldberg, 1994; 1997). Therefore more than a teaching approach this is an approach that targets parents.

Cued speech, another method proposed, is basically a sound-based hand supplement to speech-reading, designed to improve the literacy development of deaf children. It can be used by both parents and teachers to teach students phonics and articulation. The system is easy to learn and can be used to teach words for which there is no sign language equivalent (Caldwell, 1997). According to research by Wandel (quoted in Caldwell, 1997), students taught using this method read at the same grade level as their non-deaf peers.

A different option is using a *sign language* (Gustasson, 1997). Like spoken languages, sign languages differ from country to country, American Sign Language for example differing from British Sign Language. Most sign languages have developed naturally in the deaf community, but some have been specifically developed to more closely resemble the spoken version of the language, adding grammatical features of that language to the sign language. These specifically developed systems are often used by parents and teachers to teach deaf children, as they allow them more easily to learn English or whatever their home language is. However, some deaf parents feel this practice negates their culture.

No single intervention that is successful with all *autistic* children has been identified. However, a number of educationally and behaviourally orientated methods have shown some success. Overall, autistic children benefit from a highly structured environment with very clear guidelines for appropriate and inappropriate behaviour. This environment should include materials that help autistic people to clearly comprehend the sequence of events and activities that will occur, such as written or picture schedules. Skills taught should be geared towards helping the autistic person to function day to day, such as communication, language and social skills (Dunlap *et al.*, 1994; Dunlap and Fox, 1999).

For students with *mental retardation*, especially younger students, use of hands-on materials is often the most suitable teaching method, and use of pictures may be more appropriate than verbal directions. It is a good idea to break down tasks into small steps, and to proceed from simpler to more difficult tasks. Learning should take place in short sessions, and life-skills instruction could be crucial to these students' adaptive development (Hawkins-Shepard, 1994).

When dealing with students with *Tourette's syndrome*, it is important to remember that however annoying the tics they may be showing, they are not done on purpose and are involuntary. Peers must be encouraged to accept the child. Giving the Tourette sufferer private time and space to relax can help lessen the occurrence of tics in the classroom. Providing a private space to do testing can prevent the tics disrupting other students' concentration during exams (Knoblauch, 1998). If the student has language, learning or attention problems these need to be dealt with in the ways mentioned above.

Summary

Special needs is a broad term that includes gifted students who will be discussed in Chapter 12.

Among the most prevalent of special needs are learning disabilities. Learning disabilities are connected to problems with linking information in different parts of the brain. Learning disabilities take a number of different forms, which according to the American *Diagnostic and Statistical Manual of Mental Disorders* can be broadly categorized into three main subparts (APA, 1994): developmental speech and language disorders, academic skills disorders and coordination disorders and other learning handicaps.

A disability that appears to be becoming increasingly prevalent is attention disorder. Students with attention disorders tend to pay little attention to tasks, have short attention spans, do not listen when spoken to directly, do not follow instructions, have difficulty organizing tasks, avoid tasks that require sustained mental effort, are easily distracted, lose things and are forgetful in daily activities. In some people, attention disorders are combined with hyperactivity, a phenomenon known as ADHD. Other more or less prevalent disabilities include hearing loss, autism, mental retardation and behavioural disorders.

For social and philosophical reasons, there has been a move away from teaching disabled students in separate schools and classrooms and towards integrating them into regular classrooms, a process known as 'inclusion'. A question that has been asked is whether this is beneficial to their academic development. Most studies seem to point to positive effects of mainstreaming over full-time and, to a lesser extent, part-time placement in special units, although the amount of studies is small and many are methodologically flawed.

One of the main problems for students with reading difficulties appears to be a lack of phonemic awareness. These students therefore need to receive explicit phonics instruction. Bad readers have also been found to have problems self-monitoring while reading, and these skills need to be improved as well.

Students with attention disorders can be helped by using attention grabbers, using a variety of visual aids, proceeding in small steps and using a variety of teaching methods. As these students are often disorganised, enhancing their organizational skills can be necessary.

A variety of approaches has been proposed for the teaching of deaf and hard of hearing students. The auditory oral approach attempts to get hearing disabled children to acquire spoken language in an environment in which spoken language is used exclusively. In the auditory–verbal approach the idea is to identify the child's problems as soon as possible and to intervene by teaching the necessary strategies to the parents of young children. The cued speech approach is basically a sound-based hand supplement to speech-reading, designed to improve the literacy development of deaf children, while in the sign language approach a sign language that is closer grammatically to verbal English than existing sign languages is used to allow students to more easily learn English.

Autistic children benefit from a highly structured environment with very clear guidelines for appropriate and inappropriate behaviour, while mentally retarded students benefit from short lessons proceeding in small steps.

Self-study questions

1. Can you describe the main types of learning disabilities?
2. What teaching methods work best for students with learning disabilities?
3. Does inclusion harm the academic achievement of learning disabled children?
4. What can teachers do to accommodate students with behavioural disorders?
5. Describe the main teaching methods for teaching students with hearing problems.
6. What are the main symptoms of Tourette's syndrome and what can be done to accommodate these students in the classroom?
7. What is ADHD, and how does it manifest itself in the classroom?
8. Is there one best method of treating children suffering from autism?
9. How could one identify children with mental retardation and what can be done to help these children?
10. What can parents do to help children with learning disabilities?

12

Teaching Gifted Students

Advance organizers

In this chapter you will learn:

- How to identify gifted children, and what distinguishes them from bright children.
- How to help gifted students fulfil their potential through a variety of methods.
- The advantages and disadvantages of these methods, including ability grouping, curricular enrichment, co-operative learning and acceleration.
- What parents can do to help their gifted offspring.
- The characteristics of gifted learning disabled students.

Introduction

As was mentioned in Chapter 11, where we discussed learning disabled students, the school system is inevitably geared towards the majority of students, which means that special additional provisions need to be made for learning disabled students. Another group that differs from the norm, and that therefore may need special provisions, is gifted or highly able students. In this chapter we will discuss how best to teach these students.

First, though, it is necessary to define exactly what is meant by gifted, especially compared with 'merely' bright students. The term 'gifted' is usually used to refer to students who score significantly above average on ability tests such as the WISC III, Raven's Progressive Matrices or the Cognitive Ability Test. As a rule of thumb, a score in the top 2 per cent of the range of these tests (usually corresponding to a score of over 125) is considered to indicate giftedness. Within schools, a number of other factors are also taken into account in decision-making on whether or not to include a certain student in 'gifted' programmes (more on these later). These include students' grades, teachers' professional opinion and sometimes views of parents and students themselves. A number of elements that have been proposed as distinguishing bright and gifted children are listed in Figure 12.1.

While use of tests is probably the best way of identifying gifted students at present, it can be important to identify gifted students early on in their school career. For kindergarten aged students, sitting a cognitive

Bright child	Gifted child
– Knows the answers	– Asks the questions
– Interested	– Extremely curious
– Pays attention	– Gets involved physically and mentally
– Works hard	– Plays around, but still gets good test scores
– Answers questions	– Questions the answers
– Enjoys same-age peers	– Prefers adults or older children
– Good at memorization	– Good at guessing
– Learns easily	– Easily gets bored because she or he already knows the answers
– Listens well	– Shows strong feelings and opinions
– Self-satisfied	– Highly perfectionist and self-critical

Figure 12.1 Bright versus gifted children

ability test would obviously not be practical, and therefore a number of signs indicating giftedness in young students have been proposed:

1. The child uses an advanced vocabulary for her or his age.
2. The child has the ability to make interesting or unusual shapes or patterns using various media.
3. The child has an early understanding of abstract concepts such as death and time.
4. The child can master new skills with few repetitions.
5. The child demonstrates advanced physical skills.
6. The child demonstrates advanced reasoning skills through explanation of occurrences.
7. The child uses spontaneous verbal elaboration with new experiences.
8. The child demonstrates a sense of humour during normal conversation. (Silverman, 1992)

It is, however, important to remember that children do develop at different rates and that therefore scores on a test taken at one particular time are not set in stone. Giftedness at a particular age can be merely the result of more rapid development which ceases to exist once other children's development has caught up. One also has to remember that scores on ability tests do not simply reflect innate ability, but also result from environmental influences such as parents' possession of cultural capital such as books and their ability to provide their children with an intellectually stimulating environment. Scores on ability tests can also be influenced by a child's education. Identification of giftedness is therefore an empirical question at one particular moment in time, and will need to be reviewed.

Giftedness can be general, extending to a wide range of school subjects, or specific, limited to one particular area such as mathematics, creative writing or science. These students will achieve very well in that subject, while being average or able in other subjects. They will usually also be particularly interested in the area they are particularly good at.

Apart from being intellectually gifted, students can be gifted in a number of other ways. Typical examples include students who are artistically gifted, or who are gifted footballers. These students are not necessarily intellectual high achievers, but obviously do have specific gifts. However, in this chapter we will concentrate on academically gifted students.

Gifted students in classroom and school

As has probably become clear from the above, teaching gifted students in regular classrooms can lead to a number of problems. Such students are liable to find the content of the lesson unchallenging and boring, and will not be stretched by the regular curriculum. They will not benefit to the full from their classroom experience, and will not be able to work to their potential. Their boredom can make them lose interest in school altogether, in some cases leading to truancy and disruptive behaviour, and more often to gifted students underachieving. Research has shown that for these students a lot of what they learn in school can be a waste of time, as they already know large parts of the curriculum (Ness and Latessa, 1979; Kantrowitz and Wingert, 1992; Parke, 1992). A number of measures have therefore been proposed to deal with gifted students, which will be discussed below.

A first way of offering gifted students an education more suited to their ability is through *ability grouping*. Many studies (discussed in more detail in Chapter 14) have looked at the effect of ability grouping on students' achievement. The conclusion most reach is that ability grouping overall does not significantly affect achievement, but that it does according to some studies have a small negative effect on the achievement of low-ability students and a small positive effect on the achievement of high-ability students. It is therefore not surprising that this method has been advocated as a way of teaching gifted students. Obviously, being taught in a high-ability set will allow the teacher to teach higher-level content at greater speed, and thus counter some of the problems with regular whole-class teaching of gifted children such as student boredom. However, research has shown (see Chapter 14) that this practice can be detrimental to lower achieving students.

A variation on ability grouping is *cluster grouping*. This means that the small number of gifted students in a year are put in the same class. The other students in the class remain of mixed ability. This will more easily allow the teacher to provide the gifted students with the learning opportunities they need (e.g. an enriched curriculum, see below) than when they are all in separate classes. Another advantage is the fact that the gifted students will have the chance to interact with other students of the same ability. For the other teachers it obviates the need to have to deal with the one precocious child in their class (Winebrenner and Devlin, 1996). Disadvantages can be pressure from parents to have their children placed in a 'cluster' class, and the fact that dealing with a cluster of gifted students in a mixed-ability classroom can make classroom management more complex. Therefore, this should only be considered if the teacher who will teach this class has strong classroom management abilities and receives some training and support on teaching gifted students.

Another practice that has been posited as helpful to gifted students is *co-operative learning*. Co-operative group work was discussed in Chapters 3 and 8, but it is posited to have specific advantages for gifted students. The main advantage is said to be the fact that gifted students can work as mentors to their less able peers, thus allowing them to take on responsible roles in the class, which will make them less likely to get bored by the lesson content as they are busy 'teaching' others. Learning something with the expectation of teaching it to others is also said to lead to learning at a higher cognitive level (Johnson and Johnson, 1989). However, this approach is not without problems. Gifted students can start to dominate the group to the extent that they start to take over rather than co-operate. Also they can end up doing all the work themselves, not allowing lower ability students to experience the full benefits of co-operative group work. Gifted students can also find it difficult to understand why other students do not grasp the material, and can get impatient with them (Rogers, 1991; Robinson, 1993). Therefore, if this approach is used it is best not to let the co-operative groups become too heterogeneous.

The problem of gifted students mastering the curriculum faster than average students and not needing to revisit learned parts of the curriculum as much can be countered through *curriculum compacting*. This means that curricular material that has already been learned is eliminated from the curriculum and replaced by more demanding new material for students identified as gifted or highly able. Reis *et al.* (1998) found that they were able to eliminate up to half of the curriculum in this way in their study of gifted primary age students. Using a basic skills test, they found that this practice did not harm students' achievement, as achievement of students who had used the compacted curriculum did not differ from achievement of matched students who had used the full curriculum. Another curriculum adjustment is the use of an *enriched curriculum*. This means that the curriculum is adapted to the needs of gifted students by adding activities that require more higher-level thinking, enquiry, exploration and discovery. An enriched curriculum should include more elaborate, complex and in-depth study of major ideas or themes and should encourage students to generate new knowledge or to reconceptualize existing knowledge. It has also been recommended that a curriculum for the gifted and talented should include a large knowledge base, be inter-disciplinary wherever possible and explore new developments in the field (Van Tassel-Baska, 1994). Some studies have shown that gifted students in enriched classes significantly outperform gifted students in non-enriched classes (Kulik, 1992).

While enrichment and curriculum compacting can sometimes occur in the regular classroom, use is often made of some form of *withdrawal group*, whereby the gifted students will be withdrawn from their regular class-room for some part of the day to enable them to participate in enrichment activities there.

An enrichment activity that shows some promise is *peer tutoring*. The gifted student will be linked to an expert or a person experienced in a particular field from outside the school. This is particularly suited to students who have shown strong independent learning abilities and are highly motivated to work on a particular project or programme. The mentor, apart from being knowledgeable in her or his field, will have to be enthusiastic about the subject, have good communication skills, and be willing and able to work with young people. Mentors can be parents, former students, or contacts from the community, such as members of local arts organizations or businesses. When these conditions are met, a mentoring arrangement can be a highly enriching experience for the student.

Accelerated learning is another option for gifted students. This concept usually refers to the practice of allowing gifted students to move through the curriculum at a faster rate than their peers. This can take a number of forms, such as early entrance to school or to secondary school or univer-sity, grade-skipping or grade advancement, placing the student with stu-dents in a higher grade for part of the day for one or more subjects, placing students in a class in which one or more grades are combined, or advanced placement in which primary students are placed in a course at a local secondary school where they can study a more advanced topic for part of the week. Alternatively, secondary students can be placed in a course in a higher education institution (Gallagher, 1985; Southern and Jones, 1991). This range of practices means that it is difficult to reach overall conclusions on the effectiveness of acceleration. However, a num-ber of advantages have been proposed (Davis and Rimm, 1988; Southern and Jones, 1991). These include:

- increased learning efficiency;
- increased learning effectiveness;
- matching the curriculum to students' needs;
- exposure of the student to a new (more mature) peer group;
- increased time for careers;
- increased options for academic exploration;
- avoiding boredom; and
- avoiding alienation from less gifted peers.

Gifted, learning disabled students

A paradoxical finding is the existence of students who are both gifted and learning disabled at the same time. These students exhibit great talents or strengths in one area, while simultaneously showing disabling weaknesses in others.

Baum (1990) identified three categories of gifted, learning disabled students: (1) identified gifted students who have subtle learning disabilities; (2) unidentified students whose gifts and disabilities may be masked by average achievement; and (3) identified learning disabled students who are also gifted.

Identified gifted students with subtle learning difficulties are usually high achievers, or students with high IQ scores marking them out as gifted. However, as they grow older, their actual performance may increasingly fail to live up to their talents. In many cases this can be because their spelling or handwriting do not live up to their verbal ability. These students will often be told that they are not putting enough effort in, but sometimes teachers may be overlooking subtle learning difficulties which have not been diagnosed due to the student's overall giftedness. This, however, does not mean that underachievement in gifted students necessarily results from subtle learning difficulties. More often the cause will be motivational issues.

In *unidentified students* their disability and gifts mask each other, These students may often be struggling to achieve at their grade level, their giftedness compensating for their learning difficulties. An example of such a disability can be dyslexia. These students are often only identified when their giftedness comes out in a different context, often at a later age.

Identified learning disabled students who are also gifted are usually failing at school and have been identified as learning disabled. However, sometimes their talent can be discovered by teachers or other adults. More often, though, little attention is paid to the student's strengths as attention is focused on her or his problems.

However, outside school these students often demonstrate high-level interests, the ability to deal with complex matters or high levels of creativity. Because of this, they tend to be acutely aware of their problems at school and can become increasingly pessimistic and negative about their school experience.

Some guidelines to help these students in the classroom are the following:

- Focus attention on the development of the gift. As well as providing students with the remediation needed to overcome their learning disability, it is important to focus on their talent as well. This will help improve their self-esteem, and can in some cases lead to stronger gains than focusing on their disability (Whitmore and Maker, 1985).
- Encourage compensation strategies. While remediation will help the learner improve her or his skills in the area of weakness, it will usually not totally overcome them. Thus, students who have difficulty spelling can be encouraged to use computer spellchecks and students who have problems writing can be encouraged to use different means of expressing their ideas.
- Students who are gifted and learning disabled should be helped to understand what their abilities and gifts, as well as their weaknesses, are. This can help them make the right choices with respect to education and career.

Disadvantages have also been proposed, however. One of the most important of these is that although students may be academically more advanced than students of their age, they may not necessarily be equally advanced socially. Therefore, putting them in a group with older peers may have negative social consequences, with the gifted child finding it difficult to fit into the group. Older students may also be less likely to allow the younger, grade-advanced child to participate in their peer groups, as associating with younger children does not convey prestige in the peer group. Another issue is that giftedness can in some cases be the result of temporary faster development rather than permanent student characteristics. Acceleration can also be organizationally complicated for schools, especially with respect to timetabling.

A number of studies have found acceleration to have positive effects on the achievement of gifted students, both in the short term and in the long term (Benbow, 1991; Brody and Stanley, 1991; Van Tassel-Baska, 1992). There is not much evidence that acceleration has negative effects on students' social-emotional development either, although it is reasonable to expect that these effects will differ somewhat depending on which form of acceleration is used. Thus, advanced placement is unlikely to have detrimental effects, whereas grade skipping may, depending on the child. However, many gifted students have been found to be more socially mature as well and often seek older friends (Gallagher, 1985; Janos and Robinson, 1985; Robinson and Noble, 1991; Southern and Jones, 1991).

A number of researchers (e.g. Benbow, 1991) have proposed guidelines to take into account before a decision to accelerate is taken:

- The child's intellectual abilities should be comprehensively examined, using a variety of measures including ability tests and academic achievement tests to make sure that the child is intellectually capable of being accelerated.
- The child's social-emotional readiness should be assessed by a psychologist. The child should have demonstrated an absence of adjustment problems and a high motivation to learn.
- Both the child and her or his parents should be involved in the decision to accelerate. Both must be willing to do this, and there must be no coercion.
- The receiving teacher must be enthusiastic about acceleration and be willing to help the child adjust.
- Grade advancement should occur at a natural transition point, such as the start of a new school year.
- Grade advancement should be arranged on a trial basis (e.g. one to two months). After the trial period the child should be able to return to her or his original grade if she or he wants to do so.
- Teachers should try not to create excessive expectations of grade advancement, so if it does not work out the child does not consider her or himself to have failed.
- Sometimes grade advancement can lead to gaps in students' knowledge where they have missed certain topics. Arrangements need to be made to cover these. However, as most curricula revisit topics and gifted children learn fast, this is not usually a major problem.

Summary

As well as providing for students with learning difficulties, schools also have to take the needs of gifted students into account.

Gifted students are usually defined as students who score strongly above average on standardized achievement tests, who achieve much higher than their peers, and who are identified by teachers as gifted. Giftedness can be global or limited to a specific subject. Apart from being academically gifted, students can also be gifted in a number of non-academic fields, such as arts and sports.

Parents and gifted children

Parenting a gifted child can be quite a challenge as these children often have different interests from their peers, and will constantly ask questions from an early age. They can also challenge parental authority and it will be necessary to explain the reasons for decisions as 'because I said so' does not hold much water with gifted children.

Spending time reading to children from an early age and offering them an intellectually stimulating environment will help them both intellectually and emotionally. Children should be encouraged to develop their interests, even if they may seem unusual for a child of that age. Exposing them to the parents' own interests can also help them.

Gifted infants have been found to sleep less than other babies, and require extra stimulation when awake. This can obviously be very tiring for parents, who may need some other family member to help them at times (Silverman, 1992).

Parents can also help by placing their child in a school with good provision for gifted children.

A caveat here is that it is easy to overestimate the ability of one's own children, and therefore it is important to take into account all the elements of giftedness mentioned above before putting pressure on teachers to treat your child as gifted.

It is also important to remember that students develop at different rates and that one student's advantage over peers can be temporary.

Gifted students in regular classrooms are often insufficiently challenged by the regular curriculum. They can become bored and disenchanted with school, which can lead to underachievement.

For these reasons, a number of strategies have been proposed to cater for the needs of gifted students.

Ability grouping has been found to slightly improve the achievement of high-achieving students in some studies, but may be detrimental to low-achieving students. A variant of this is cluster grouping, in which gifted students are grouped in one class, which is mixed ability for the rest. This can have the advantage that it allows gifted students to interact with one another and that the teacher can more easily cater to their needs. However, classroom management may become more complicated.

Co-operative learning has also been proposed as a strategy. The advantages of this lie in the monitoring role that gifted students can assume in co-operative groups. Possible disadvantages are that gifted students become too dominating in the group, and that their presence can lead to free-rider effects occurring.

Other approaches have looked at adjustments to the curriculum. Curriculum compacting is the practice whereby parts of the curriculum are skipped for gifted students. This can be done because a large part of the curriculum consists of low-level practice and revisiting of previously learnt material, which may be unnecessary for gifted students. Curriculum enrichment on the other hand means adding more challenging content to the curriculum. An enriched curriculum should include more elaborate, complex and in-depth study of major ideas or themes and should encourage students to generate new knowledge or reconceptualize existing knowledge. This practice has been found to improve the achievement of gifted students, and can be combined with curriculum compacting.

Acceleration is the practice of allowing gifted students to move through the curriculum faster than their peers. This can take a number of forms, such as early entrance to school or to secondary school or university, grade skipping or grade advancement, placing the student with students in a higher grade for part of the day for one or more subjects, placing students in a class in which one or more grades are combined and advanced placement in which primary students are placed on a course in a local secondary school for part of the week. This approach has been found to be quite effective, as long as certain conditions are met. These include ensuring that the student is not only intellectually but also socially and emotionally sufficiently advanced to be able to cope with acceleration, and that the student, her parents and the receiving teacher are all motivated to make acceleration work.

Self-study questions

1. What are the possible disadvantages of acceleration, and what could you do to alleviate them?
2. How can one distinguish gifted from bright students?
3. What strategy would you choose to help gifted students in your school?
4. What adjustments to the curriculum can be made to help gifted students?
5. Why could gifted students pose a problem for teachers if nothing is done to cater to their needs?
6. What can parents do to help their gifted children?
7. Describe cluster grouping, its advantages and disadvantages.

13

Teaching in the Early Years

Advance organizers

In this chapter you will learn:

- The importance of early childhood education.
- Differing views on how to teach in pre-school, and what research has to say about these methods.
- How best to promote students' school-readiness in pre-school settings.
- The importance of play and what children learn from it.
- The main features of two influential early years programmes, the American High/Scope project and the Italian Reggio Emilia approach.

The importance of early years education

The early years of childhood are probably the most important developmental period in human life. Childhood experience shapes development in a large number of ways, one of these being cognitive development. As we mentioned in Chapter 8 according to most learning theories important cognitive developments take place in the early years, such as the transition from the sensori-motor stage to the pre-operational stage in Piagetian theory. Young children are learning all the time through interaction with their parents and their environment long before they enter any kind of formal schooling. Brain research has shown that up to 85 per cent of all the neurological pathways that people acquire develop during the first six years of life (Rutter and Rutter, 1992).

At this age large differences start to emerge between children caused by their social background. An excellent example of this is a longitudinal study by Hart and Risley (1995), which found that by the age of 48 months children of parents from a professional background would have heard their parents use five times as many words as children of parents living on welfare benefits, and almost twice as many words as children of parents from a working-class background. By the age of four children of parents from a professional background would also have received 560,000 more instances of encouraging than of discouraging feedback, children of working-class parents 100,000 more instances of encouraging than discouraging feedback, and children from parents on welfare 125,000 more instances of discouraging feedback than of encouraging feedback. This means that differences between children from different social backgrounds will have already accrued, both with respect to self-esteem and ability. If no intervention happens these disparities will increase, leading to large differences once students enter primary school.

This is clearly an argument to intervene before primary school, and to encourage in particular children from lower social backgrounds to enter some form of pre-primary schooling. This has led most countries to encourage pre-school education, with enrolment in nursery education being almost universal in France, Belgium and the Scandinavian countries. This still leaves us with the issue of how formal this schooling should be. This question will be discussed below.

Early years teaching: what research has to say

That pre-school education does indeed have positive effects on students' subsequent achievement in primary school is demonstrated by research showing that children who take part in pre-school education perform better at primary school than students who have had no pre-school education. Some research even suggests that students benefit most if pre-school education starts before the age of 3 (the age that pre-school educations starts in most countries) (Wylie, 1998).

Students starting nursery education have often been found to have difficulty with the transition from home to kindergarten. A survey of over 3,500 teachers in the USA found that almost half of all children entering kindergarten had difficulties with this transition, problems being reported in such areas as following directions, academic skills, working independently, working in a group and communicating. These are clearly crucial skills that children will need during the course of their education from primary school onwards, and getting students ready for primary school therefore has to be one of the main goals of pre-school education (Wylie, 1998).

The main discussion among early years educators is whether to go for a mainly formal academic approach, starting early with the teaching of basic skills through instruction, or a more informal approach that stresses children learning from interacting with their environment and other adults and children. According to Egertson (1997) early years teaching in the USA has moved away from a play and group orientation to more direct teaching of basic skills in recent decades. A similar change is also taking place in the UK, as a result of government strategies (Siraj-Blatchford, 1999). A focus on learning basic skills has been shown to be positively related to achievement on standardized tests, and it has been argued that this method is particularly important for children from less advantaged backgrounds in light of the fact that they in particular may be lacking these basic skills. Doubts have been expressed over whether this method is the best one over the long term, however, as a number of studies show that this type of instruction is not suitable for students of this age as it may lessen their disposition to learn and cause these young students too much stress (Katz, 1999; Schweinhart and Weikart, 1997). In order to promote school-readiness it may well be better to focus on social skills, creating a disposition to learn and developing 'school-readiness' skills. A number of studies have shown that over the long term young children taught in this more child-centred way (known as a developmentally appropriate practice) performed better (Miller and Bizzell, 1983; Schweinhart and Weikart, 1997). A longitudinal study comparing the active learning model devised in the High/Scope programme with an academic approach likewise found better results for the High/Scope approach, which persisted up to age 23. Students in this type of classroom have also been found to score higher on measures of creative thinking (Hirsch-Pasek, Hyson and Recorla, 1990) and to show better language development (Marcon, 1992). However, this does not mean that teaching of basic skills should not take place at all. In general though, it can be said that the younger the child the more informal the learning environment should be. Such an environment should encourage spontaneous play and construction, which does need to be combined with more demanding exercises (Katz, 1999).

In a number of non-Anglo-Saxon countries the 'academic' approach to nursery education is far less prevalent. Thus, in Flanders (one of the highest scoring European regions in most international comparisons) most nursery education centres around play, and literacy and numeracy teaching are not started until primary school. In Hungary, another educationally high-ranking country, formal numeracy and literacy teaching is likewise only started in primary school, nursery teaching concentrating on school readiness skills such as listening, paying attention and shape and space. In both Hungary and Flanders primary education only starts at age 6. A similar approach is taken in Scandinavia, where children are encouraged to learn by play and discovery.

Research has shown that young children learn best when they are actively interacting with others and their environment rather than being passive recipients of information (Wood and Bennet, 1999). This means that early years teaching should be highly interactive, and students should be allowed to explore their environment. They should have the chance to record their learning in a variety of ways, verbally, written, through painting, drawing and building things (Katz, 1999). Early years education needs to balance student discovery of their environment with structured activity designed to get the most educationally from these experiences. Teachers should emphasize the connections between the classroom and students' everyday experiences. As young children learn best through hands-on activities, these should be plentiful in the nursery classroom. A wide variety of easily accessible resources need to be provided. Children enjoy imitating adults, therefore activities such as peeling potatoes, washing the pots or cooking can be used to great effect. Siraj-Blatchford (1999) identifies three main elements necessary for effective early years teaching:

1. Creating the learning environment. This includes organizing materials and resources, providing relevant, interesting and novel experiences, and providing opportunities for active exploration and questioning, including a lot of student–student and student–adult talk in order to allow linguistic competency to develop.
2. Direct instruction, including demonstration, description, answering questions, directing the child's attention and constructive criticism and reinforcement.
3. Scaffolding, including directing attention to new aspects of a situation, helping the child to sequence activities and managing complex tasks by breaking them down into smaller, more manageable parts.

Research thus seems to indicate that the prime purpose of pre-school education is to promote school-readiness, focusing on skills rather than academic content. Key school-readiness skills include the following:

- social skills, such as the ability to respect others, to work co-operatively, to express emotions and feelings in an appropriate way, to listen to others, to follow rules and procedures, to sit attentively and to work independently;
- communication skills, such as asking for assistance in an appropriate way, verbalising thoughts and feelings, answering open and closed questions, participating in class discussion and relating ideas and experiences; and
- task-related behaviours such as not disrupting other students during the lesson, monitoring one's own behaviour, finding materials necessary to complete a task, following teacher directions, generalising skills across situations, being on task during whole-class work, making choices, beginning and completing work at an appropriate time without teacher direction and trying different problem-solving strategies.

Some ways of developing school-readiness skills are the following:

1. One of the main aspects of early years education is play. Teachers should provide students with an environment where they can play with each other, using a variety of materials designed to facilitate their learning and development. Teachers can in some cases usefully join in children's play in order to extend it. The teacher needs to make sure that all students are joining in the activities, and needs to introduce students to new ideas and situations. This can sometimes be done in the course of play, by observing children's problems and helping them to overcome them. For example, when building using blocks children will initially pile them on each other, and will find that their structure quickly falls down. The teacher can point to how the walls of the classroom are built to help them pile the blocks better (Edelman Borden, 1997).
2. Small group or class discussion is another method that has been proposed for early years education. One way to do this is for teachers to

introduce an idea or topic, and then allow the children to give all the possible answers, ideas and relevant words they can come up with. All students should be encouraged to participate and should be made to listen to others. This will develop listening skills and the skills to generate ideas, to verbalize ideas and to respect one another's opinions. The main ideas can then be written down on the board. These discussions can be more or less guided by the teacher depending on the topic and goals of the discussion.

3. Categorizing objects, like toys or other materials in the classroom according to criteria such as colour, shape or size will help students to develop their classification skills and mathematical ability. The teacher needs to make sure that students explain the criteria they have used to classify the objects and that all students understand what criteria can be used.

4. Paired or group work, in which students work together on a project or assignment has been successfully employed in nursery schools as well. To ensure effectiveness it is necessary to make sure that all students have to contribute to be able to complete the task. The teacher needs to closely monitor student interaction, modelling co-operative behaviour and correcting behaviour where necessary. This should help develop students' co-operative learning skills, help them verbalize what they are doing, and develop their problem-solving skills. Working in large groups is not always suitable with very young children.

5. At the beginning of the lesson the teacher can start with a discussion of a particular topic (known as 'circle time'). This can be a project they are going to work on or are working on, but may also be a game to help students learn each other's names at the beginning of the year, a discussion of objects brought into the class by students, singing, or discussing students' recent out-of-school experiences. This will help students to learn to organize their thinking, and verbalize experiences in a structured way (i.e. telling a story with a beginning, middle and end).

Some research has shown that if the child has not achieved minimal social competence by age 6, she or he will find it hard to develop that competence later in life (Katz, 1997). Children can easily slip into negative recursive relationships, in that their own behaviour patterns will cause reactions in others that will strengthen those patterns. It is therefore important that teachers try to counteract these forces by having high expectations of all students and by trying to draw out shy and socially dysfunctional students and develop their competences, for example through role-play and group activities.

As in primary and secondary education, activities need to be matched to the child's capabilities. This necessitates that teachers are aware of what these capabilities are for each individual student and for their class as a whole. Standardized testing can be unsuitable for young children, whose performance on standardized tests can change from day to day, leading to highly unreliable results. Therefore, alternative methods have

---

What children learn from play

As has been mentioned above, a lot of countries use a play-based approach to pre-school education. That this does not mean that no learning takes place is illustrated by the following examples, taken from Edelman Borden (1997).

As most play activities involve verbal interaction with other students, they can aid the development of social skills, verbal skills and co-operation, although teacher input will be necessary to develop these skills.

Outdoor play, such as running, digging and climbing, refines a child's gross-motor skills, including cross-lateral movements (using right arm with left leg, for example) that are important to later writing and reading. It also gives children the chance to manipulate their environment.

Indoor play activities, which are often more structured as the environment has usually been designed by the teacher for teaching purposes, likewise offers children a wide range of learning opportunities.

Block building develops children's small motor skills, and can help them learn about mathematical concepts like depth, width, height, volume, area and measurement, as well scientific concepts like gravity, stability and weight. Shape recognition, differentiation of shapes and size are also involved in block building.

Dramatic play, such as dressing up, cooking, or having a little shop helps students make sense of the adult world and helps develop children's vocabulary. Dramatic play helps students to concentrate, to be attentive and to use self-control. For example, when setting up a shop, the child must set up the counter, invite friends to shop, use the 'cash register' and bag the groceries, all of which develop children's concept of sequential acts. Imaginative play can contribute to children learning how to express their emotions and think abstractly. Imaginative play provides an important role in developing children's creativity.

Solving *puzzles* requires abstract thinking to enable students to know where to fit the pieces and fine motor skills to allow them to actually do this.

Playing with *manipulative toys* such as Lego likewise develops children's fine motor skills and sometimes their abstract thinking as well. This type of play can encourage children's creativity, being incorporated into imaginative play in novel ways.

In contrast to adults, young children will also consider *cleaning up* after play to be a fun activity. Doing this is a useful educational activity, requiring children to sort, classify, match and organize when they put building blocks, toys and other materials in place.

A *sand or water basin* with containers that students can fill up and empty will allow students to develop further pre-mathematical skills such as fractions, as well as developing fine motor skills.

---

been proposed to assess the progress of young children. One of these methods is structured observation of children's behaviour. For example, in the High/Scope programme teachers use a child observation record on which they take daily notes of children's developmentally significant behaviours. Another possibility is the use of portfolios. These contain a record of a child's work at different times of the year, including the child's drawings, teachers' notes, or photographs of the child's work such as block structures. This allows the teacher to look at student progress over time, and can also help students develop forms of self-reflection, by allowing them to look at their own progress with the help of the teacher, who can ask questions such as 'what would you do differently if you did it now?' In order for this effect to be strongest portfolios must be easily accessible to students (Cohen, 1999).

High/Scope and Reggio Emilia, two influential early years programmes

The High/Scope project

The High/Scope project, developed in the USA, is based on principles of active learning emphasizing direct experience with real objects. Through active learning children are supposed to engage in 58 key experiences set out by the High/Scope programme. These are grouped into ten categories: creative representation, language and literacy, initiative and social relations, movement, music, classification, seriation, number, space and time. The school day is organized around the 'plan–do–review sequence'. The children plan what to do during that session, do the activity and then reflect on the results. Adults are supposed to interact with the children, taking part in the activities and generally helping to facilitate students' learning and interactions. The physical environment is organised around a number of 'interest areas', each focusing on a specific kind of play such as block play or art activities. Materials are made suitably accessible so children can work with them independently.

In High/Scope academic skills are not directly taught. Rather, experiences and an environment are provided that help children develop broad abilities which can form the basis of academic learning in primary school. This is done by providing them with relevant experiences (based on the 58 key experiences identified) through, for example, providing materials that allow children to use their beginning skills in counting (High/Scope, 2000).

Reggio Emilia

Another influential programme has been that adopted by the district of Reggio Emilia in Italy.

Nursery schools in this district follow a thematic, project-based approach developing an emergent curriculum that follows from the interaction between teachers and students. Teachers record students' discussions on a topic and their reactions to questions put to them by the teacher, and develop the curriculum based on their transcript of the tapes. This means that each year the curriculum is adapted to students' interests. Usually students work in groups on a particular project over a number of days or weeks, not necessarily working on it everyday, but returning to the project at regular intervals (Siraj-Blatchford, 1999).

An important aspect of the programme is documentation, which is seen as an important aid to students' learning. Children are encouraged to express the feelings and experiences they have during their work through drawings, in written form or through three-dimensional representations. These are then displayed, providing parents with a chance to see their children's work and what is being done in school, and allowing students to revisit past experiences and see themselves and their peers from a different point of view. Seeing their work displayed in this way also validates it for the children and can thus enhance their self-esteem. Looking at this documentation can also help teachers to refine their own work (Edwards, Gandini and Forman, 1993).

The programme is well resourced, with schools employing specialist staff such as an 'atelierista' (resident artist) and a 'pedagogista' (child development specialist). Teachers usually work in teams of two.

Summary

In this chapter we have learnt the crucial importance of an early start to education, especially in the light of the big differences emerging at an early age between students of differing social backgrounds as a result of such factors as the amount of vocabulary they are exposed to and the number of encouraging as opposed to discouraging comments they receive from their parents. Therefore, pre-school education is encouraged in most countries, with participation rates near to 100 per cent in a number of them.

A discussion point in early years education is whether it should be mainly academic and geared to teaching basic skills, an approach increasingly taken in the USA and the UK, or use more informal, often play-based methods in order to foster school-readiness skills, leaving the actual acquisition of numeracy and literacy until later. The academic option does tend to show some positive short-term results on standardized tests. However, longitudinal studies show more positive effects for students taught in less academic ways in nursery school, such as those enrolled in settings taking part in the High/Scope project.

A number of ways to encourage the acquisition of school-readiness skills, which include social skills, communication skills and appropriate task-related behaviour, have been proposed. These include the use of more or less structured play, which can enhance students' social skills, verbal skills, co-operation, pre-numeracy and literacy skills and motor skills; small group or class discussion, which can help develop listening skills and the skills to generate ideas, to verbalize, and to respect each other's opinions and ideas; paired or group work, which could help develop students' co-operative learning skills, help them verbalize what they are doing, and develop their problem-solving skills; and circle time, which will help students to learn to organize their thinking, and verbalize experiences in a structured way (i.e. telling a story with a beginning, middle and end).

Assessment is another issue in early years, in that standardized testing is not suitable for students of this age group. Therefore, alternative forms of assessment need to be used, such as observation of students' behaviour in the classroom or portfolios of students' work.

Two programmes which have been influential in recent years are the High/Scope project in the USA and the Reggio Emilia project in Italy. The High/Scope project is based on principles of active learning, emphasizing direct experience with real objects. The school day is organized around the 'plan–do–review sequence'. The children plan what to do during that session, do the activity and then reflect on the results.

The Reggio Emilia approach is thematic and project-based and developing an emergent curriculum that follows from the interaction between teachers and students. An important element of the project is documenting students' work.

Self-study questions

1. At what age do you think children should receive their first out-of-home education, and why?
2. How could you assess students learning in pre-school?
3. What do children learn from play?
4. Describe the main features of the High/Scope approach.
5. What are the advantages and disadvantages of an academic approach to pre-school education?
6. What school-readiness skills should children acquire in pre-school?
7. Can you name some teaching strategies that can help children to acquire these school-readiness skills?

14

Taking Account of Individual Differences

Advance organizers

In this chapter you will learn about various ways of dealing with individual student differences such as:

- The advantages and disadvantages of different grouping methods.
- How to limit the negative effects of setting if it is used.
- Various ways of individualizing instruction, their advantages and disadvantages.
- Kolb's theory of learning, and how it applies to teaching.
- Gardner's theory of multiple intelligences, and how it applies to teaching.
- Other theories of learning differences, and how they apply to teaching.
- Evidence on the effectiveness of teaching to different learning styles.

Introduction

One of the most controversial aspects of teaching is dealing with the many differences between students in the classroom. Traditionally these differences have mainly been conceptualized in terms of differences in ability.

Initial research into individual differences in ability was based on the theory that people possess such a thing as 'global intelligence' which is an accurate predictor of students' performance in school subjects. However, this view has been increasingly challenged. Research has, for example, shown that students can exhibit different levels of achievement in different subjects, thus challenging the view of the primacy of global intelligence or IQ (e.g. Gould, 1996). More recently, this has led to the theory of multiple intelligences which posits that rather than there being a single intelligence, which is related mainly to cognitive ability, there exist a variety of intelligences including emotional intelligence, verbal intelligence and spatial intelligence which are all important to people's lives (Gardner, 1983). Also, rather than look at intelligence or ability, researchers (e.g. Kolb, 1973) have increasingly started to focus on differences in learning styles which are posited to affect the way people prefer to learn, some people for example preferring a visual and others a verbal approach to learning.

In this chapter we will look first at the main ways in which educators have tried to deal with differences in 'ability', and then explore how research on multiple intelligences and learning styles could affect classroom practice.

Streaming, setting and selection

A first traditional method to deal with the fact that students may differ in ability is selection. This can be done in two ways. In some countries the whole education system is selective. This means that at some point in the student's school career she or he will be tested on a national test which will determine her or his entry into different types of schools. The '11-plus' examination, used in Northern Ireland and in the past in the whole of the UK, is an example of this. A second method is for individual schools to select their students by interview or testing.

There is not much reliable research comparing systems using selection to those that do not, but what research there is does not seem to suggest that selection leads to higher achievement once students' prior achievement has been taken into account. There are a number of reasons to suspect that selection is not the best approach to take for dealing with student differences. The first issue is that selection may lead to a waste of talent. In a selective system the basic underlying principle is one of allowing only a minority of the school population to enter the 'academic' schools which will lead to higher education, based on their perceived innate ability. This is essentially contradictory to the needs of societies in the information age which will require an ever larger proportion of people to acquire higher order skills and go through higher education. Furthermore, there is a clear equity issue here in that students from lower socio-economic status backgrounds who tend to do worse on national tests are likely to be excluded from the chance to participate in academic education and, therefore, in higher education. In essence, this argues against the thesis that schools can make a difference and can improve the skills of students from all social backgrounds. It has in fact been found that students at the bottom end of the achievement spectrum in selective schools will tend to do worse than if they studied at non-selective schools. Selection is also likely to be inefficient, as no selection mechanism will be 100 per cent accurate (some estimates suggest that any selection mechanism will inaccurately include 10 per cent and inaccurately exclude another 10 per cent). Finally, the idea that one could select students who are to receive an academic education is based on the view that students' ability is both unidimensional and fixed. Both positions have been contradicted by research. First, it has become increasingly clear that intelligence is a multidimensional concept, and that it might even be possible to talk about the existence of multiple intelligences (see below). Furthermore, the idea that intelligence in any area is fixed and unchanging has likewise been disproved by research (Gould, 1996). One of the factors that affects

intelligence as measured through a variety of tests is education. Therefore, it would seem that selection is not the best way to deal with student
differences.

A second way of dealing with student differences is streaming. This is a
procedure whereby within a school students are segregated into different
classes according to ability. This could have the advantage of allowing
teachers to teach students of similar ability which makes it easier to pitch
lessons at the right level and provide experiences of success for all
students.

However, there are a number of problems associated with streaming.
Still underlying streaming is the assumption that intelligence is unidimensional enough to be able to predict students' achievement in all
subjects based on some prior measure. This is not supported by research,
which points to differences in student performance over different subjects. More recent research supports the view that intelligence is a multidimensional concept. While correlations between performance in
different subjects are significant, they are not high enough to suggest that
one is measuring the same underlying concept, the average correlation
between mathematics and English being only about 0.5 to 0.6 according to
a recent study (Muijs, 1998b). Like selection, streaming also assumes that
ability is basically fixed and unchanging, which, especially among rapidly
changing teenagers, is a questionable assumption.

Furthermore, both streaming and selection assume that ability is *the*
determining factor in achievement. However, while this view is strongly
engrained in our culture, this is not necessarily the case in non-Western
societies. Thus, in other cultures, such as a number of South-East Asian
countries, effort is stressed more strongly, and the belief that anyone who
puts in the effort can succeed is often cited as a major reason for the
educational success of these South-East Asian countries (Reynolds and
Farrell, 1996). Other aspects, such as motivation and self-esteem, have
also been found to affect achievement quite strongly, and a large number
of studies show that being streamed into the lower streams has a negative
effect on students' self-esteem (Hansell and Karweit, 1983; Muijs, 1997).
This can clearly lead to self-fulfilling prophecies, as low self-esteem leads
to low achievement and disaffection from school.

Research has also shown that students in lower streams are often
taught an 'impoverished' curriculum, which does not attempt to engage
students' thinking or understanding and is limited to simple drill and
practice exercises (e.g. Hansell and Karweit, 1983). While in theory designed to teach students at their level, this practice can further widen the
gap between the high and low streams, and fails to give all students
access to a rich, full curriculum, thus creating equity issues. This is an
unfortunate consequence of streaming as many educators have found
that 'low-ability' students can pleasantly surprise them when allowed to
engage with a high-level curriculum. Furthermore, critical thinking skills
are crucial to all in modern society, not just to a 'high ability élite'. Some

studies have also found that high-ability students receive the better teachers and support, thus furthering inequality (Hallinan and Sorenson, 1985).

As with selection, a further problem with streaming is that according to research there is a tendency for students from lower socio-economic status backgrounds and from ethnic minorities to be put in the lower streams whether or not they are able. (Hallinan and Sorenson, 1985; Secada, 1992).

Overall, then, streaming does not seem to be a particularly effective way of dealing with student differences.

A third way of dealing with student differences is through setting. In contrast to streaming, in setting students are assigned to 'same ability' groups on a subject by subject basis. Setting solves a number of the problems associated with streaming, in that in setting students it is acknowledged that students can be at different levels in different subjects. Thus, depending on her or his results a student can be in the top group for maths and in one of the lower groups for English. However, a number of problems do remain. The possibility of harming a student's self-concept in a certain subject still exists when that student is put into a lower set, although if that student is in a higher set for other subjects this should not necessarily harm her or his overall attitude to school. Also, as with streaming, it is extremely difficult for teachers to have high expectations (identified in Chapter 6 as a crucial aspect in helping students perform better) of classes which they know to have been formed explicitly from students who are not particularly good at the subject. This can in turn lead to these students suffering expectancy effects and receiving an impoverished curriculum in that subject. Furthermore, setting does not allow lower-ability students to benefit by learning from higher-ability students.

On the positive side, setting can make teaching more easy, as the attenuation of the range of ability in the lesson will make it easier for the teacher to pitch the lesson at the right level for students. This will also mean that lower-ability students will not be left behind through not understanding the lesson and becoming demoralized. Higher-ability students are on the other hand less likely to become bored in a group of a similar achievement level, as the lesson is more likely to be sufficiently challenging for them. This is particularly relevant when whole-class teaching is employed in schools with a particularly heterogeneous intake with regards to student performance, which is often the case in the most deprived areas.

Looking at the effects of setting on student achievement, the results are somewhat indecisive and do not seem to be uniform across subjects. Most research in mathematics, for example, shows small positive effects (Askew and William, 1995). However, when the data are studied more closely, this seems to result from the fact the high-ability students perform better in sets than in mixed-ability classrooms, while low-ability students do worse in sets than in mixed-ability classrooms. There is no

---

Streaming in secondary schools

One of the first major studies of the effects of streaming in schools occurred in England in the 1960s. This ethnographic study looked at the effect of both selection between schools, one school studied being for students who had passed an IQ test at 11 years of age, the other catering for students who had failed this test, and at the effects of streaming within the schools. Both had similar effects, called 'differentiation and polarisation' by the two authors, Lacey (1970) and Hargreaves (1967).

Lacey's (1970) analysis of peer relations in a boys' grammar school (secondary school to which the students who performed best at '11+ examinations' usually went) revealed the development of an anti-school subculture in the lower streams by the end of the second year, friendship choices being made almost exclusively within either the highest two or the lowest two streams, antagonism choices being made almost exclusively from the higher to the lower streams and vice versa. Lower-stream students were more strongly orientated to the out-of-school adolescent subculture and expected to leave school earlier than higher-stream students. This process was even more strongly evident in the third year. Students who failed to ally themselves to either group became isolates. Extreme anti-school behaviour was not evident in this (élite) school, as students who went too far could be removed from school. This was not the case in the secondary modern school (for students with poorer results on the 11+ examination) studied by Hargreaves (1967), where the lower streams were much more extreme in their anti-school attitudes resulting in the formation of a delinquent group among the anti-school group. The four streams in that school in general were differentiated in a similar way to those in the grammar school, the highest stream boys valuing academic norms and neat dressing, and being opposed to fighting, 'messing' in class and copying. They also tended to attend organized leisure time activities and more often visited the public library. Students from the lower streams considered school to be a waste of time and valued aggression and messing around in class. They were more likely to attend unorganised clubs, such as billiard halls and the 'beat' club. The two streams differed strongly in absenteeism, late arrivals and general school commitment. As in the grammar school studied by Lacey (1970), there was clear antagonism between the groups as evidenced by the friendship choices made.

In two more recent studies the same processes were seen to operate. Thus, Hallinan and Williams (1990) found the same tendency of differentiation between high and low streams, friendship dyads formed mainly within one's own stream among 1,500 high school and college students, and Berends (1995) using data from a sample of 25,000 US high school students reports significant differences between college-bound, general and vocational stream members on several measures of school bonding, such as absenteeism, engagement with school and disciplinary problems in school. Hallinan and Sorenson (1985) remark on the similar performance expectations for a certain group created by streaming both among the teachers and the students themselves. In a study of Belgian primary school children, Muijs (1997) found similar results.

---

strong effect for average students. For English the overall effect is usually slightly negative, but with similar results for high- and low-ability students.

All this means that whether or not to set is a difficult decision, for which there are arguments both for and against which need to be weighed against each other in each individual case.

If setting is to be used, there are a number of things that can be done to alleviate the most negative effects resulting from this practice. First, to be effective, setting needs to be flexible with students being able to change from one group to another when their achievement seems to call for this. This can help teachers keep in mind that ability is not fixed, and can also stop setting becoming too much of a self-fulfilling prophecy.

Another way of helping to avoid teacher expectancy effects, and also of preserving some of the advantages of having students of different ability levels helping one another in class while simultaneously decreasing the ability range in a subject, is using the 'zip method'. This method works as follows: students in a subject are listed by achievement in that subject (for example, on a standardized test) from high to low, and groups are then formed as shown in Figure 14.1. While the range of ability in each of these three groups is reduced, in every case there is at least one student who has scored higher than the lowest scoring student in the other groups. This means that teachers can less easily assume that these are the 'worst' students.

Student 1
Student 2
Student 3
Student 4
Student 5
Student 6
Student 7
Student 8
Student 9
Student 10
Student 11
Student 12
Student 13
Student 14
Student 15
Student 16
Student 17
Student 18
Student 19
Student 20

GROUP 1, *GROUP 2*, **GROUP 3**

Figure 14.1   Setting using the 'zip method'

Individual learning

Rather than changing grouping arrangements in the school, teachers can also try to take individual differences into account as much as possible in their classroom teaching.

One way to do this is to allow all students to work through previously prepared schemes or worksheets at their own tempo, going on to the next worksheet/page/exercise when they are ready. The teacher's role is then primarily one of facilitating this individual learning by going round the class helping students with problems and answering their questions. This approach has been tried, in particular in Anglo-Saxon countries, but has not been found to be an effective teaching strategy. A large number of studies, discussed in Chapter 1, have found that when too much time is spent letting students work on their own, their achievement is lower (e.g. Rosenshine, 1979; Brophy and Good, 1986; Mortimore *et al.*, 1988). This is largely the result of the fact that this style of instruction does not allow many teacher–student contacts, or indeed student–student contacts (research has shown that the number of contacts is lower in this type of classroom than in classrooms in which whole-class teaching predominates), and thus does not allow students to express and articulate their ideas. Scaffolding by either the teacher or other students is also less likely to occur. Using this method as the main part of classroom teaching is therefore not usually effective. However, using some individualized work in which students can progress at different rates during the seatwork part of the lesson may be useful.

The use of 'individual learning plans' is another variant of individual learning strategies. In this strategy, used in several countries for students with special needs or learning difficulties, teachers will develop specific 'individual learning plans' for students, which set out the goals that students should be able to acquire and the means by which teachers can help students acquire these goals. This can be a very useful exercise, but a number of caveats need to be taken into account. First, this process takes a lot of time and effort, and probably if applied to all students would require more staff than is usual in schools at present. Second, focusing too much on individual plans may disadvantage some students who are not able to access a full and rich curriculum, and may also exacerbate possible negative expectation effects.

Splitting the class into a number of small groups engaged in different tasks can also help the teacher to deal with student differences. This solves some of the problems involved with individualized instruction as it allows students to interact with each other and allows the teacher to teach different groups in turn, thus allowing more student–teacher and student–student contacts. However, arrangements in which different groups are engaged in different activities are complex from a classroom management point of view, and usually lead to more time being spent on routine classroom management activities at the expense of academic learning time. Teachers still have less contact with each individual student than in whole class teaching. It is therefore not surprising that Mortimore *et al.* (1988) found that classrooms in which more time was spent teaching different small groups had lower gains in achievement than classrooms in which more time was spent teaching the whole class. Differentiated group work can be useful during seatwork sessions, however.

Finally, during whole-class teaching teachers should differentiate questions to students according to their performance in the subject taught, and possibly differentiate seatwork tasks for different students or groups of students.

Teaching to different learning styles

While previously we have discussed student differences mainly in terms of differences in 'ability', recently increasing attention has focused on differences in students' learning styles. While this concept is often evoked, what exactly is meant by different learning styles is not always clear.

One of the most clearly elucidated theories of learning styles is that of Kolb (1995), according to whom learning styles can be ranked along a continuum running from

1. concrete experience (being involved in a new experience) through
2. reflective observation (watching others or developing observations about our own experience) and
3. abstract conceptualization (creating theories to explain observations) to
4. active experimentation (using theories to solve problems and make decisions).

As is clear from the above, Kolb saw these different styles as a cycle through which all learners should move over time. However, more recently learning theorists have conceptualized these styles as ones which learners come to prefer and rely on, most learners thus preferring one of these four styles. Litzinger and Osif (1993) called these different types of learners *accommodators*, *divergers*, *convergers* and *assimilators*, and arranged them along Kolb's continuum as depicted in Figure 14.2.

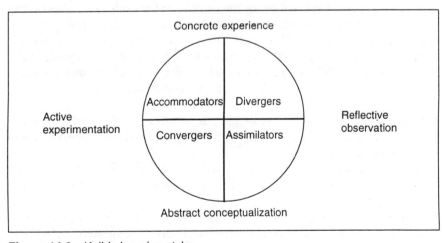

Figure 14.2 Kolb's learning styles
Source: Litzinger and Osif (1993)

Accommodators prefer an active learning style. They tend to rely on intuition rather than on logic and like to connect learning to personal meaning and experiences. They enjoy applying their knowledge to real-life situations and do not like to analyse too much. When teaching these learners it is recommended to encourage independent discovery and to let learners participate actively in their learning. Interpersonal aspects are important to accommodators, so they will tend to enjoy co-operative learning and group work.

Assimilators like accurate, organized delivery of knowledge and tend to respect the views of those they consider to be experts on the subject. They think logically and prefer abstract ideas. Logic is more important to them than a practical explanation. They will prefer lecture-style lessons or carefully prepared exercises which they will follow closely. However, they also enjoy independent analysis of data and research.

Convergers are mainly interested in the relevancy of information. They want to understand in detail how something operates, so they can use it in practice. These learners prefer technical information and are not very interested in social and interpersonal issues. Lessons that suit these learners are interactive, and it can be useful to provide them with real-life problems to explore. Convergers will enjoy doing hands-on tasks, use manipulatives, etc.

Divergers are mainly interested in the 'why' of a system. They like to reason from specific information and to explore what a system has to offer. They like to see things from a variety of viewpoints and like categorizing information. These learners like to use their imagination when solving problems. Divergers enjoy self-directed learning and like independent study, simulations and role-play. Information should be presented to them in a detailed, systematic manner.

Kolb's theory is far from being the only learning styles classification in existence. Other classifications look at students' different sensory preferences. According to this theory, learners can be classified as preferring either visual, auditory or tactile/kinaesthetic learning (Dunn and Dunn, 1978; Benzwie, 1987), while others add print, interactive and olfactory learners to this typology, leading to the following typology:

- Visual learners learn best by looking at pictures, graphs, slides, demonstrations, films, etc. Colourful, bright graphics can help these learners retain information.
- Auditory learners like to learn through listening both to others speaking and to audiotapes. They will benefit, for example, from preparing listening tapes for review.
- Tactile/kinaesthetic learners learn best through touch and movement, and will therefore like to work with hands-on manipulatives. They will also like role-plays and activities which employ body parts as an mnemonic device, such as hand-signals.
- Print-oriented learners prefer to learn through reading.
- Interactive learners enjoy discussions with other students in small groups or during paired work.
- Olfactory learners benefit from the use of smell during learning. Associating certain lessons to particular smells can benefit these learners.

Multiple intelligences

One of the most popular recent theories on intelligence and learning styles is Howard Gardner's theory of 'multiple intelligences'. Gardner's theory suggest that there are a number of distinct forms of intelligence which everyone possesses to different degrees. According to Gardner there are seven primary intelligences (and a large number of secondary ones). These primary intelligences are:

- linguistic intelligence;
- musical intelligence;
- logical-mathematical intelligence;
- visual/spatial intelligence;
- body-kinaesthetic intelligence;
- intrapersonal intelligence (focusing on self-knowledge and metacognition); and
- interpersonal intelligence (relationships with others).

Doing different tasks may involve different combinations of these intelligences, but very rarely involves only one of these. Different intelligences are also emphasized more or less in different cultures, Gardner (1983) for example pointing to the high spatial abilities of the Puluwat people of the Caroline Islands, who use this ability to navigate their canoes on the Ocean.

According to Gardner (1983; 1993) teaching and learning should focus on the particular intelligence of each individual, who should be encouraged to develop this particular ability.

Thus, people with a strong linguistic ability should be given the opportunity to read, see and hear words associated with the topic/skill they need to learn. Logical/mathematical students should be given the opportunity to classify, categorize and work with abstractions and relations of different concepts to one another. Students with a strong visual/spatial intelligence can best be presented with visual information, maps, charts and colours. Musically intelligent learners should be given the opportunity to learn through melodies, musical notation and rhythms, using singing and clapping in delivering new information. Students with a strong body-kinaesthetic intelligence should be allowed to interact with their environment while learning, through movement, acting and use of body parts to help information retention. Interpersonally intelligent learners should be given the opportunity to interact with others, to compare and contrast information, to share ideas and to cooperate. Finally, students who are intrapersonally intelligent learn better on their own. Individual, self-paced activities will be most beneficial to these learners.

A problem with applying this theory is, firstly, the lack of evidence that teaching to these different abilities actually aids students learning. As mentioned below, most studies find no positive effects for doing this. Secondly, developing those abilities that a student already seems to possess may leave other abilities underdeveloped, and can put the student at a disadvantage in later life in society, where some abilities will have more widespread application than others.

The distinction between inductive and deductive learners has also been looked at by learning styles researchers (Hodges, 1994). Inductive learners begin with observations or data and then infer governing rules and principles from these observations. They work from particulars to general principles, and want to know: (1) what will the results to be derived help me know; (2) what are the results; and (3) how do I derive them. Deductive learners begin with general principles, then deduce consequences and phenomena from these. They work from generalities to particulars and want to know: (1) what are the results to be derived; (2) how do I derive them; and (3) how do I use them.

A final distinction that is sometimes made is that between sequential and global learners. Sequential learners learn one thing at a time. They function well with partial understanding, are good at analysis and convergent thinking, but may sometimes miss the big picture. Global learners on the other hand learn in large chunks, do not function well with partial understanding, are good at synthesis and innovation, but are fuzzy on details and may appear to learn more slowly, especially at the beginning of a topic.

As can be seen from the above there are a whole number of learning styles that teachers are advised to take into account. There are a number of commercial tools on the market designed to measure learning styles among students of various ages (e.g. the Learning Style Inventory (Dunn, Dunn and Price, 1985)). However, while a number of these tips make intuitive sense there is very little research that suggests that teaching to different learning styles actually improves students' achievement. Thus, Stahl (1999, p. 29), reviewing a number of studies on the effects of teaching different learning styles, concluded that: 'These five research reviews, published in well-regarded journals found the same thing. One cannot reliably measure children's learning styles and even if one could, matching children to reading programs by learning styles does not improve their learning.'

However, as mentioned in previous chapters, a good lesson needs to be varied and interesting, and use different types of materials and explanations. Mixing verbal, visual and tactile elements can obviously aid students' attention, while at the same time addressing possible different learning preferences. Also, varying teaching styles in different lessons according to lesson goals and topics will automatically cater for different learning styles. Spending a lot of time, effort (and money) on instruments designed to measure different styles, and then trying to match teaching to each student's individual learning preferences, is probably not worth the effort.

Summary

In this chapter we have learnt about the major ways of dealing with individual differences between students.

A number of grouping practices have been proposed to deal with differences in ability.

Selection is the grouping of students into different schools which are supposed to cater for students of different aptitude. Selection is usually based on students' performance on a test of ability. This presupposes that ability is both fixed and unchanging, a theory that has been widely disproved, and that access to higher education should be limited to an élite of highly able students, which is not in accordance with the needs of the modern 'knowledge society'.

Streaming refers to selection within schools, where students are put into classes according to their 'ability'. While giving more students a chance, this method suffers from many of the disadvantages of selection, leading to self-fulfilling prophecies, low self-esteem and disaffection with school in the lower streams, and also presupposes that ability is unidimensional and essentially stable.

A final grouping method is setting, in which students are put in different classes for different subjects according to ability. This still has a number of the disadvantages associated with streaming, but does allow different levels for different subjects, and can more easily be used in a flexible manner.

A second way of accommodating difference is through individualized learning approaches, whereby different students learn individually at their own tempo. Similarly, in differentiated group learning, different groups in a class are taught and work on different subjects. The evidence does not support this approach, various studies finding that too much individual or group learning is negatively related to student performance.

Recently, much attention has been given to different learning styles. One learning styles theory is that of Kolb, adapted by Litzinger and Osif. They define four types of learners. Assimilators think logically, prefer abstract ideas, and respect the views of experts. Convergers are mainly interested in the relevancy of information. Divergers are mainly interested in the 'why' of a system. They like to reason from concrete specific information. Accommodators prefer an active learning style, tend to rely on intuition rather than on logic, and like to connect learning to personal meaning and experiences.

Gardner (1983) suggests that there are a number of different intelligences, which different learners possess in different amounts. While some tasks rely more strongly on one intelligence, they rarely rely solely on one. He proposes seven primary intelligences: linguistic intelligence, musical intelligence, logical-mathematical intelligence, visual/spatial intelligence, body-kinaesthetic intelligence, intrapersonal intelligence (focusing on self-knowledge and metacognition) and interpersonal intelligence (relationships with others). According to Gardner, teaching should be geared to students' specific intelligence.

All these categorizations come with recommendations for teaching to these styles, by first measuring students' learning styles/preferences and then adapting teaching to the individual preferences of students. This is not supported by research, most studies not finding positive effects for this approach. Using a varied teaching style and employing a range of explanations and methods is part of effective teaching, however, and this will usually cater to most learning styles as well.

Self-study questions

1. What are the advantages and disadvantages of streaming and selection?
2. What are the four main learning styles according to Kolb?
3. How would you teach students with different primary intelligences according to Gardner?
4. Why could using a variety of teaching aids, such as visual aids, manipulatives and writing, address different learning styles?
5. How could you help to dispel some of the negative effects of setting?
6. Why do you think individual learning is not usually found to be effective?
7. Would you set your class, under which circumstances and why?

PART 3

TEACHING SPECIFIC SUBJECTS AND ASSESSMENT

15

Literacy

Advance organizers

In this chapter you will learn:

- How children learn to read.
- The main characteristics of the phonics approach to reading instruction.
- The main characteristics of the whole-language approach to reading instruction.
- Some examples of collaborative approaches to reading instruction.
- The main findings of the large-scale National Institute for Child Health and Development reading studies.
- The main findings of the largest review of reading research undertaken to date.
- The main characteristics of two popular early reading intervention strategies.
- The importance of a balanced approach to reading instruction.

Introduction

The most important skill children acquire at school is learning to read. Literacy forms the basis of most other learning. Children and adults who cannot read proficiently will experience significant difficulties at school and will often fail to reach their potential both at school and in life (Basic Skills Agency, 1997). Although some commentators have posited that the growth of television and ICT will lead to a 'post-literate' society, this can easily be overstated. Most technology, even if not explicitly literate, assumes that literacy is there as a prior condition, and the importance of reading and language has certainly not diminished through the advent of largely language-based information and communication technologies.

In light of the crucial importance of literacy it is not surprising that many different approaches to teaching reading have been developed and that controversy is rife in this area. While it falls outside of the province of this book to discuss in detail all the existing literacy teaching strategies, we will discuss a number of key ones and the controversy surrounding them.

Main approaches to teaching children to read

The main debate in literacy instruction in recent years has been between two approaches known as *phonics* and *whole language*. This debate has often been so heated (in particular in the USA) that it has been described as a 'language war'. In this section we will discuss the main features of these two approaches, while in the next section we will review some research on this matter. However, while the phonics–whole language debate has been fierce, we will also discuss the collaborative approach, the merits of which should not be ignored.

How children learn to read

A first important thing to note is that reading, in contrast to oral speech development, is not a process that develops naturally through interaction with significant others. Most children have to be explicitly taught to read. Learning to read is a process that starts early in children's development, before they enter formal schooling in most cases, and takes a long time to complete. Frequent exposure to language and literacy from the earliest age is crucial to literacy development.

Two main features of reading development are the acquisition of phonemic awareness and the acquisition of the alphabetic principle. Phonetic awareness refers to the knowledge that words and syllables are made up of small units of sound (phonemes). The problem with acquiring this awareness is that in speech specific phonemes often cannot be heard, e.g. the word 'cat' is made up of three phonemes c/a/t, but sounds like one. Learning readers therefore need to learn that spoken words can be divided into phonemes, letters and combinations of letters that represent these phonemes, and that written words have the same number and sequence of sounds as are heard in spoken words (Ehri, 1987; Adams, 1990; Torgesen, 1993; Foorman, Fletcher and Francis, 1996; Lyon, 1999). The alphabetic principle refers to the knowledge that the 26 letters of the Western alphabet correspond to specific phonemes, in English 44. These principles must become automatic and fluent for reading with comprehension to occur. Research by the National Institute for Child Health and Development (NICHD) in the USA has shown that poor readers often have difficulty developing these principles (Lyon and Kameenui, 2000).

Other factors that influence reading comprehension are the reader's vocabulary and background knowledge of the text.

Reading problems are often related to home background. Children who enter school with reading difficulties have often had limited exposure to language at home. They are often from poor backgrounds and have parents who themselves are not proficient readers. Therefore, raising parents' awareness of the importance of reading to their children and engaging in language-based play through rhymes, storybooks and, later, early writing activities is crucial. Talking out loud to children will help develop their vocabulary and background knowledge, both important to reading development (Foorman, Fletcher and Francis, 1996; Lyon, 1999).

The *phonics instruction* approach is supported by theories derived from cognitive psychology, research into the way pupils learn to read and research on the differences between pupils with and without reading difficulties. The basic supposition is that children learn to read by first making sense of the smallest component of the language and then progressing to larger wholes (Adams, 1990; Stahl, Duffy-Hester and Stahl, 1998). Phonics instruction focuses on teaching pupils sound–word correspondences, i.e. the correspondence of the 44 *phonemes* of the English language to the 26 alphabetic characters that represent them. There are a number of related approaches in phonics instruction.

In the *analytic phonics method* the student first learns a number of words which encompass common phonic components, such as /p/ in pill, park and pot. This element is ideally discovered by the student her or himself, as she or he reads a number of words with the particular phoneme. During a second phase students then learn to discriminate this phoneme from a number of other phonemes, e.g. they read the words pan, bad, pop and then decide whether these begin with the same sound as the original words (in this example, pill, park and pot). Students will then be asked to generate words that begin with the phoneme they are learning. Once students have mastered these steps, they will need to learn how to generalize from these known words to new words, and eventually apply this learning in actual reading situations, going on to sentences rather than single words. In this approach the focus is on learning phonics through building up a bank of known words and creating new ones. Rather than learning the sounds in isolation they are learned in context. This approach is *systematic* in that it consists of teaching children a planned sequence of phonics elements, rather than touching on phonics elements as and when they appear in a text.

Synthetic phonics instruction consists of teaching students to explicitly convert letters into phonemes and then blend the phonemes to form words. This is done through the use of *word families*, which are parts of a word that contain a vowel and a consonant element, to which one can add another consonant element to form different words. An example is the word family (or *grapheme*) 'it', which can become bit, hit, sit and so on. The basic principle here is that once a student has learned the phonemic principle and its relationship to the alphabet, she or he can use this principle to decode unknown words, thus helping her or him to learn to read. The teacher will usually start with a known word, the phonemic elements of which are explored. The word family can then be combined with new consonants to generate new words and sounds (nonsense words are also encouraged, as they can be sounds that form elements of larger words that the student may encounter later). The word family may be used as an end, beginning or middle of newly formed words. As well as starting off with a number of known words, students must know or be made aware of the rhyming principle, i.e. the fact that words can sound the same at the end, and be able to recognize that words which look the same at the end usually sound the same. There are a large number of commercial schemes available which can aid teachers in phonics teaching.

In contrast to phonics, which is a reading strategy based on research on reading and cognitive psychology, *whole language* is a philosophy that largely draws on knowledge of child development. Advocates of this approach believe that children learn to read and write, as well as speak and listen, through trial and error and practical and authentic uses of language. They believe that rather than going from the smallest element to the whole, learning to read progresses from the whole to the part and from the familiar to the unfamiliar (Goodman and Goodman, 1982). As language is an aggregate of many language functions, these are best learnt as a whole rather than being disaggregated. Learning in this view is not about learning to read words, but about learning to make meaning from text. Therefore, rather than having specific lessons focusing on decoding skills teaching, reading will occur through communication and natural activities throughout the day. Any phonics instruction (which can be included in a whole-language approach if necessary) should take place in the context of a particular meaningful text and not on its own (Goodman and Goodman, 1982; Tierney and Readence, 2000).

One of the main factors to influence reading development is seen to be internal motivation, which means that building up children's enthusiasm and motivation is crucial. Whole language is essentially a meaning-based approach, which sees reading as finding meaning in written language. This is evident, for example, when children can read a word in a familiar book but not outside that context. Skilful readers, according to this philosophy, 'skip, skim and guess' rather than reading exactly what is on the page. Both children's motivation and their learning through context are enhanced by letting them read interesting, authentic literature, and not artificial 'basal readers'. Word recognition skills should be picked up by the child in the context of actual reading, writing and immersion in a print-rich classroom. Learning to read should occur through pupil discovery, not teacher instruction, and learning in school should in this respect not be different from learning outside of school. Silent and oral reading are encouraged (Goodman and Goodman, 1982; Church, 1994; Weaver, 1990). However, the view that skilled readers skim and guess what's on the page has been disputed by eye-movement and brain scan research, that has shown that skilled readers tend to read meticulously, word to word and line by line, and translate print to speech while they are doing this (Adams, 1990).

Whole-language teachers will attempt to provide a stimulating classroom environment, consisting of a variety of print resources and artwork, designed to stimulate children's interest. Reading areas, literature circles and writing centres are often in evidence. Shared book experiences (children gather round an oversized 'big book' which they read and discuss co-operatively) are considered important, and children will be encouraged to write stories themselves and to read real literature and each other's writing (Tierney and Readence, 2000) There are a number of similar holistic reading instruction approaches, such as the 'real books' approach, which also focuses on learning to read by reading literature rather than using basal readers. A criticism of this approach is the fact that children can encounter a word in context, but then not encounter that word again for a long time. This is obviously not the case in basal readers, where words are introduced systematically.

While most of the recent debates on teaching reading have focused on the phonics–whole language divide, a number of other interesting approaches exist. One of the methods that is best supported by research is teaching reading in collaborative small groups. There are a wide number of collaborative programmes in existence (e.g. CIRC, Discussion Web, Language Circles). As an example, two collaborative approaches are discussed here.

One of these is *Collaborative Strategic Reading* (CSR). In this approach, pupils are taught reading comprehension strategies while working collaboratively. The first step consists of the teacher presenting the comprehension strategies to the whole class using direct instruction, modelling and role-playing. After practice has shown that the pupils have attained a sufficient level of mastery of the strategies they are then asked to form groups (of heterogeneous composition) in which the students collaboratively implement the strategies, each student fulfilling a particular role (Palincsar and Brown, 1984; Johnson and Johnson, 1989). The approach has shown good results both with pupils with reading difficulties and with average and high-achieving students (Klinger *et al.*, 1996). The main comprehension strategies taught are:

1. *Preview*. This phase takes place before reading. Students have to discuss what they already know about the topic and then predict what they think they will learn about it.
2. *'Click and clunk.'* Students have to reflect which parts of the text were hard to understand, and what they can do to 'fix' these 'clunks' by, for example, rereading the sentence and the sentences before and after the one they are having difficulty with, or breaking the word down into smaller parts.
3. *Get the gist* by reflecting on what the most important ideas, persons or places in the text were, and what is most important about these places, persons or things.
4. *Wrap up*. After reading students should ask questions showing they understand what the most important information in the text is, give the answers to those questions, and finally review what they have learnt from the text.

Another example of a co-operative approach is *Jigsaw*, in which students are supposed to become experts on a particular aspect of the text or lesson and then teach it to their peers, a method that is known as *peer tutoring*. Each student receives an expert sheet that tells them what they are to read, gives them some questions and tells them which group (which should be heterogeneous with respect to gender and ability) they will work with. They will then read their assigned text, and discuss with their expert group (other pupils from different co-operative groups who are to become experts on the same subject) what the most important aspects of that topic are. Then they return to their co-operative group to tell the other children what they have learnt in their expert group. At the end of the activity, the teacher should give a short test (Slavin, 1983).

In general, co-operative learning has proved an effective teaching method in a wide variety of studies conducted over several decades (Slavin, 1983; 1996; Johnson and Johnson, 2000).

Finally, it is important to point out that many of the studies on effective teaching reviewed in Chapters 1, 2 and 3 were conducted in language classrooms. This means that the direct instruction approach which was found to be most effective in these studies is likely to be effective in teaching children to read. Phonics-based direct instruction approaches to teaching reading have indeed been found to be highly effective in a number of studies (Carnine, Silbert and Kameenui, 1996).

The NICHD studies and the evidence for phonics

Probably the most extensive body of research on reading has come from studies conducted under the auspices of the National Institute of Child Health and Human Development in the USA. This organisation has, since 1965, systematically studied reading development through a network of 41 research sites across North America, Europe and Asia. Over the last decades researchers working with NICHD have studied the reading development of almost 35,000 children and adults, both with (about 1/3) and without (about 2/3) reading difficulties. This research has led to the development of a number of intervention projects, in which almost 8,000 children have participated since the mid-1980s.

A number of important findings on effective teaching of literacy have emerged from these studies. First, both for parents and teachers, reading out loud to children is highly effective in developing vocabulary, language expression, and expressive and receptive language skills (Lyon, 1999). Early intervention with pupils with reading difficulties is highly important.

Direct and systematic instruction in phoneme awareness and phonics skills was likewise found to be important, and should be continued until children can automatically process this information. Direct instruction in reading comprehension strategies was found to be effective, and children's reading development is also aided by a literature-rich environment and practice in reading authentic literature and familiar materials. While important, authentic literature and rich contexts are not a suitable replacement for explicit teaching of phonics decoding skills according to this research (Moats, 1996; Lyon, 1999). The NICHD research has shown that guessing words from their context (the text in which they are embedded) is only accurate about 10–20 per cent of the time. Thus, according to Lyon and Kameenui (2000) children need to be taught:

1. Phonemic awareness (the sounds that make up words such as c/a/t).
2. The sound-spelling relationships in words.
3. How to say the sounds that make up words.
4. By using texts that are made up of words that use the sound–spelling correspondences children have learnt.

5. By using interesting and authentic stories to develop vocabulary and language comprehension.

Early intervention with pupils with reading difficulties is paramount as the intensity and duration of reading interventions need to increase exponentially as children get older (Lyon, 1999). While some research shows that for the majority of children sound–word correspondence will be learnt through most teaching methods, for between 30 per cent and 40 per cent of children this is not the case. Explicit phonics instruction is particularly beneficial for this group (Foorman, Fletcher and Francis, 1996).

Recently, the NICHD, at the behest of the American Congress, reviewed the scientific literature on the most effective strategies to teach children to read. Out of more than 100,000 studies published, the panel reviewed those that followed an experimental or quasi-experimental approach and reached rigorous scientific criteria.

The panel concluded that research strongly supported the explicit and systematic teaching of the manipulation of phonemes and phonemic awareness (the knowledge that words are made up of small segments of sound, e.g. go = two phonemes). There was also clear evidence that phonics teaching was beneficial for children from preschool through to 6th grade, as well as for older children who are having reading problems. For most children, *systematic phonics teaching* showed the strongest effects, but for low-achieving children and pupils with learning disabilities improvement could best be combined with *synthetic phonics teaching*. Synthetic phonics teaching was also found to be effective with pupils from low socio-economic status backgrounds and improves all pupils' spelling ability (NICHD, 2000).

Guided oral reading, where students read out loud to the teacher, a classmate or another adult who corrects their mistakes and provides feedback, was found to develop students' reading fluency and helped students to recognize new words, read accurately and improve their reading comprehension. The results on *silent reading* were inconclusive (NICHD, 2000).

The panel also looked at research on reading comprehension, focusing in particular on how best to teach vocabulary, text comprehension and comprehension strategies. According to their review, *vocabulary* can best be taught both directly (apart from a particular text) and indirectly (as words occur in a particular text). Repetition and multiple exposure will help develop vocabulary, and use of ICT was also found to be effective. No single best teaching method could be identified, suggesting that a combination of methods is more appropriate. *Reading comprehension* itself can best be facilitated by teaching students a variety of techniques and systematic strategies to assist them with recall of information, question generation and summarizing information (NICHD, 2000).

This research thus clearly supports the explicit teaching of phonics, while evidence supporting a whole language approach does not seem to be this clear (Tierney and Readence, 2000). However, whole-language advocates reject these results, arguing that the standardized tests used in this type of research lack validity. They support a view of evaluation that focuses on student self-evaluation, teacher observation of classroom processes, periodic performance samples and dialogue journals (Church, 1994). It is clear, however, that the subjectivity inherent in this type of assessment precludes any scientific evaluation of the effectiveness of programmes and any objective assessment of students' progress.

A balanced approach

The research summarized above clearly points to the crucial importance of direct instruction in phonics in developing students' reading ability. This is especially important for pupils from lower socio-economic status backgrounds and pupils who are having difficulties reading. Both phonemic awareness and the alphabetic principle need to be explicitly taught until they become automatic.

Likewise, generating enthusiasm for reading and developing students' contextual understanding through exposure to interesting, authentic literature has clear merits. Spending too much time doing phonics in one session can be boring, and the materials used to teach it need to be as attractive and interesting as possible. Phonics teaching must not be reduced to meaningless skill and drill.

A balanced approach, in which both authentic, rich contexts and environments and explicit teaching of phonics coexist, is therefore both possible and desirable. However, it has become clear that explicit phonics teaching must underlie teaching to read. Therefore, a balanced approach needs to consist of four components:

1. Explicit instruction in phonics skills and other skills such as spelling.
2. Direct and indirect teaching of reading comprehension strategies.
3. A focus on literature, language and authentic text in a text-rich environment.
4. An effective early intervention programme for readers with problems, such as Reading Recovery (Chall, 1995). This type of balanced approach is becoming more and more common, and the English government's National Literacy Strategy is an example of such a balanced approach.

Amidst all the thunder of the phonics–whole language debate it is easy to lose sight of other promising approaches, particularly in the field of collaborative learning. Hopefully literacy instruction can move on from this debate and towards a more balanced and possibly more collaborative approach.

Early intervention programmes

As mentioned above, early intervention with students who are experiencing reading problems is crucial if these students are not to fall further behind other children in all subjects as they go through school. Two of the most successful intervention programmes are Reading Recovery and Success for All.

Reading Recovery, a programme devised in New Zealand by Marie Clay, combines direct phonics instruction with a rich whole-language style environment. The programme runs for an average of 16 weeks, during which period specially trained teachers work with individual students for 30 minutes a day. Students are exposed to books that get gradually more difficult, mini writing lessons and plastic letters that they use to form words. Reading Recovery lessons have seven components:

1. Rereading two or more familiar texts, stories the student knows (but does not know by heart). The focus during this part is on comprehension of the text.
2. Running record on the previous day's new story. The teacher observes the child reading the text.
3. Letter identification and word formation using magnetic letters.
4. Writing a story and developing phonemic awareness. The student writes a story and phonics is used when children come up to a difficult word. Students are encouraged to divide words into their component sounds.
5. Students then are encouraged to cut up the story into its component parts, such as phrases, words, clusters of letters and single letters.
6. New book introduction. A new book is introduced which is not too difficult for the student to master, but should contain a minimum of new elements the child needs to learn.
7. Read the new book with help from the teacher (Clay, 1993).

In general, Reading Recovery, now used in most English-speaking countries, has proved effective with a wide range of students with learning difficulties. However, as up to a quarter of students may fail to make the necessary progress some have doubted the cost-effectiveness of the method (Geeke, 1988; Center *et al.*, 1995; Haen, 2000)

Success for All (SFA) is a highly successful school-wide programme designed for schools with disadvantaged intakes. As with Reading Recovery, SFA emphasizes both meaning and authentic texts and systematic phonics instruction. Direct instruction of reading strategies is another component of the programme.

The main programme components are:

1. Trained reading tutors give one-to-one tutoring to students who are not performing up to the reading standards of their peers in 20-minute sessions. They also help teach the class during reading or literacy sessions, thus helping to reduce class sizes (see below). Students are continually assessed by their tutor.
2. A 90-minute reading period is given every day, during which time the students are grouped by reading ability (possibly cross-age) in classes of, at most, 20 students. Direct instruction of phonics is used as are big books and reading stories to the class. By the time kindergarten children can read to primer level, they start co-operative work on reading and composition activities.
3. Every eight weeks students' progress is assessed, and tutor groups are re-evaluated.
4. SFA schools provide half-day preschool and a full-day kindergarten, where students receive developmentally appropriate learning experiences and language development activities.

> 5. A family support team works with students' families and provides what assistance is deemed necessary (Slavin, 1993; Madden *et al.*, 1993; Tierney and Readence, 2000).
>
> Success for All has been extensively evaluated, and has shown considerable success in raising reading levels and overall academic achievement compared to matched control schools (Wasik and Slavin, 1993; Slavin, 1995; Slavin *et al.*, 1997).

Summary

Learning to read is probably the most important skill that children will pick up during the early years of schooling.

A range of approaches exist in reading instruction, but most controversy recently has focused on phonics instruction and the whole-language approach.

Phonics instruction focuses on teaching children the correspondence between the 44 phonemes (sounds) in the English language and the 26 letters of the alphabet. This is seen as essential to decoding language, the assumption being that the best way to learn to read is to proceed from the part to the whole. This approach is supported by research into how children learn to read, phonemic awareness and awareness of the alphabetic principle having been found to underlie successful reading.

The whole-language approach focuses on the importance of making meaning from texts. Motivation is seen as paramount, and using authentic, interesting literature and a text-rich environment to encourage students' motivation to read are seen to be crucial. According to the whole-language view explicit teaching of phonics is usually unnecessary, as learning to read goes from the whole to the part, with guessing from context and skimming being prime strategies in reading.

The National Institute of Child Health and Development in the USA has conducted a series of studies over three decades, accumulating what is probably the most extensive evidence base on reading in the world. Their research clearly supports the importance of teaching phonics in an explicit way, although reading comprehension strategies were also found to be important. Teaching phonics is especially important to pupils experiencing difficulties reading and to pupils from deprived backgrounds.

However, while this research clearly supports the importance of teaching phonics; meaning, motivation and the joy of reading as stressed by whole-language advocates are important as well. This realization has led many to advocate a balanced approach, containing both phonics instruction and elements of the whole language philosophy.

The vehemence of the whole-language–phonics discussion should not distract our attention from other approaches that may prove fruitful, especially collaborative learning methods such as Jigsaw and CSR, which have strong research support.

Self-study questions

1. What are the main factors that distinguish pupils with learning difficulties from their peers?
2. What are the main elements of the whole language philosophy, and how could they fit in a balanced approach to reading instruction?
3. What is synthetic phonics instruction?
4. Does the NICHD research support the whole language approach?
5. What are the main components of Reading Recovery?
6. Is Success for All a balanced approach? Why?
7. Describe a collaborative approach to reading instruction.
8. What does research have to say about the effectiveness of oral and silent reading?

16

Mathematics

Advance organizers

In this chapter you will learn:

- Some findings from international studies on the mathematics achievement of children and adolescents.
- What we know about how children learn mathematics.
- The implications of research on how children learn mathematics to mathematics teaching.
- Other factors that can enhance the effectiveness of mathematics teaching.

Introduction

Mathematics, though one of the most important subjects in the curriculum of most countries, is also commonly seen as one of the most difficult subjects by students and adults. In a number of studies conducted by the Basic Skills Agency, for example, a large proportion of English adults were found not to possess basic numeracy skills (Bynner and Steedman, 1995; Bynner and Parsons, 1997), a proportion that is larger than that of illiterate adults. In schools a lot of students seem to become disenchanted with mathematics, and often question the relevance of the large amount of time spent teaching mathematics. This notwithstanding, research has shown the importance of mathematics in adult daily life. Thus, according to the Basic Skills Agency Studies mentioned above, lack of numeracy was related to unemployment and low incomes among adults, over and above the effects of poor literacy among these same adults. Likewise, adults with a higher secondary school mathematics qualification (the 'A'-level) in England had average earnings 10 per cent higher than people without this qualification (*Times*, 1999). Mathematics has importance over and above the application of basic numeracy skills. It is also the prime vehicle for developing students' logical thinking and higher-order cognitive skills. Mathematics also plays a major role in a number of other scientific fields, such as physics, engineering and statistics.

In view of both the significance and the problems involved with learning maths it is not surprising that there is a lot of research into students' mathematical thinking and learning. In this chapter we will review some of the main findings of this research.

What we know about the way children learn mathematics

Children come to school with mathematical knowledge, skills and misconceptions

Even before they come to school, children engage in a number of activities that appear to be mathematical. They count, share out (things like sweets), and often manage to do simple addition and subtraction. However, the relationship between this prior out-of-school knowledge and children's mathematics learning in school is not straightforward (Aubrey, 1993; Anghileri, 1995).

The International Mathematics and Science Study (TIMMS)

Starting in the 1960s, the International Education Association has studied the performance of children from a large number of countries in mathematics on three occasions. The First International Mathematics Study (FIMS) took place in the 1960s. More recently, the Second International Mathematics Study (SIMS) study in the 1980s and the TIMSS (Third International Mathematics and Science Study) study carried out in the 1990s have produced valuable data on the comparative performance of children in different countries in various aspects of mathematics.

Most political interest has focused on the ranking of countries in the tests, which tend to show high performance by students from a number of South-East Asian countries, such as Singapore, Korea and Hong Kong, and above average performance from Flanders (Belgium) and the Czech Republic. In the USA and the UK there is a perception that their students have done particularly badly. This is only partly true. In fact, students from both countries tend to get mediocre scores. Furthermore, these global rankings obscure some interesting differences in performance on different subsets of the tests. When one looks at these subsets it appears that English students, for example, do quite well in geometry and very well in problem-solving, but very poorly in basic number skills and arithmetic.

In both SIMS and TIMSS researchers have attempted to look at factors that could explain these differences between countries, as well as the (usually larger) differences within countries. The main school-related factor that was found to be significant was opportunity to learn, i.e. the extent to which students in those countries and schools had encountered the questions on the test in their curriculum.

For example, while children can already to a large extent *count* before they come to school their grasp of the meaning of number words and of *cardinality* (knowing that numbers are absolute amounts, and thus that for example 4 green sweets are as much as 4 red sweets) is shaky. *Sharing* is another activity that children master before they enter school, and in this case they seem to understand the concept well. Children have also been found to be able to *add and subtract* small numbers, though research has not yet established whether they understand that the two operations are *inverse*.

This early knowledge is important to children's learning and teaching in the primary school as counting, sharing, adding and subtracting form the basis of much early in-school teaching and learning. Students build upon their existing knowledge to build up their mathematical competence and extend the breadth and understanding of that knowledge. Once students get older they will continue to garner mathematical knowledge outside school through such activities as shopping and reading the paper, and *this out-of-school learning* can usefully be incorporated into teaching. In this way students will learn the relevance of maths to 'real life', and be able to *transfer* knowledge learned in the classroom to the outside world so they can actually use their maths in everyday situations.

While students' externally garnered knowledge forms one basis of their numeracy, it is important to remember that external knowledge may also provide them with misconceptions about the meaning of mathematical terms. Common-sense meanings of mathematical terms such as the '=' sign are not necessarily exactly the same as the mathematical meaning of these terms (Anghileri, 1995; Bryant, 1997; Thompson, 1997).

Numeracy is based on the application of logic

It seems like stating a truism to say that children need to be able to *think logically* to do mathematics. After all, do they not need this for whatever subject they do? However, logic is particularly important to mathematics learning. Even basic numerical operations such as counting rely on the application of logic.

One of the logical operations children must understand is *ordinality*, the fact that numbers are arranged in ascending order of magnitude (3>2, 2>1). This means that they need to understand not just this order, but also the fact that if 3>2, and 2>1, then 3>1 as well. They also need to know that if they are counting something (e.g. the number of sweets in a packet) they can count each one only once, that the order in which they are counted makes no difference, and that the final number they have counted to is the total number of objects in a *set* (in this case the total number of sweets in the packet). These are all logical rules, and you can see that even a relatively simple operation like counting involves a lot of logical thinking on the part of the student!

Logic is equally important to more complex numerical operations. An example of this, taken from Piaget, is the following. Two children do a gardening job. One has worked for 10 hours, the other for 4 hours. They receive £10 between them. How to share this money? A fair share would clearly involve giving one child a larger share of the money than the other. Solving this kind of problem does not require much more advanced arithmetic than a simple sharing problem. However, as Piaget stated, the logic underlying this operation is far more complex, involving keeping the relationship between time and money constant. According to Piaget, this requires a *second order operation*, or an operation on an operation (Nunes and Bryant, 1996; Verschaffel and De Corte, 1993).

Numeracy means learning a conventional system

Numeracy does not just involve application of logic, however. It also involves learning a set of conventions that are needed for mastering mathematical techniques (like long division, for example). These conventions provide us with ways of representing concepts, such as the *number set* (= the set of all possible numbers). These can therefore differ between cultures, e.g. our base ten number set or our measurement system differs from those in other cultures (an example of this is the difference between the imperial and the metric measurement systems). These differences are essentially arbitrary. However, what they do share is that they encompass the logic needed to do mathematics. Both the metric and the imperial system share the concept of ordinality, for example.

Children obviously need to learn how to use these systems as well as master the logic behind mathematics. Initially they may experience problems doing this. According to Bryant (1994) learning the conventional system may actually increase children's ability to think logically as well. An example he gives of this is use of a base number system, such as our base ten system, in which ten units make a decade, ten decades a hundred etc. Such a base system is not inevitable, but number systems that have a base have been found to be more efficient than non-base systems. If a child has to learn number words in a fixed order (e.g. 0, 1, 2, etc.) in a non-base system, she or he will have to learn as many words as she or he can, the number of which is inevitably limited due to limitations in the capacity of memory. In a base ten system, however, the children need to memorise all the words from one to ten, all the teen words (11, 12, etc.) and decade words (20, 30 . . .), as well as words such as 100 and 1,000, but they will then be able to combine these to form new words. This allows them to easily count to high numbers without having to memorise a huge number of words. Therefore, once we have a base system, we possess a powerful tool for thought (Nunes and Bryant, 1996).

Effective teaching: mathematics-specific factors

Using effective teaching strategies

When discussing mathematics learning above, it was posited that the first thing one needs to do is look at applying what we know about learning in general. Similarly, when looking at how to teach mathematics, the first thing to do is to look at what have generally been found to be effective teaching strategies. These were discussed in Chapters 1, 2 and 3 (Brophy and Good, 1986; Reynolds and Muijs, 1999a).

It is important to point out here that this research is of particular relevance to mathematics. Many of the American teacher effectiveness studies were carried out in mathematics classrooms and in many cases when we are saying that a certain behaviour is linked to achievement it is therefore mathematics achievement that we are talking about.

The structured teaching style advocated by the effective teaching researchers also corresponds well to the structured nature of mathematical knowledge as discussed above, and the emphasis on mastering relatively small chunks of content well before going on to the next step could help counter the fear of maths and uncertainty about their mathematical ability that many people feel. It also ties in well with the hierarchical nature of the subject itself.

From the above it is also clear that effective maths teaching involves *both* teaching for understanding, using problem-solving, etc. and an element of rote learning, in that students need to master the conventional systems of maths and gain automaticity in the use of skills such as multiplication facts and times tables in order to allow them to work efficiently and free memory space for more meaningful work (Merttens, 1996).

Mathematics and calculators

The issue of calculator use in mathematics lessons has caused a lot of controversy in recent years. Some experts advocate banning their use in the primary school, while others on the contrary express great hopes for the positive effects of calculator use in the classroom, in part because of the time that can be saved by their use.

The evidence, first, does not show that calculators are very widely used in most countries, but does show that they are less widely used in a number of the most successful countries according to the TIMSS study. That this difference in performance is due to the use of calculators is doubtful, however. Research on the effects of calculator use on students' achievement supports neither the pro- nor the anti-calculator lobby. Most studies indicate that calculator use does not have any negative effects on students' achievement in mathematics (as long as it does not replace mental or written calculation strategies). Some studies report some small positive effects of calculator use in the short term, but no effects are significant in the long term (Hembree and Dessart, 1986, 1992; Ruthven, Rousham and Chaplin, 1998).

In view of this evidence, the fact that this issue has caused so much controversy is surprising.

Correcting misconceptions

As mentioned above, children can easily develop misconceptions about the meaning of mathematical concepts. It is important for teachers to address these from the start (Hiebert and Carpenter, 1992).

This implies the necessity of letting students explain how they come to their answers, whether right or wrong, and in the second case to correct the wrong answer explicitly. This is especially important in mathematics as even right answers can sometimes result from inefficient or incorrect methods (which are incorrect because they can sometimes lead to the wrong answer). Teachers should also provide detailed justifications of the solutions they are using.

An example of a misconception that often occurs in the primary school is that students will acquire a rule and then overgeneralize it to situations in which it is not applicable. For example, students often acquire the rule that when multiplying a number by ten, one adds a zero. They will then use this rule in situations in which it is not correct, e.g. when multiplying decimals (e.g. $5.6 \times 10 = 5.60$). Also, students will often think that multiplication always makes things bigger, while division always makes things smaller and then choose wrongly to apply division or multiplication based on their perception of whether numbers need to get smaller or bigger.

As these misconceptions tend to be shared by a relatively large number of students addressing them can improve students' mathematical achievement. It has been found to be more effective to let students make the mistake first and then to discuss it afterwards, rather than giving students examples of the misconception beforehand (Askew and William, 1995).

One way of avoiding future misconceptions is to teach the exact meaning of mathematical terms right from the start. This may not seem immediately obvious, as in the lower years a less than exact definition or understanding of a term or symbol such as the '=' sign may be sufficient for children's mathematical problem-solving at that stage. However, once they reach a higher stage of learning and need to know the exact mathematical meaning of the term, they will find it difficult to unlearn inexact meanings they have internalized. It is far more difficult to change students' understanding of a term later on than to teach them correctly in the first case (Askew and William, 1995).

Using real-life contexts

A specific difficulty of mathematics knowledge for students lies in its *abstract nature*. Students often find it hard to link the mathematics learnt in the classroom to real-life situations, and also have difficulties making the connections between the mathematics knowledge they already possess and what they learn at school. These problems can be remedied by using real-life examples as much as possible and by validating students' existing mathematics knowledge. Use of real-life materials such as, for the younger students, shopping bills can enhance the making of these connections and the generation of informal mathematical knowledge. These materials can be brought to class by the students themselves, furthering involvement in the lesson (Gravemeijer, 1997).

One possible model that has been proposed is one in which the teacher starts off with a realistic example or situation, turns this into a mathematical model leading to mathematical solutions, which are then reinterpreted as a realistic solution. This strategy would certainly be useful in linking mathematical and real world knowledge and applications (Askew and Williams, 1995).

Examples given by the teacher should be as close as possible to the real world, and new mathematical concepts should be explained using a variety of representations, e.g. symbolic, graphic, through the use of materials, etc. In this way the student can learn to think of the mathematical concept apart from its physical representation.

It is important to take into account here that using real-life examples is more than just using words from everyday life in a word problem that is, as a whole, unrealistic. An example of this is the following problem, taken from a teacher's worksheet observed by the author: 'Two bees working together can gather nectar from 100 hollyhock blossoms in 30 minutes. Assuming that each bee works the standard eight-hour day, five days a week, how many blossoms do these bees gather nectar from in a summer season of fifteen weeks?' It is clear that this problem does not actually connect in any way to students' real-life experience, notwithstanding the fact that the calculations are embedded in a word problem. Use of this type of problem will not aid students' application of mathematics, or help them to connect their informal mathematics learnt outside the classroom to what they have to learn in school.

While this example may appear exaggerated, many word problems resemble it, using a *context* which only at first sight appears realistic. To be effective, a real-life example needs to connect far more to students' actual experience (Gravemeijer, 1997).

Making connections

A subject already touched on in the chapter on students' learning is clearly linking different parts of the lesson and the curriculum. This has been found to be particularly important for mathematics. New knowledge needs to be linked to concepts learnt earlier and different parts of the lesson should be linked to each other, to earlier learnt knowledge and to the curriculum. Mathematical ideas should not be taught in isolation; a strong focus should be put on the relationship between ideas. This will enable students to be better able to retrieve knowledge from memory and to understand the hierarchical nature of mathematical knowledge. These linkages must be explicitly taught to students. Teachers can also use questions that ask a student to relate a newly taught concept to a previously learnt idea (Hiebert and Carpenter, 1992; Askew *et al.*, 1997).

This means that teachers must themselves be aware of the connections between different aspects of the mathematics curriculum and the use and application of mathematics in different fields, and thus requires good subject knowledge from the teacher, which has been found to be linked to higher student achievement (Mandeville and Liu, 1997).

Summary

Mathematics and numeracy are an important part of schooling due to the importance of basic numeracy skills in everyday life, the role of mathematics in the acquisition of logical thinking skills and the role of mathematics as a crucial component of other scientific fields.

Children come to school already possessing mathematical skills such as counting, simple addition and subtraction and cardinality, which need to be built on once they enter a formal school environment. From the earliest age, doing mathematics also requires use of logic, such as ordinality, and use of a formal system, such as the base ten system. Children explicitly need to learn how to master these systems and develop their logical thinking.

Teaching mathematics involves first and foremost use of the effective whole class interactive strategies mentioned in Chapters 1–3. Much of the research on which these findings on effective teaching are based was done in mathematics, so they are highly relevant to this subject. However, there are a number of additional aspects that are particularly important to mathematics teaching. As mentioned above, children come to school already possessing mathematical kills and knowledge. Not all that they know is correct, however, and students are often found to have misconceptions about maths which impede their learning of the subject. These need to be made explicit and need to be tackled in mathematics teaching. The abstract nature of mathematics often causes problems both to students' learning and in their attitudes towards mathematics. This problem can be counteracted by using real-life contexts and examples as much as possible and by stressing the relevance of mathematics to daily life. Finally, it is particularly important to make sure that mathematical knowledge is suitably linked and connected in students' minds.

An issue that has led to a lot of controversy in mathematics education is the question of whether or not to use calculators in teaching mathematics. Notwithstanding the often heated debate on this matter, most research shows that calculator use has neither strong negative or positive effects on students' mathematics achievement.

Self-study questions

1. In what ways can children's prior knowledge help or harm their classroom mathematics learning? And what do teachers need to do about the latter?
2. Why is teacher effectiveness research particularly relevant to mathematics?
3. Why is logic so important in mathematics learning?
4. Describe some specific problems that children face when learning mathematics, and make some suggestions to address these.
5. Why do children need to learn mathematical conventions?
6. Should mathematics teaching focus on understanding or on rote learning of basic skills?
7. Is using calculators in mathematics lessons harmful?

17

Information and Communication Technology Skills

Advance organizers

In this chapter you will learn:

- The main ways in which ICT can help student learning.
- Some ways of using ICT in the classroom.
- Some of the problems and pitfalls of ICT use.

Introduction

In a sector that has developed and is developing as quickly as information and communication technology it is always hard to predict what exactly will be the skills that today's youngsters will need in their adult life. Those of us who grew up in the 1980s can testify to this, having been taught such skills as programming in Basic, now largely obsolete.

One development that is likely to continue in future is the ever increasing user-friendliness of computer appliances. This means that simple usage of the computer is likely to be no more baffling to future generations brought up with ICT than using the television is for today's adults. None the less, the importance of ICT in society, both currently and in the future, make it necessary to look at its consequences to education, both with regards to the teaching of ICT skills to students and to their use in teaching other parts of the curriculum, although evidence on what is actually effective in the use of ICT is surprisingly limited (Higgins and Muijs, 1999). What research does exist tends to be quite positive though, a large-scale British study for example finding that use of ICT made a positive contribution to student outcomes although its effects were not consistent over subject or age group. Information and communication technology was also found to be a good motivator, students working on the computer showing high levels of enthusiasm and on-task behaviour, and often wanting to continue school work after the task had finished (Watson, 1993).

How can ICT help students' learning?

If ICT can make a positive contribution to students' learning, the question of course is why this is the case. The following uses of ICT may be particularly beneficial to student learning.

Presenting information

Information and communication technology can clearly make a difference to students' presentation of their ideas. At a superficial level this can refer to the increased attractiveness of presentations designed using the sophisticated word processing software now available, which allows students to easily include graphics and tables in their work. This can have a motivating effect on students. At a deeper level use of this type of software allows students to cut and paste and make changes to their work easily and speedily. This tends to encourage more risk-taking from students in the production of their texts than if they had to write everything down or remember the whole text. According to some authors, this way of working also provides students with some 'mental distance' from the text, encouraging reflection on their own work.

Use of ICT in producing documents also allows more co-operative work in preparing the text, as it is easier to share a computer screen than a book, and it is easy for students to add their ideas to the text of one another and communicate electronically with each other while writing (Somekh and Davis, 1997; Bucher, 1998; Higgins and Muijs, 1999).

Quick and automatic completion of routine tasks

Computers can easily and quickly complete routine tasks, which could otherwise engage students for a long period of time without adding to their understanding or learning.

An example can be gleaned from mathematics lessons. As any primary mathematics teacher will tell you, teaching students about graphs at present often involves them drawing the graph in some detail. Purely writing the information down and drawing the graph can easily take the whole of two lessons, during which time little of substance is learned. Allowing the computer to do this instead can save time which can be spent on activities that better develop mathematical understanding.

The computer can also be used for calculations in subjects such as physics and biology in the higher years once again freeing up time to engage in more cognitively rewarding activities (Somekh and Davis, 1997; Bucher, 1998).

Accessing and handling information

Accessing and handling information is one of the most important contributions ICT can make to students' learning. Through such tools as the World Wide Web, interactive compact discs – read only memory (CD-ROMs) and CD-ROM encyclopaedias, students now have access to a greater wealth of information than ever before.

The amount of CD-ROM titles is increasing rapidly, and they provide a wealth of information on a wide variety of topics. Examples of this include the encyclopaedic Encarta program as well as specific series on curriculum topics in mathematics and sciences.

An increasing number of schools also have access to the World Wide Web. The amount of information on the web is vast, but also often anarchic and of variable quality. Therefore, just letting students loose on the web is not necessarily a useful strategy, especially in view of the relatively easy access to unsuitable materials which may be tempting to students especially at the secondary level. There are, however, a number of organizations that provide a useful 'portal' through which schools can access the web and reach directly relevant material. In the UK, for example, the National Grid for Learning (http://www.ngfl.gov.uk) provides an obvious and useful starting point in this respect. There also exists a large number of other sites that provide useful resources on such topics as fractals, history and other subjects, as well as a number of other general school resource sites.

It is important, however, to remember that most of what is available on the web has, in contrast to books for example, not been edited. It is therefore necessary to instil in students a certain degree of scepticism about what they read on the web.

Difficult ideas can often be made more readily understandable by being made visible through ICT. A concept such as the flow of electronic current can be drawn on a blackboard, but an animation of same on the computer can clearly aid students' understanding of this and other concepts.

Modelling and control

Computer modelling is one of the most powerful uses of ICT in the classroom. It is possible to, for example, set up a model in science using a spreadsheet. Using formulae, one can calculate and recalculate results as data are added, thus allowing students to study the effect of changes in the values of one or more variables on the outcomes under study.

This way of working allows users to be creative in adding factors or changing relationships, while working at quite an abstract level. Modelling also allows students to answer 'what if . . .' questions relatively easily by, for example, entering the value 0 for gravity in a model.

Another form of modelling that students can now access via the computer are simulations. The best known of these are flight simulators.

Others also exist, however, including simulators that help students design a city or dissect a frog. These programs are likely to increase in quantity and sophistication in future (Somekh and Davis, 1997; Bucher, 1998; Ager, 1999).

Interactivity

A further advantage of ICT is the interactivity it allows. An example of this can be found in integrated learning systems (ILS), in which a student solves a question and gets immediate feedback on whether or not this response is correct. This interactivity has been found to motivate students and as such stimulate learning.

This interactivity also features to a certain extent in CD-ROM encyclopaedias and other applications which involve search processes in that once children have searched using one word the software will lead them to search using a more refined and narrowed-down process by suggesting they add words to their search, or suggesting areas they might like to search in.

Finally, interactivity can also refer to interacting with other students or adults through ICT, such as in chat groups, via e-mail or using web-cams through which students can contact other students. Computer use clearly also expands possibilities for distance learning from experts, and can be successfully used as a homework tool, several Internet sites and service providers such as America Online (AOL) providing expert homework help to students.

Extending the school to the student's home

A further use of ICT can lie in easily extending learning from the school to the home. An example of this is the use of the Internet observed in a Hong Kong primary school. The school's mathematics curriculum and exercises are stored on a website, which can be downloaded by students at home allowing them to complete homework and exercises and receive immediate feedback, as exercises are marked by the software program (Muijs, 2000). The parent-teacher association at this school has provided a number of computers to those parents who cannot afford to purchase one.

In one American school district a different solution has been found. There school work has been put on to a CD that can be loaded on a Playstation games console and can easily be carried around by students. The use of the Playstation not only has a positive motivational function for students but also widens access, as more students have a games console than a personal computer (PC) at home (Mann, 2000).

Buying software in school: how to decide what to buy?

When deciding to use computing software in the classroom, teachers and administrators in school can often be confronted with both a lack of knowledge about what software exists to attain their goals, and by a somewhat bewildering array of software and claims as to its effectiveness by manufacturers.

A number of steps can be followed, however, that could lead to a more ordered approach to software purchasing. These may sound obvious, but taking these steps into account can prevent a lot of problems later on.

1. Develop an initial list of software required. Often this can be little more than a listing of subjects by grade and software function (e.g. 'a number practice program for 3rd-grade mathematics'). This needs to be based on an analysis of the goals that the software is supposed to fulfil.
2. Try and find information about what software is available and what the quality of that software is. It is a good idea to consult the relevant press, websites and experts from the local education authority or university. Ask other schools what they are using, and how happy they are with that software.
3. Consider, if you have the necessary technology in place, purchasing programs that have a local area network (LAN) version, as these will provide maximum spread across the school at minimum cost compared with stand-alone computer software, for which the licence will be valid for only one machine.
4. Make sure that whatever software you purchase will work on the available machines. Often computers available in school will not be the newest, so make sure the software works on these older machines as well.
5. Another important factor to take into account is the amount of after-sales support provided by the software developers, the clarity of manuals and the user-friendliness of the software. If all three are present, staff in the school or the department will be more likely to make use of the software.

Using ICT in teaching

Finding teaching resources on the Internet

In the last section, we mentioned the way students can benefit from ICT by being able to find materials on the World Wide Web. In much the same way it is becoming more and more interesting for teachers to use the World Wide Web themselves. It is now possible to download teaching resources, from worksheets and resource materials to ready-made lessons.

In England, the National Grid for Learning has been explicitly designed to help teachers do this, through the dissemination of lesson plans and optional teaching materials. The Government, which is a trend-setter in many of these areas, wishes in future to increasingly disseminate good practice through this channel by making available model lesson plans in various National Curriculum subjects. Apart from government websites and those sponsored by universities, web-sites set up by classroom teachers can often provide useful resources as well.

Using the computer instead of the blackboard in whole-class interactive settings

Computer screen images can be projected on to a large screen in front of the classroom, in order to present information to the class, either by the teacher or by students in response to teacher exercises.

Using a computer in this way has a number of advantages over and above more traditional means of communication such as black/whiteboards. One of these is the ease of changing what is on the screen. For example, in geography lessons one can produce a blank map and superimpose geographical or other features on to it. As discussed earlier, computers can also instantly produce a graph with information provided by students.

Adding illustrations is also easy and motivating for young students. In general, presentations on the computer can more easily be made attractive than on the black/whiteboard, which may contribute to a pleasant classroom environment and student motivation (Higgins and Muijs, 1999).

Integrated learning systems and drill-and-practice programs

One of the main uses of ICT in schools at this moment is integrated learning systems. These are systems which are made up of content, a system for recording and reacting to individual responses and a management system. Basically, they are drill-and-practice programs, with the children sitting in front of the computer answering questions on screen and receiving immediate feedback from the computer. The system also records all the answers a student has given, allowing it to produce a report on the progress of the child. What ILS can do that simple drill and practice programs cannot is manage students' learning in that, if a child has answered a series of questions correctly, the system can take her or him to the next level or topic while occasionally putting in revision questions on the previous topic. Furthermore, the program can give children a more detailed response on a certain topic if they appear to be having difficulty with it based on their answers to the questions, and a briefer response if the topic appears to be understood.

As such ILS's work as a sort of tutor, giving the students individual learning support. The degree to which these systems allow students to learn independently must not be overestimated, however. The program can obviously only give pre-programmed answers, and cannot assess the reasons for a student's wrong answer, or address misconceptions.

An advantage of ILS is the fact that if students appear to understand a concept they can move on to the next one rather than having to answer a load of additional questions on the same topic. This can alleviate boredom, and working on the computer in general still seems to have a motivating effect on students.

Nevertheless, a recent large-scale study in Britain did not find clear evidence that this approach improves student achievement, and it is becoming increasingly clear that these systems can by no means replace the teacher in the classroom (Wood, 1998). Integrated learning systems can be a useful resource, however, especially for remediation among low-achieving students which has been found to be one of their most effective uses.

Smaller-scale drill-and-practice program may also be a useful teaching resource. The weakest of these, however, are not much more than computerized worksheets and one needs to look carefully at the quality of the program on offer.

Using the web in student projects

As mentioned earlier, the World Wide Web is a veritable treasure trove of information, with sites providing material relevant to virtually all subjects. Therefore, for any project that involves student research having them access the web could be one of the most fruitful strategies.

However, apart from the problems mentioned earlier, one also needs to make sure that this type of activity does not harm students from less advantaged backgrounds. Teaching students how to use the web for research will obviously encourage students with access to a computer and Internet connection to do this at home as well, possibly leading to higher-quality work from these students compared with those who do not have this resource at home. It would therefore be advisable to provide web access to these students in after-school homework clubs, for example.

A further use of the web is communication, both with peers and with experts. The web allows students to contact students in other schools, in other countries and even in other continents, in order to engage in common projects or gather information about each other's country and culture. A number of projects using such tools as a web-cam have generated considerable student enthusiasm and long-term contacts between schools in different parts of the world.

Problems and pitfalls

In order to make all this work, however, a number of problems and pitfalls need to be overcome.

First, the ICT skills of many (particularly older) teachers are poor, leading to an inability to effectively use ICT and a general aversion and lack of confidence when faced with ICT. This may lead to some resistance to and anxiety about ICT from the 'old guard'. Continual professional development should clearly include elements of ICT training for these teachers.

Furthermore, the number of computers in schools needs to be drastically increased. At present in the average primary classroom there is often only one computer. This makes many effective uses of ICT impractical. Having more than two children working on a computer at any one time may lead to frustration and free-rider effects, and having some children work on the computer while others are doing something else may lead to exactly the kind of classroom management problems that whole-class teaching strategies seek to avoid (Green, 1998).

One also needs to beware of some of the claims made by software manufacturers. The software industry is a competitive one, and software manufacturers are basically trying to sell their products rather than produce objective research. Therefore, software manufacturers may exaggerate the evidence for the effectiveness of their products.

All in all, ICT provides teachers and students with a range of exciting new possibilities for teaching and learning. However, choosing how and when to use ICT, and what software to purchase, is something which requires a good deal of thought.

Summary

Information and communication technology is a rapidly developing and promising field in education (as in society more generally) which does, however, make it more difficult to provide firm guidance on its most effective uses.

Information and communication technology has been hypothesized to help students' learning in a number of ways, such as by allowing students to cut and paste texts in a way previously impossible and by enhancing possibilities for co-operative learning. Computers can also complete routine tasks faster and more efficiently than the human brain (e.g. computing), thus freeing up student time to concentrate on higher-level cognitive skills. As in society more generally, ICT in education provides students with unprecedented access to information on a range of topics through the use of the Internet and CD-ROM encyclopaedias. Interactivity and immediate feedback are further advantages of ICT in the classroom. Finally, ICT allows easy extension of learning from the classroom to the home. In the classroom, typical applications are use of the Internet for collecting information, use of an interactive whiteboard in whole class teaching, and use of integrated learning systems.

When deciding to purchase software, it is important to start from an analysis of the goals the software is to fulfil. A number of steps can be followed, taking into the account such factors as the availability of a local area network system and after-sales support.

Self-study questions

1. How can the World Wide Web be used in teaching, and what are the advantages and problems associated with this?
2. What are integrated learning systems, and what are their advantages and disadvantages?
3. In what ways can ICT help students' learning?
4. How important is it for students to learn how to use specific computer programs?
5. In what ways do you think computer use could be integrated into a direct instruction style lesson?
6. What do you need to take into account when purchasing educational software?
7. Can you describe some ways in which ICT use can extend learning into the home?

18

Assessment

Advance organizers
In this chapter you will learn about:
• The main types of assessment used in schools and classrooms today.
• The main characteristics of standardized tests, such as reliability and validity.
• The advantages and disadvantages of using teacher-made tests.
• The advantages and disadvantages of multiple choice and open essay-style questions.
• The most common forms of alternative assessment: performance assessment and portfolio assessment.

Introduction

Assessment is probably one of the most important but also most contentious activities teachers engage in. Assessment occupies up to one third of teacher time according to research by Stiggins (1987). This time spent is one of the reasons for criticism, as some commentators have said that this time could be better spent on actual teaching. Many types of assessment, in particular standardized tests, have been criticized as concentrating too strongly on basic skills (e.g. Wiggins, 1989). However, as we shall see below, assessment is an invaluable tool for teachers and education systems, allowing teachers to better plan their lessons by taking into account the strengths and weaknesses of their students and allowing teachers and schools to see whether students are actually learning what has been taught and to adjust their teaching if this is not the case. Assessment can also allow teachers to see how well their students are doing relative to national norms and can serve as quality control of schools, teachers and curriculum by the education system.

The term 'assessment' refers to all information gathered about students in the classroom by their teachers, either through formal testing, essays and homework or informally through observation or interaction (Arends, 1998). In this chapter we will focus on formal assessment. The related term of 'evaluation' refers to the process of judging, valuing and ranking students (Arends, 1998; Scriven, 1999). In practice, giving a test is assessment (collecting data on a particular student), while assigning a grade or mark is evaluation. There are two main types of evaluation: *formative* and *summative* evaluation. *Formative* evaluation is designed to inform the teacher about their students' performance, prior knowledge and skills, and this information is then used to plan lessons or remediation to improve students' performance. *Summative* evaluation is meant to give a picture of how well a student (or group of students) has done over a time period on a set of learning goals in a particular subject. Formative evaluation has been found to have a strong positive effect on achievement (Black and William, 1998). Summative evaluation is more useful for systemic quality control.

The three main types of assessment in use today are standardized tests, teacher-made tests and alternative forms of assessment such as performance assessment and portfolio assessment. We will discuss each of these in turn.

Standardized tests

Standardized tests have been developed by professional test developers (as opposed to classroom teachers) and have been designed to produce reliable results in a variety of settings. Examples include the California Achievement Test and the Texas Assessment of Academic Skills (TAAS) in the USA, and the Centraal Instituut voor Toetsontwikkeling (CITO) Schoolvorderingentoets in the Netherlands.

Standardized tests are widely used at the school, local education authority, school board, state or nation levels, often for purposes of accountability. These tests cover a wide range of subjects and can be commercially purchased or developed specifically for state or national testing purposes. In many systems, the results of testing are used to make judgements on the effectiveness of schools and teachers.

Two main types of standardized tests exist: *norm-referenced* and *criterion-referenced* tests. Norm-referenced tests are essentially comparative in that they rank students and are designed to allow comparison of students' performance relative to that of other students, usually a national sample. This means that these tests must be designed to discriminate students from one another, and thus must have enough different scores to allow this to happen. Usually as well as the actual score of the student on the test (the *raw score*) this type of test also provides users with an *age standardized score*, which has a mean of 100, corresponding to the average score of students of that age on the test, a minimum of 70 and a maximum of 130. In order for this standardization to be reliable the sample on which the test was originally *normed* must be representative of the population (for example all grade 4 elementary school children in the Netherlands). This means the sample must include a percentage of students of low socio-economic status, different genders, different types of school and so on that corresponds to the distribution of these characteristics in the population.

Criterion-referenced tests are not designed to compare students with each other but to measure the performance of students on a particular pre-chosen criterion, for example being able to reach a particular level of mastery in a subject. This means that criterion-referenced tests need to be more specific than norm-referenced tests with respect to content, but will be less effective at distinguishing students from each other. For example, if the goal of the test is to measure whether students have mastered a particular topic in the curriculum, the test should be designed in such a way that the large majority of students will pass the test if they have understood the topic. A good criterion referenced test will give information on students' mastery on one or more topics in a subject or curriculum, such as addition with three-digit numbers, place value or mental arithmetic in mathematics.

It is obviously important to decide before purchasing or designing a test what it is that you want it to do. For classroom use and for formative assessment more generally, criterion-referenced tests are usually most useful as they will allow the teacher to see whether students have attained specific learning goals. For some summative assessment purposes, especially where the performance of students is to be compared with that of peers, or where schools' or teachers' performance is to be compared, norm-referenced tests are more useful. It is important not to confuse the two, as designing tests for both purposes simultaneously leads to bad test design.

It is important when choosing to use either a norm-referenced or a criterion-referenced test that the test has been either recently designed or recently re-normed (i.e. within the last five years). This is necessary because both students and teaching change over time, which means that older tests will have norms that may no longer be valid for the current cohort of students. Furthermore, curricula and textbooks change over time, so old criteria may no longer reflect schools' current curriculum.

A further distinction within standardized testing is that between *achievement tests* and *aptitude tests*. Achievement tests measure students' performance in a particular school subject or topic at a given time. Aptitude tests cover a broader area and are less closely tied to the school curriculum. They are designed to give an indication of the knowledge that a student brings to a situation, and of the likelihood that that student will be academically successful during the course of the year (Macklem, 1990). As such they can be a helpful diagnostic tool for teachers, giving a picture of the strengths and weaknesses of students and helping teachers to set (individual) targets for these students and the class as a whole.

Two other criteria, derived from what is known as *classical test theory*, are *reliability* and *validity*. A test is reliable when the scores it produces are consistent and dependable, i.e. if a student took the same test on two occasions, she or he should obtain similar results. All standardized tests should come with a manual in which reliability measures are provided. The main measures of reliability are test-retest reliability (students are tested twice on the same test at different time points) and Cronbach's Alpha (a measure of internal consistency). These measures should be above 0.8.

Validity is a concept that is related to the content of the test. A test is valid if it measures what it purports to measure. *Content validity* means that the test questions measure what they are supposed to. For example, if a test claims to measure the English mathematics curriculum at age 4 the items of the test should reflect the content of the mathematics National Curriculum for that age group. This can be tested by looking at the items and relating them to the content of the curriculum. *Predictive validity* refers to the relationship of the test to other variables that it is supposed to predict. For example, if a test is supposed to measure mathematical ability, the results on the test should be correlated with those on (other) mathematics tests and to national high stakes tests (such as GCSEs in England) in that subject. This information should be available from the test developers. Finally, *construct validity* refers to the internal structure of the test. For example, if a cognitive ability test is supposed to measure verbal, non-verbal and quantitative ability, each item should *load* on one of these three factors. This can be determined using exploratory and (preferably) confirmatory factor analysis, and this information should also be provided by the test developers.

More recently, a new paradigm in measurement has taken hold, known as *Item Response Theory*. This theory posits that all items on a test are indicators of some *latent* underlying construct, such as mathematical ability or mathematical achievement. Using sophisticated software one can determine how well items fit with this model, how difficult they are and how well they discriminate between students of differing ability. Preferably a test should have been evaluated using an Item Response Model, and those items that did not fit should have been removed.

Another important criterion for test quality is that it should be unbiased. This means that the test should not disadvantage any ethnic groups or gender. This can be tested using a method called *differential item functioning* and test developers should be able to prove that no items in their test are biased, and that the test as a whole is unbiased as well (differential test functioning).

The main advantages of standardized tests lie in the high quality of the items written by specialists in the subject and in item construction, the standardization of administration and scoring procedures, the fact that standardized tests allow comparison with national norms and students, and the good psychometric qualities (reliability and validity) of the test. Standardized multiple choice tests in particular cover a wide range of topics, thus giving a good overview of students' knowledge of the curriculum (Sanders and Horn, 1994, 1995). Disadvantages lie in a possible mismatch between what students have learnt in class and what is measured by the test, and in the lack of flexibility of these tests. They also offer less insight into students' thought processes than do a number of alternative assessment methods.

As mentioned above, standardized tests are also often used for large-scale state-mandated assessments meant for accountability purposes (making sure schools and teachers are reaching mandated levels) and for measuring student achievement across the region in a standardized way. This use of 'high-stakes testing' is highly controversial, with proponents and opponents making strong claims for the benefits and dangers of this practice. Actual research on the results of high stakes testing is not widespread, however, and findings are mixed. There is some evidence that testing influences teaching ('teaching to the test'), though not to the extent that some opponents claim. There is also evidence that students' scores on standardized tests increase over time, which suggests, if the tests are reliable and valid, that they can increase achievement. On the other hand, high-stakes testing has been found to lead to stress among teachers and students (Mehrens, 1998).

Computer adaptive testing

One of the most exciting developments in testing is the advent of computer adaptive testing. Computer adaptive tests are, as the name suggests, performed on a computer, either via a connection to the World Wide Web or off-line using software packages or CD-ROMs. Essentially these tests are standardized multiple choice tests with the added advantage that, using so-called screening items, students will be presented with a selection of items suited to their ability level. The students will answer a number of preliminary questions, and on the basis of their performance on these items they will take a test that is neither too easy nor too difficult for them, a problem that can often occur with written tests.

Computer adaptive tests also allow test developers to constantly update and add items to the test, so items of similar difficulty can be randomly selected from large *item banks*. This means that tests are constantly changing and can be sat on several occasions without becoming unreliable through familiarity with the test items. Tests can also be immediately scored.

Technically, Item Response Models are used in order to calibrate new items and make sure that the difficulty levels of items are accurately known.

As technology develops, these tests will increasingly include multimedia presentations and film. Audio versions for students with reading difficulties and touch-screens for people with impaired sight have already been developed.

Teacher-made tests

Often, rather than use standardized tests, teachers will want to design their own tests, which may be better matched to their curriculum and their students' level of progress. Teacher-made tests also allow for more frequent testing than most standardized tests which can only be used occasionally because of item familiarity setting in and because the large range of topics covered makes them unsuitable to assess whether a particular recently taught topic has been learnt.

Gronlund (1991) suggests the following principles for effective teacher made tests:

1. Tests should be constructed to measure (as much as possible) all the learning goals that students are meant to reach, and not just a subset of these.
2. A good test should encompass different types of knowledge, such as factual knowledge, procedural knowledge and thinking skills.
3. Different types of test item are suitable for different purposes. Therefore teachers need to consider whether they want to use open questions, multiple choice questions or some other format based on their objectives.
4. Teachers should try to maximize reliability and validity in their tests. Using unambiguous items and making sure the test contains a sufficient number of items will enhance reliability. Calculating a reliability measure such as Cronbach's Alpha is relatively straightforward and can be done in a number of spreadsheet packages.
5. Tests should be used diagnostically. Students should be provided with feedback, and the teacher should go over problems in the test with students. Testing should be integrated with teaching. This is essential and far more important than giving marks or grades to students according to a review of research by Black and William (1998). Feedback should be helpful and aim to improve students' learning rather than encouraging competition and comparison between students. If these guidelines are followed then this type of formative assessment has a strong positive effect on learning, especially among low achievers.

A major distinction in testing is between tests using *closed*, often *multiple choice*, questions and questions that are open, often requiring students to write a type of essay. Both formats have advantages and disadvantages. The main advantage of multiple choice tests is that they are easy and quick to score, allow objective marking (as there is only one possible right answer) and the ease of varying questions according to difficulty based on statistical criteria. This type of test can also easily contain a large number of items, as multiple choice items take less time for students to answer than do open questions. This means that a larger proportion of the topic can be covered. A disadvantage is that students are not able to explain their thinking, leading to a focus on outcomes rather than processes in scoring. A further problem is guessing the answer, although this problem can be lessened by techniques such as subtracting a point for a wrong answer. Also, some statistical techniques exist that can take guessing behaviour into account (the three-parameter Item Response Model), although these are by no means foolproof. Multiple choice tests, while fast to administer and score, take a long time to prepare. The first part of the multiple choice question is called the *stem* (e.g. King Leopold's rule over the Congo Freestate was highly controversial because . . .). This should be clear and unambiguous, and provide sufficient context. The various (usually three) wrong answers are called *the distractors*. They need to be sufficiently plausible to be selected by students and should not contain formal clues that they are wrong, such as being significantly shorter than the right answer, being nonsensical and having a different grammatical structure (Arends, 1998; Borich, 1996).

Different forms of closed tests also exist, such as matching sets of items (an example of this is a vocabulary test in a foreign language, in which a list of words in the mother tongue needs to be matched to a list of words in the target language presented in a different order) and *cloze* tests, in which students have to fill in the blanks, for example 'The capital of France is _____'.

Open questions have the advantage of allowing space for students to explain their answers and working out, and thus can be more useful diagnostically because teachers can see exactly where misconceptions are occurring. Open questions can cover a wider area or concept than multiple choice questions. It has often been argued that multiple choice questions do not allow process or higher-order questions. This argument is not entirely accurate, however, as multiple choice tests covering a variety of learning objectives (and not just factual recall) have been successfully developed (Sanders and Horn, 1995). Usually essay tests are better suited to testing higher-order thinking than multiple choice tests though. Disadvantages of open questions include that they take longer to mark and that they are more difficult to mark objectively. In order to lessen this problem, clear and highly detailed marking schemes outlining exactly what elements are expected to be present or absent and how each element is to be marked are essential. 'Blind marking', where the teacher does not know whose test is being marked, can further enhance objectivity. This can be done by having students write their roll number rather than their name on the test, or by having them write their name on the back of the test sheet. In a classroom in which the teacher knows all the children personally and recognizes their handwriting this can be problematic, however. Having a colleague mark the tests may be a solution here. Finally, it can be easy to mistake fluent and correct writing for knowledge and understanding of the topic to be assessed. Teachers need to make sure essay tests are not turned into literacy tests, and should make sure they are not too strongly influenced by factors such as length and good handwriting, which can disadvantage students from low socio-economic status backgrounds (Sanders and Horn, 1995; Borich, 1996).

In order for open essay-style questions to be effective, they need to be clear and explain in a sufficiently detailed way exactly what is expected of students. If the goal of assessing higher-order thinking skills is to be reached, open questions need to require more than factual recall from students and preferably need to have more than one possible solution. Marking needs to set more store by the processes than by the outcomes of the question (Badger and Thomas, 1992).

Teacher-made tests are clearly suited to everyday classroom assessment. They can be made to fit exactly with the topics covered during lessons and the levels of students in a particular class. The main disadvantages are that it is harder to achieve good psychometric properties than with standardized tests designed over long periods of time and at some expense by a large team of experts, and the lack of a benchmark to compare the performance of students in the class to national norms. Usually some combination of teacher-made tests and standardized tests is advisable.

Alternative assessment methods

More recently a number of other assessment methods which aim to provide what is known as a more 'authentic' measure of students' learning have gained in popularity. Authentic in this context is usually taken to mean that student performance is measured directly on a realistic task, rather than indirectly using proxy items designed to measure an underlying latent trait (Wiggins, 1989). These types of assessment are intended to occur in a natural classroom context.

The aim of *performance assessment* is to measure learning or performance directly instead of using a paper-and-pencil test. An obvious example of this can be found in physical education where performance is judged directly by the teacher in many instances. This method can also be used to measure higher-order cognitive processes. To do this the teacher needs to establish a particular situation and then observe students solving problems, co-operating with other students and carrying out the tasks that the teacher wants to assess. The advantage of doing this is that it allows teachers to observe student behaviours in realistic situations rather than in the artificial test situation. This will enable teachers to study behaviours that may not occur under testing conditions, either because they are not explicitly tested or because test anxiety makes students not do them. An example is rating students while they are conducting a conversation in a foreign language or while they are conducting an experiment. Performance assessment can easily take place during a regular lesson (Brualdi, 1998; Moskal, 2000).

Developing a performance assessment is a deliberate and structured process that must go further than casual observation of students. When preparing a performance assessment the teacher needs to start off by formulating the outcomes that she or he wants to measure, both at the cognitive and affective levels. Then a task needs to be designed that will allow students to use the skills, behaviours or performance the teacher wants to measure. These can include role-plays, experiments or discussions. These tasks should be complex, allowing the teacher to assess a variety of skills, and do not necessarily have to lead to one particular 'right' outcome. The task should be sufficiently representative that it allows the teacher to make generalizations about the student's skills that are being assessed. As most performance assessments are administered to a single or small group of students, it is important that some standard procedure for presenting the task to the students is developed. In order to assess students' performance, the teacher needs to develop a *scoring rubric* that clearly lists those elements that the teacher is wanting to assess, such as attitudes, skills and cognitive processes. If the assessment is on clearly observable behaviours, a checklist on which the teacher notes whether the behaviour has or has not occurred will be most suitable. For more complex cognitive assessment a rating scale may be more effective. The fact that there is a clear list of descriptions of what is expected can be very useful in providing feedback to students for formative purposes (Elliott, 1995; Roeber, 1996; Brualdi, 1998; Borich, 1996; Moskal, 2000). Rather than formally setting up a performance assessment situation, some authors have suggested that it may be better to informally assess a student doing work in the classroom (Brualdi, 1998). While heightening authenticity, this can exacerbate problems of unreliability and bias, and it may be hard to compare the performance of different students when the situation observed is not standardized.

Performance assessments lack the reliability and validity of pencil-and-paper tests and are by their nature somewhat subjective, which means that teacher bias can be a problem. On the other hand, the ability to measure behaviours in realistic contexts and to assess processes that cannot easily be measured on paper (e.g. students' co-operative behaviour) makes this form of assessment potentially very powerful. Preparing and executing a performance assessment is very time-consuming, however, which means that usually only a few assignments can be graded. Performance assessment thus gives great depth, but not much breadth in assessing students' performance (Sanders and Horn, 1995).

While performance assessment gives a picture of the student at one particular point in time *portfolio assessment* is designed to give a picture of a student's performance over a longer period of time, such as a school year, by collating a collection of student work. As well as the finished essays, exercises and other specimens of student work, portfolios should also include drafts, early ideas and some indication of the processes the student used to arrive at the finished work.

As with performance assessment, the goals of the portfolio and what needs to be included in it need to be carefully defined at the outset and clearly agreed with the student. The contents of the portfolio need to match the goals that have been set out, and the teacher needs to prepare the student to be able to complete the portfolio successfully. The teacher needs to prepare a scoring rubric that outlines what criteria make for good, bad or average performance on each predefined goal and for each draft and final product in the portfolio. Finally, these grades will need to be aggregated, for example by adding the scores and averaging them, or by weighting one aspect (e.g. final products, structure) higher than others (e.g. drafts, spelling) (Borich, 1996).

One of the advantages of portfolios is that they show not just how students think and the processes they use to get to certain results, but also how they, and their work, have evolved over the year. Portfolios are also more than any other assessment a collaborative effort between students and teachers (and hopefully parents) who need to consult on the goals and content of the portfolio (Dietel, Herman and Knuth, 1991). The main disadvantages lie in the considerable amount of work this involves from both teacher and students, problems with establishing reliability of this assessment method and the high demands portfolio assessment places on students' self-motivation. As with performance assessment, teacher bias can occur (Sanders and Horn, 1995; Madaus and O'Dwyer, 1999). Some evidence of the 'construct validity' of both forms of alternative testing was found by Shavelson and Baxter (1992), who reported that a battery of alternative tests had a similar correlation to an aptitude test as had a standardized achievement test.

Data-rich schools

In view of the large amount of assessment conducted, it is often surprising how little data is used at the school level. It could, however, be beneficial if schools were to become 'data-rich organizations' using student data to inform a range of school and department-level decisions, something that has been piloted in the 'High Reliability Schools' project in the UK. If test data on a variety of measures, from teacher-made tests to standardized tests and other achievement measures, are centrally stored and accessed, teachers, headteachers and heads of department will be able to immediately collect information, for example on a child that is having problems in her or his class. The teacher will be able to see whether the child is having problems in other subjects, has reading difficulties based on scores on a reading test, has performed well in her or his previous school and in previous classes, has scored well on aptitude tests or has self-esteem or school commitment problems as measured by attitude tests. This will help the teacher diagnose the problem.

At the school level data can be used to set students in different subjects, to identify students who are underperforming relative to their potential as measured by the aptitude tests, to identify students with reading problems and to identify problems in the performance of subgroups of students (such as ethnic groups). Data can be used to look at the relative performance of different departments and subjects using value-added systems such as the YELLIS system in the UK.

In order for this to be possible schools need to collect and store all data centrally on an accessible database and teachers need to be trained both in data management and interpretation.

Summary

Assessment is one of the main parts of the teacher's job, taking up almost one-third of teacher time according to one study. There are three main types of assessment: standardized tests, teacher-made tests and alternative assessment methods. Formative assessment is designed to inform the teacher about their students' performance, prior knowledge and skills, and this information is then used to plan lessons or remediation to improve students' achievement. Formative assessment has been found to have a positive effect on students' achievement. Summative evaluation is meant to give a picture of how well a student (or group of students) has done over a time period on a set of learning goals in a particular subject.

Standardized tests have been developed by professional test developers and have been designed to produce reliable results in a variety of settings. There are two main types of standardized tests. Norm-referenced tests compare the performance of students to each other. Criterion-referenced tests assess whether students have reached a predefined level of mastery in a particular subject or topic.

Standardized tests should be reliable (dependable, giving the same result over time), valid (measure what they are supposed to measure) and recently designed or normed. The main advantages of standardized tests lie in their good psychometric properties, their easy scoring and use, the possibility of comparison with national standards and samples of students, and the breadth of coverage they can provide. Disadvantages include a lack of fit with the curriculum and a lack of flexibility.

Teacher-made tests can be made to link closely with the curriculum as covered in a particular classroom and can be tailored to the level of students in a particular class. They are usually less psychometrically sound than standardized tests and do not allow comparison with national norms or samples.

When designing a test, or indeed purchasing one, it is necessary to decide whether to use multiple choice questions, open questions or a combination of the two. Multiple choice questions have the advantage of being quick and unambiguous to mark and allow a large breadth of coverage as they can also be answered quickly. They do not allow assessment of processes, however, and are often less suited to assessment of higher level cognitive thinking. Open questions allow students to write down their thought processes and working out, and allow greater depth of coverage (but less breadth). Teacher bias and lack of standardization of scoring can be a problem with this type of test.

Recently, authentic assessment has gained in popularity. This type of assessment aims to study performance in natural circumstances rather than the contrived pencil-and-paper test situation.

In performance assessment, students are given a particular task (such as a discussion or experiment) that is observed and assessed by the teacher. The teacher needs to set out clear goals (what is to be assessed) and devise a detailed scoring rubric (how the goals are to be assessed) for this assessment method to be successful. This method allows the teacher to assess a wide range of processes, such as interactions with other students and affective factors that cannot be assessed easily in paper-and-pencil tests. This method is very time-consuming, allows little breadth (though great depth) and suffers from reliability problems.

In portfolio assessment students assemble a portfolio of their work, both finished products and drafts, over the year. This allows teachers to get a picture of a student's performance and growth over the year rather than assessing performance at one particular point in time. Goals need to be clearly articulated from the outset and a scoring rubric prepared. This method may also lack reliability.

Overall when deciding which of these assessment methods to use the teacher needs to weigh the greater breadth, higher objectivity, ease of administration, reliability and validity of standardized tests and some teacher made tests against the depth, authenticity and ability to assess higher non-cognitive processes in alternative assessment procedures such as performance assessment. As all forms of assessment have advantages and disadvantages, a combination of methods would appear to be the best approach.

Self-study questions

1. What are the main advantages and disadvantages of using standardized tests?
2. For what purposes would you use a norm-referenced test?
3. How can the reliability of grading answers to essay-style questions be enhanced?
4. What criteria should one take into account when deciding to purchase a standardized test?
5. What is portfolio assessment?
6. Why is a detailed scoring rubric important in performance assessment?
7. What are the advantages of authentic assessment methods?
8. What is computer adaptive testing and in what way does it differ from pencil-and-paper standardized tests?

19

Professional Development and Peer Classroom Observation

Advance organizers

In this chapter you will learn:

- Why classroom observation can be a powerful staff development tool.
- The main types of classroom observation.
- Some examples of the use of general and specific classroom observation instruments.
- Factors that determine the effectiveness of classroom observation.
- The use of classroom observation in educational research.

Introduction

In many countries teaching has traditionally taken place 'behind closed doors'. While collegial discussion between teachers has always existed in the staffroom, teachers have rarely observed colleagues teach. In many schools even management has traditionally not observed teachers teach. Recently this has changed significantly, however. Outside agencies, usually school inspection bodies sent out to observe lessons for purposes of accountability by state or national government, have invaded the classroom, leading management of schools to start to observe their teachers as a quality control measure. This is good management practice, as seeing what is actually going on in classrooms will allow management to put in place tailored interventions aimed at improving teaching. Managers will be able to see whether new programmes and approaches are being implemented effectively, and whether teaching is consistent within (and across) subjects.

Outsiders observing lessons can give a wider perspective having observed teaching in a variety of schools and classrooms and should be able to give useful comparative information to teachers. However, this type of observation, especially high-stakes observation by school inspection agencies, can be somewhat problematic. Teacher stress is likely to be considerable and feedback based on observations of just one (or, in some cases, just a part of one) not necessarily representative lesson is not necessarily valid. Unsurprisingly, where observations are likely to have practical consequences for the school and teachers, such as in the

197

OFSTED inspections in the UK, observed lessons can become 'performances' that are carefully set up for the benefit of the observer in an attempt to incorporate all the criteria used by the inspection agency in its judgments on teaching quality. It is clear that the formative advantages of observations conducted under these circumstances will be very limited. These problems can exist to a greater or lesser extent when observations are done by the school management depending on relations in the school and the goal of the observation (e.g. controlling teacher quality v. staff development).

While classroom observation by management (and sometimes by inspectors) can be effective, it is a shame that in many schools this has become the dominant form of classroom observation, largely 'crowding out' observation by peers of one anothers' teaching. Peer observation can be highly beneficial to both observer and observed. For the observed, peer observation can provide highly useful information on his or her strengths and weaknesses, which should help improve his or her teaching. For the observer, watching colleagues teach can provide ideas to use in her or his own classroom, and help the observer reflect on the strengths and weaknesses in her or his own practice. Peer classroom observation can also encourage discussion on classroom practice between teachers. Both peer and management observations can be used to help prepare teachers for external observations by, for example, school inspection bodies. However, while peer observation is the most useful form of observation for formative professional development, using it for public accountability or performance assessment purposes is likely to be less effective as some research has shown that the ratings vary strongly between colleagues, correlations being only .26. in one study. Peer ratings have also been found to show a positive bias, peers generally rating colleagues more positively than neutral observers (Centra, 1975).

A particularly interesting form of classroom observation is the use of 'research lessons' in Japan. In that country teachers will regularly present research lessons to colleagues, in which they demonstrate some innovative practice in the subject they are teaching. Colleagues and the teacher will then discuss the lesson. These lessons are very well prepared beforehand, teachers usually collaborating in this preparation. Usually the entire school faculty is invited to attend. Some schools are designated 'research schools' in a particular subject, and will present research lessons to teachers from schools in the area or, in some cases, nationally (Lewis and Tsuchida, 1997).

To be effective, classroom observation needs to be done using some kind of standard instrument on which the observer notes those things she or he is meant to observe. This is essential in view of the complexity of the classroom and the many activities occurring in it, which makes it unrealistic to try and observe (and remember) everything. Therefore, at the outset a number of decisions need to be made. Who is going to be observed? The teacher or the students, or maybe a classroom auxiliary? What is going to be observed? The overall quality of the lesson? Teachers' questioning behaviour? Classroom management? Whether or not boys and girls participate equally? Once these decisions have been made, an observation instrument needs to be chosen that fits in with these goals. All aspects of teaching can form the object of classroom observation.

One of the main distinctions in classroom observation is that between behaviourally orientated observation instruments and instruments that require value judgements from the observer (*value-orientated instruments*). *Behavioural instruments* are designed to look at the occurrence, or not, of often very specific behaviours without passing global judgements on whether the teaching or the behaviour observed was 'good' or otherwise. At the opposite end are instruments which aim to provide global value judgements on large parts of the lesson. Many instruments fall in between these two extremes. When instruments require too much subjective judgement from the observer (such as when observers need to judge the overall quality of the lesson on a scale from 'excellent' to 'inadequate') they can become highly problematic. The reliability of these judgement will be hard to establish even with extended training of the observers, and the meaning of the judgements (what is 'good') will make this type of observation hard to use formatively. For professional development purposes, this kind of global measure also provides too little detail for teachers to use to improve their practice. A particularly bad example of a highly subjective judgement is the practice in the English school inspections carried out by OFSTED of judging whether and what students have learnt during an observed lesson, a task which presupposes telepathic ability on the part of the observer.

A related distinction is that between *high and low inference measures*. Low inference measures require the minimum of judgement from the observer. An example of this is to count the number of times a teacher asks a question or to count the number of seconds that the teacher waits for the student to answer after asking a question. High inference measures require more judgement from the observer. An example of this is 'the teacher gave clear explanations'. The observer needs to make a judgement on whether explanations were clear, and ultimately what 'clear' means in this case. High inference scales are often rating scales and will require training of the observer on the meaning of the items (e.g. 'behaviour has occurred frequently' to 'behaviour did not occur').

A final distinction is that between *general instruments*, which aim to look at a wide range of teaching behaviours, and *specific instruments*, which look at one particular part of teaching such as classroom management. One possible sequence in peer classroom observation is to start off with a relatively general measure and then, based on what that has revealed with respect to the main problems, proceed to more detailed schedules looking at those particular areas.

Some examples of classroom observation instruments

Global classroom observation schedules aim to look at the totality of classroom practices of a particular teacher. This can help to pinpoint general strong and weak points of a teacher's teaching which can form the basis of a conversation about suggested improvements or professional development activities. Alternatively, one can move on from the findings of this observation to observing certain areas (such as questioning or classroom management) in more detail using a specific instrument. As an example we will discuss two global classroom observation instruments in this chapter, Quality of instruction, Appropriate level of interaction, Incentive and Time (QAIT) and Mathematics Enhancement Classroom Observation Record Scale (MECORS).

The MECORS scale (Schaffer *et al.*, 1998) was designed for the evaluation of a primary mathematics programme in the UK, but most items refer to more general teaching characteristics and the scale can therefore easily be adapted to other subjects. The scale was inspired by the SSOS and Virgilio scales (Schaffer *et al.*, 1998). It is a high inference scale that contains both qualitative and quantitative components.

The first part of the instrument is the actual observation sheet (Figure 19.1). This is filled in during the observation. Every time the teacher does a particular activity the observer writes down the time that activity starts. On the left of the form the observer fills in a code indicating whether teaching of that activity was whole-class interactive (direct instruction), whole-class lecture, individual review and practice, assessment or classroom management (i.e. students moving from one part of the classroom to the other, distribution of worksheets and purely administrative activities such as collecting school trip money). If the activity involves co-operative group work, the code 'b' is added. Observers then write down exactly what is occurring during that part of lesson in the mid section of the sheet. The observer also needs to count the number of students on task or off task every 5 minutes, a method known as 'time sampling'. The results are filled in on the right-hand side of the sheet. Only students visibly off task (who are, for example, looking outside, fiddling with displays or talking about yesterday's television with peers) are rated off task, as the assumption is that observers cannot look inside the heads of students. The category 'waiting' refers to students waiting for the teacher to help them. An average on-task rate of over 80 per cent is adequate, over 90 per cent is good in most cases although lower rates are more frequently observed in secondary school.

The second section of the instrument is the actual rating scale (Figure 19.2). This comprises 59 items, based on the effective teaching research discussed in Chapters 1 to 6. Observers are asked to rate whether behaviours occurred rarely, occasionally, often, frequently or constantly. Training is necessary to ensure that observers rate consistently. When trained, observers have been found to produce reliable ratings (inter-observer reliability being high) (Muijs and Reynolds, 2000a; 2000b). This

Activity Code	Time	Descriptive Notes	Time on Task (every 5 mins)	
			Category	Number
			Time: On task: Off task: Waiting: Out of class:	
			Time: On task: Off task: Waiting: Out of class:	
			Time: On task: Off task: Waiting: Out of class:	

Activity Key:
1 = Whole-class interactive
2 = Whole-class lecture
3 = Individual/group work
4 = Classroom management
5 = Testing/assessment

a = Calculators
b = Collaborative

Figure 19.1 The MECORS classroom observation schedule

1 = behaviour rarely observed
2 = behaviour occasionally observed
3 = behaviour often observed
4 = behaviour frequently observed
5 = behaviour consistently observed
na = not applicable

Classroom Management Techniques

1.	Rules and consequences are clearly understood	1 2 3 4 5 na
2.	The teacher starts a lesson on time (within 1 minute)	1 2 3 4 5 na
3.	The teacher uses time during class transitions effectively	1 2 3 4 5 na
4.	The teacher takes care that tasks/materials are ready and papers and papers and materials are collected and distributed effectively	1 2 3 4 5 na
5.	There are limited disruptions in the class	1 2 3 4 5 na

Maintain Appropriate Classroom Behaviour

6.	The teacher uses a reward system to manage student behaviour	1 2 3 4 5 na
7.	The teacher corrects behaviour immediately	1 2 3 4 5 na
8.	The teacher corrects behaviour accurately	1 2 3 4 5 na
9.	The teacher corrects behaviour constructively	1 2 3 4 5 na
10.	The teacher monitors the entire classroom	1 2 3 4 5 na

Focus and Maintain Attention on Lesson

11.	The teacher clearly states objectives/purposes of the lesson	1 2 3 4 5 na
12.	The teacher checks for prior knowledge	1 2 3 4 5 na
13.	The teacher presents material accurately	1 2 3 4 5 na
14.	The teacher presents material clearly	1 2 3 4 5 na
15.	The teacher gives detailed directions and explanations	1 2 3 4 5 na
16.	The teacher emphasises key points of the lesson	1 2 3 4 5 na
17.	The teacher has an academic focus	1 2 3 4 5 na
18.	The teacher uses a brisk pace	1 2 3 4 5 na

Provides Students with Review and Practice

19.	The teacher clearly explains tasks	1 2 3 4 5 na
20.	The teacher offers effective assistance to individuals/groups	1 2 3 4 5 na
21.	The teacher checks for understanding	1 2 3 4 5 na
22.	The teacher or students summarize the lesson	1 2 3 4 5 na
23.	The teacher reteaches if error rate is high	1 2 3 4 5 na
24.	The teacher is approachable for students with problems	1 2 3 4 5 na

Demonstrates Skills in Questioning

25.	The teacher uses a high frequency of questions	1 2 3 4 5 na
26.	The teacher asks academic questions	1 2 3 4 5 na
27.	The teacher asks open-ended questions	1 2 3 4 5 na
28.	The teacher probes further when responses are incorrect	1 2 3 4 5 na
29.	The teacher elaborates on answers	1 2 3 4 5 na
30.	The teacher asks students to explain how they reached their solution	1 2 3 4 5 na
31.	Students are asked for more than one solution	1 2 3 4 5 na
32.	The teacher uses appropriate wait time between questions and responses	1 2 3 4 5 na
33.	The teacher notes students' mistakes	1 2 3 4 5 na
34.	The teacher guides students through errors	1 2 3 4 5 na
35.	The teacher clears up misconceptions	1 2 3 4 5 na
36.	The teacher gives immediate academic feedback	1 2 3 4 5 na
37.	The teacher gives accurate academic feedback	1 2 3 4 5 na
38.	The teacher gives positive academic feedback	1 2 3 4 5 na

Demonstrates MEP Strategies						
39. The teacher uses realistic problems and examples	1	2	3	4	5	na
40. The teacher encourages/teaches students to use a variety of problem-solving strategies	1	2	3	4	5	na
41. The teacher uses correct mathematical language	1	2	3	4	5	na
42. The teacher encourages students to use correct mathematical language	1	2	3	4	5	na
43. The teacher allows students to use their own problem-solving strategies	1	2	3	4	5	na
44. The teacher implements quick-fire mental questions strategy	1	2	3	4	5	na
45. The teacher connects new material to previously learnt material	1	2	3	4	5	na
46. The teacher connects new material to other areas of mathematics	1	2	3	4	5	na
Demonstrates a Variety of Teaching Methods						
47. The teacher uses a variety of explanations that differ in complexity	1	2	3	4	5	na
48. The teacher uses a variety of instructional methods	1	2	3	4	5	na
49. The teacher uses manipulative materials/instructional aids/resources (e.g. number lines, coins)	1	2	3	4	5	na
Establishes a Positive Classroom Climate						
50. The teacher communicates high expectations for students	1	2	3	4	5	na
51. The teacher exhibits personal enthusiasm	1	2	3	4	5	na
52. The teacher displays a positive tone	1	2	3	4	5	na
53. The teacher encourages student interaction and communication	1	2	3	4	5	na
54. The teacher conveys genuine concern for students (empathic, understanding, warm, friendly)	1	2	3	4	5	na
55. The teacher knows and uses student names	1	2	3	4	5	na
56. The teacher displays students' work in the classroom (ample amount, attractively displayed, current)	1	2	3	4	5	na
57. The teacher prepares an inviting and cheering classroom	1	2	3	4	5	na

Figure 19.2   The MECORS rating scale

scale can be used to highlight general strengths and weaknesses of teachers, although the level of detail may be insufficient for specific interventions. Once problems have been identified using this scale one can use a more fine-grained and specific scale to look at the particular area.

One of the instruments that MECORS is based on is QAIT (the acronym refers to the different elements of the scale). This instrument is similar to MECORS in that it consists of two parts, a qualitative part and a rating scale. The qualitative part is similar to MECORS, the only difference being that there are 15 instead of seven activity codes (teacher presentation of content, recitation/discussion, directions for assignment, small group work, tests, checking, individual seatwork, pairs or group seatwork, student presentations, procedural behavioural presentation, administrative routines, transitions, non-academic activities, waiting time and discipline). The items in the rating scales are given in Figure 19.3. This scale has been successfully used in international research, supporting its cross-cultural validity (Schaffer, Nesselrodt and Stringfield, 1994). As can be

	Unlike this class			Like this class

I. Quality of Instruction
A. Lessons make sense to students. The teacher:

1. Organises information in an orderly way	1	2	3	4	5
2. Notes transitions to new topics	1	2	3	4	5
3. Uses many vivid images and examples	1	2	3	4	5
4. Frequently restates essential principles	1	2	3	4	5

B. Lessons relate to students' background. The teacher:

1. Uses devices such as advanced organisers	1	2	3	4	5
2. Reminds students of previously learnt material	1	2	3	4	5

C. Teacher exhibits enthusiasm	1	2	3	4	5
D. Teacher shows a sense of humour	1	2	3	4	5

E. Teacher clearly specifies objectives of the lesson. The teacher:

1. Conducts formal and/or informal assessments	1	2	3	4	5
2. Provides immediate and correct feedback	1	2	3	4	5
F. The teacher uses an appropriate pace to cover content	1	2	3	4	5

II Appropriate Level of Instruction
A. Instructional strategies match students' abilities. The teacher:

1. Accommodates students' level of prior knowledge	1	2	3	4	5
2. Accommodates students' different learning rates	1	2	3	4	5

B. Grouping strategies enable students to work together or alone. The teacher:

1. Uses in-class ability grouping	1	2	3	4	5
2. Has a class that is homogeneous in ability	1	2	3	4	5
3. Bases instruction on mastery of skills and/or concepts	1	2	3	4	5
4. Uses individualized instruction	1	2	3	4	5
5. Uses co-operative learning arrangement	1	2	3	4	5

III Incentive
A. Teacher arouses student curiosity by:

1. Presenting surprising demonstrations	1	2	3	4	5
2. Relating topics to students' lives	1	2	3	4	5
3. Allowing students to discover information	1	2	3	4	5
4. Presenting intrinsically interesting material	1	2	3	4	5

B. Teacher uses extrinsic academic incentives, such as

1. Praise and feedback	1	2	3	4	5
2. Accountability	1	2	3	4	5
3. Homework checks	1	2	3	4	5
4. Waiting for responses	1	2	3	4	5
5. Guiding partial responses	1	2	3	4	5
6. Tokens and rewards	1	2	3	4	5
7. Communicating high expectations	1	2	3	4	5
8. Small groups with individual incentives	1	2	3	4	5
9. Students encourage one another to achieve	1	2	3	4	5
10. Group contingencies	1	2	3	4	5

		Unlike this class			Like this class	
C. Teacher uses extrinsic behavioural incentives such as:						
	1. Praise	1	2	3	4	5
	2. Tokens and rewards for improvement	1	2	3	4	5
	3. Group contingencies	1	2	3	4	5
D. Teacher provides instruction appropriate for student abilities:						
	1. Effort by the student leads to success	1	2	3	4	5
IV Time						
A. Allocated time						
	1. Necessary time is allocated for instruction	1	2	3	4	5
B. Engaged rates						
	1. Teacher uses effective management	1	2	3	4	5
	2. Students attend to lessons	1	2	3	4	5

Figure 19.3   The QAIT rating scale

seen in Figure 19.3 this instrument highlights some different aspects than the MECORS scale. The scale generally uses higher inference than MECORS, requiring more observer judgement.

There are numerous other general classroom observation scales available, such as Virgilio, SSOS and the Classroom Observation Instrument, and it may be necessary to adapt one or a number of these scales to the purposes of the observation and the teaching practices prevalent in the school or school system (Schaffer, Nesselrodt and Stringfield, 1994).

Once a general classroom observation instrument has highlighted areas that could be improved, it might be useful to follow up using a more fine-grained instrument to look at that particular area. Alternatively, it could be that one has made a decision beforehand to look at a particular aspect of teaching in the school. An example of a more specific rating scale is the scale for looking at effective questioning (Figure 19.4).

Alternatively rather than using a rating scale one could use low-inference measures to look at particular behaviours. For example, if one wanted to look at the involvement of boys and girls in an interactive classroom, one could count the number of questions directed at boys and girls, measure the time boys and girls were talking during interactive sessions or discussions or count the number of higher-order questions directed at the two genders. From a general classroom observation instrument one could have concluded that classroom climate was not as good as it might be. One could then decide to look at particular behaviours, such as types of praise and criticism or expressions of low and high expectations of students by the teacher by, for example, counting the number of times positive and negative feedback occur, the number of negative and positive comments directed at student effort, the number and type of expressions of either high or low expectations and other such measures. Likewise, most of the items in the rating scale given in Figure

		Like this class		Unike this class	
1.	The teacher asks a high number of questions	5	4	3	2	1
2.	The teacher uses factual recall questions	5	4	3	2	1
3.	The teacher uses higher order questions	5	4	3	2	1
4.	The teacher asks open-ended questions	5	4	3	2	1
5.	The teacher asks closed questions	5	4	3	2	1
6.	The teacher asks product questions	5	4	3	2	1
7.	The teacher asks process questions	5	4	3	2	1
8.	The teacher acknowledges correct responses	5	4	3	2	1
9.	The teacher praises students who give the right answer	5	4	3	2	1
10.	The teacher acknowledges incorrect answers	5	4	3	2	1
11.	The teacher criticises students who give incorrect answers	5	4	3	2	1
12.	The teacher prompts the student when the answer is incorrect	5	4	3	2	1
13.	The teacher gives verbal prompts before going on to gestural or physical prompts	5	4	3	2	1
14.	The teacher acknowledges correct part of partially correct answers	5	4	3	2	1
15.	The teacher prompts the same student to answer incorrect part correctly	5	4	3	2	1
16.	The teacher uses an appropriate wait time after asking a question	5	4	3	2	1
17.	The teacher only moves on to the next step once students have demonstrated mastery over the topic during questioning	5	4	3	2	1
18.	The teacher makes sure all students are given the chance to answer questions	5	4	3	2	1
19.	The teacher makes sure students do not shout out answers	5	4	3	2	1
20.	The teacher allows students to ask questions themselves	5	4	3	2	1
21.	Students freely volunteer answers during the lesson	5	4	3	2	1

Figure 19.4   High inference effective questioning rating scale (based on effective interactive teaching behaviours, see Chapter 4)

19.4 could be made low inference by simply counting the number of times they occur.

Effective classroom observation: some pointers

For the observation to be useful to the observed teacher a number of conditions need to be met. The most important thing is to provide feedback, preferably both some brief feedback immediately after the observation and more comprehensive feedback later on (though not too much later, 48 hours seems a reasonable period). It is good practice to allow the observed teacher the opportunity to say what she or he thought about the lesson. One can start off with questions such as:

● What did you think of the lesson?
● What were your objectives, and do you think you have met them?

- Did things go as you had intended?
- What did you think were the strong points of the lesson?
- What did you think were the weak points?
- What would you have done differently?
- What caused things to go as they did?
- Was this a typical class or lesson?

These initial questions should be open (e.g. why did you send that boy out?) and the observer should avoid leading questions (e.g. did you send that boy out because he was talking all the time?) in order to receive enlightening answers (Brown, 1990).

Shadowing students

Another type of observation aims to look not at the teacher but at the experience of one or more students in school. One variant of this is for an observer to follow the school day of a particular student, following her or him from lesson to lesson. This can give valuable insights into how students experience school and can highlight problems such as impractical lesson transitions, inconsistent teaching or inconsistent behaviour management and rule enforcement. It can also allow one to see how the student reacts to different lessons and teaching styles and may help teachers deal with problem students. Teachers can find out whether the language they use is appropriate, whether there are hidden difficulties in texts or questions used, whether students are able to work independently in lessons, whether students get bored during certain parts of the lesson and what factors make particular students more likely to be on or off task during lessons.

Alternatively, the teacher can observe one or more students within her or his own lesson. Obviously this means that a colleague will need to take over teaching in the class while the teacher does the observations. The teacher can also ask a colleague to do the observing. As with observations of teaching, it is necessary to decide beforehand what it is one wants to observe: the student's interaction with other students, her or his behaviour or her or his motivation during different lessons. An observation schedule of some kind should be used here as well.

A problem with shadowing is obviously that students' behaviour is likely to be affected by the knowledge that they are being observed. When observing students in one's own class this can be partly solved by going about the observation in as subtle a way possible by sitting at the back of the class or joining a group as a kind of 'classroom assistant'. This obviously is not possible when students are actually followed through school.

The observer then needs to describe what he or she observed starting off on a positive note by highlighting the strong points found during the observation. The observer should point out what was less successful about the lesson, and allow the observed to comment on her or his observations.

Feedback needs to focus on the data collected and needs to be factual, whether delivered by peers or management. It should be concrete and focused towards practical issues, concentrating on the behaviours rather than on the person observed. Feedback should be neither anecdotal nor judgemental (Miles, 1989; Centre for Academic Practice, University of Warwick, 2000). For example, if the focus of the observation was the respective involvement of boys and girls during interactive lessons the observer will probably have counted the number of questions directed at girls and boys, the amount of times boys and girls were picked to answer questions, and possibly the length and types of questions answered by boys and girls. Observer and observed should go over and analyse the data and identify points that need to be worked on together. Observer and observed should then work out a strategy to solve these problems. It is important that the observer has some constructive suggestions to make (which can include advice on following external courses as well as practical tips), as the teacher can otherwise be left with the feeling that the criticism is purely there for its own sake and she or he can not really do anything to improve. Feedback should therefore be focused on behaviours which the observed teacher can change. Once the intervention has finished, the teacher will need to be observed again to see whether she or he has successfully changed her or his teaching practices. The feedback should concentrate on the main points and not overload the observed with information, as this can make the task of improving seem hopeless.

A relationship of trust between observer and observed is essential. The observing colleague needs to be a 'critical friend'. When using peer observation, the observer and observed should hopefully be people who trust one another and should establish a positive and supportive relationship (Aiex, 1993). The role of the observer needs to be agreed beforehand, as does the purpose of the observation. The criteria on which the observation is based need to be clear from the start and feedback needs to be constructive and positive.

During the observation, the observer needs to be as unobtrusive as possible and should not intervene in the lesson by correcting the teacher, for example. She or he should stay focused on the goals of the observation and mainly concentrate on collecting information to be used later.

Summary

Recently, as a result of increased calls for accountability, classroom observation by outside agencies such as the school inspectorate has become an increasingly common occurrence for teachers in many countries. Largely as a result of this outside pressure, observation by school management has become increasingly common as well.

While classroom observation by management has its uses, peer classroom observation during which teachers observe one another's lessons can be an even more effective tool. Peer observation can be highly beneficial to both observer and observed. For the observed, peer observation can provide highly useful formative feedback which should provide invaluable information on the teacher's strengths and weaknesses. For the observer, watching colleagues teach can provide ideas to use in her or his own classroom, and help reflection on the strengths and weaknesses in her or his own practice.

Research and classroom observation

Apart from its use as a staff development tool, classroom observation has been widely used in educational research. Many of the major effective teaching studies discussed earlier in this book used classroom observation as a major research tool. Initially, a lot of these studies employed low inference instruments, looking purely at the quantity of behaviours occurring (Stallings and Kasowitz, 1974). Later, increasing use was made of high inference instruments, with the aim of looking at quality as well as quantity of behaviours. Typically, these ratings or counts are correlated with achievement measures, usually scores on standardized tests or gain measures (change in standardized test scores over a period of time) in order to ascertain which behaviours make a difference to student outcomes. It is this research that has led to much of our knowledge on effective teaching.

Nevertheless, a number of criticisms have been levelled at this type of observation-based 'process-product' research. Thus, this type of research has been said to insufficiently take into account the context in which the observation occurs with respect to factors such as subject matter, students' socio-economic background, school-level and socio-political factors (Schaffer, Nesselrodt and Stringfield, 1994). This problem can be alleviated by collecting more data on school-level factors and student-level factors such as students' socio-economic background and ethnicity to incorporate into researchers' models, and by incorporating interviews and qualitative research to provide richer contextual knowledge.

The generalizability of the findings has also been questioned, for example whether findings from primary studies are generalizable to secondary schools and whether findings in mathematics and reading are generalizable to other subjects. More research is needed to sort these matters out.

Finally, the practical use of these results in teacher training, while some successful examples are known (e.g. Good, Grouws and Ebmaier, 1983) remains, in the words of Schaffer, Nesselrodt and Stringfield (1994, p. 74) 'spotty, inaccurate and difficult to implement'.

Classroom observation is best done using some kind of standard observation instrument. These observation instruments can be broadly ranged on a continuum between two poles. At one end, purely behavioural instruments are designed to look at the occurrence, or not, of often very specific behaviours without passing global judgements on the quality of teaching. At the opposite end are instruments which aim to provide global value judgements on large parts of the lesson. Many instruments fall between these two extremes.

A related distinction is that between high and low inference measures. Low inference measures require the minimum of judgement from the observer, usually consisting of counting behaviours or measuring time.

High inference measures require more judgement from the observer, and aim to take into account quality as well as quantity of behaviours.

Observation instruments can be either general, aiming to look at a wide range of behaviours (such as MECORS and QAIT), or specific, looking at just one aspect of classroom teaching.

For the observation to be useful to the observed teacher, a number of conditions need to be met, the most important of which is the provision of feedback, preferably both immediate feedback after the observation and more comprehensive feedback later on. This feedback needs to start off by allowing the observed teacher to comment on the lesson her or himself. Feedback needs to focus on the data collected and needs to be factual, whether delivered by peers or management. It is important that the observer makes some constructive suggestions (which can include advice on following external courses as well as practical tips) during the observation.

Self-study questions

1. What benefits could classroom observation have for the observer?
2. What factors can enhance the effectiveness of observation feedback sessions?
3. What is the difference between low and high inference measures?
4. What are the main criticisms of 'process-product' research using classroom observation?
5. What are the possible benefits of shadowing students?
6. When would you use a specific observation instrument?
7. What are the main problems associated with the use of highly 'value-based' instruments?

Conclusion: Teacher Effectiveness in the Future

What has become clear throughout this book is how much we actually know about what makes for effective teaching. The view that teaching is purely an art and can never be a science is clearly no longer tenable, as our knowledge on what makes for effective teaching becomes ever larger. This is not to say that there is no place for the teacher-artists, or for artistry and creativity in teaching. It does mean, however, that teaching needs to be firmly research based, as only this approach will maximize the effectiveness of all teachers and the learning and development of all learners. Obviously, in this book we have only been able to present a summary of the range of research findings in the various areas discussed, and we would like to point the interested reader to the References given if she or he wants to find out more. Also, there are a number of areas which we have not touched on in this work, including the effect of teacher beliefs and attitudes on pupil achievement, subject-specific research in such areas as science and modern foreign languages, and research on differences in teaching pupils from different social backgrounds and eth-nic groups. We have, however, reviewed the main findings of research in a large number of teaching-related areas.

We have summarized the research on classroom and behaviour man-agement, which has provided firm foundations for creating classroom environments in which learning can take place. Likewise, research on the direct instruction model has provided us with best practice for teaching basic skills, as well as a large amount of information on effective generic teaching behaviours in such areas as questioning, individual practice and structuring the lesson. An increasingly robust body of knowledge now exists on the teaching of higher-order thinking skills (reviewed in Chap-ter 9), and we also know a lot about student self-esteem, enhancing social skills and, to a lesser extent, teaching gifted pupils and pupils with special needs. There are robust findings on the learning and teaching of reading and literacy, and an increasingly strong research base on the learning and teaching of mathematics (although this research base remains less strong than that on teaching literacy).

Future research needs

The research base is not as robust in all areas, however. The knowledge base on generic teaching behaviours discussed in Part 1 is probably the most firmly grounded in research of all. However, most of this research was conducted in a limited number of countries (mainly the UK, the USA and the Netherlands), in a limited number of subjects (mainly mathematics and reading) and often in the primary rather than in the higher years. This clearly leaves question marks over the generalizability of this research to other subjects, grades and countries. While arguments can be made for the global nature of many of the findings, only further research will be able to resolve this question. The research base on a number of other areas, such as individual differences and classroom observation, is weak and needs much more development.

Two areas particularly in need of more research are the effective use of ICT and the cost-effectiveness of various educational strategies and interventions. While a large number of ICT interventions have been developed and ICT use is generally supported by politicians and educators alike, there is, as mentioned in Chapter 17, very little research that gives clear pointers on the most effective programmes in this area. Another area that is in need of far more research is the cost-effectiveness of educational interventions. Funding for education is not unlimited, which means that decisions about the best allocation of resources constantly have to be made at all levels. While obviously a first concern has to be to select practices and strategies that are educationally effective, attention has to be paid to the cost-effectiveness of educational strategies as well. At the systems level, policy-makers may need to choose between spending more money on providing schools with ICT or spending more on in-service training. Similarly, when providing ICT resources, how should resources be allocated between, say, software and training of users? More research needs to be done on how cost-effective (as well as educationally effective) various educational strategies are.

In those areas in which the research base is more developed there are weaknesses as well. More sophisticated methodologies need to be employed in many areas of educational research. Mixed methodologies, combining quantitative and qualitative research, seem to provide a fruitful way forward; combining quantitative rigour with qualitative depth (Tashakkori and Teddlie, 1998). Better collection of pupil background data is essential if research is to progress. Also, research in the various areas we have looked at is often done without consideration of the unintended consequences they may cause. For example, what is the effect of inclusion of pupils with special needs on the achievement of their non-disabled peers? Or how does the effective teaching of higher-order thinking skills impact on the effective teaching of basic skills? Another methodological issue is that in most research an underlying, though often not acknowledged or not even realized, assumption is that learning proceeds in a linear fashion. This is particularly the case in quantitative research, which usually applies linear models to educational phenomena, as this is the type of model underlying such common statistical methods as multiple linear regression or linear structural equation modelling. This assumption clearly does not accord with most theories and research on learning, and it is high time educational researchers started to make more use of the non-linear methods now available.

Across all the areas we have identified in this book there is also an urgent need to move beyond 'one size fits all' descriptions of effective teaching practices toward research which looks at whether there is 'context specificity' in the factors that are effective, originally shown in interesting research from California, where highly effective schools in poor catchment areas pursued policies *discouraging* parental involvement in the school, in contrast to the effective schools in more advantaged catchment areas that *encouraged* the practice (Hallinger and Murphy, 1985). While some factors apply across all social contexts (such as having high expectations of what children can achieve or 'lesson structure'), it may be that certain factors apply only in certain environmental contexts. At classroom level an example might be that the factor of 'proceeding in small steps with consolidation if necessary' is important for all children who are learning to read for the first time in all contexts, while in the contexts inhabited by lower social class or lower-attaining children it may be necessary to ensure high learning gain through the use of small 'steps' for teaching *all* knowledge and not just knowledge that is new, before moving on to other approaches.

Borich (1996) gives the following summary of teacher factors that may be necessary to attain high achievement gains in classrooms in two different social settings, those of low socio-economic status and middle/high socio-economic status. Effective practices within low socio-economic status contexts involve the teacher behaviours of:

- generating a warm and supportive affect by letting children know help is available;
- getting a response, any response, before moving on to the next bit of material;
- presenting material in small bits, with a chance to practise before moving on;
- showing how bits fit together before moving on;
- emphasizing knowledge and applications before abstraction, putting the concrete first;
- giving immediate help (through use of peers perhaps);
- generating strong structure, ground-flow and well-planned transitions;
- the use of individually differentiated material; and
- the use of the experiences of pupils.

Effective practices within middle socio-economic status contexts involve the teacher behaviours of:

- requiring extended reasoning;
- posing questions that require associations and generalizations;
- giving difficult material;
- the use of projects that require independent judgement, discovery, problem-solving and the use of original information;
- encouraging learners to take responsibility for their own learning; and
- very rich verbalizing.

We do not know as yet the extent of any 'context specificity' in the precise factors associated with gains in academic achievement. However, there are enough hints of the existence of this factor to make one wary of recommending undifferentiated methods in highly differentiated school contexts.

We also need to have teacher effectiveness studies that are aware of the need for new, more contemporary outcomes of schooling to be measured, particularly the 'learning to learn' skills that are necessary for the existence of successful learning processes (De Corte, Greer and Verschaffel, 1996). Many argue that these skills contribute to outcomes (Wang, Haertel and Walberg, 1990, 1993), although it is not clear how large their contribution actually is (Palincsar and McPhail, 1993).

Also, new perspectives on the process of learning itself (Resnick, 1987) have reconceptualized it as an active process in which students construct knowledge and skills by working with the content, which differs from the passive role of the student as to be 'instructed' that is in evidence in some teacher effectiveness research. Whereas older models of instruction aim at direct transfer, the new models consider learning as an active part of knowledge construction, in which the student plays the active part. Ideas about active learning also change the role of the teacher in that the student is responsible for learning. The teacher is seen as a manager, an orchestrator of that learning process, and is no longer seen as a person who delivers the content and the instruction, but as a supervisor and a counsellor. This implies teaching students how to learn (Weinstein and Mayer, 1986).

The new views on learning, especially the new views on the responsibilities of teachers and students in the learning process, have resulted in new models for instruction, or at least adaptations of the direct instruction model we have outlined in this book (Veenman, 1992). The new models put more emphasis on the students as active, responsible learners in co-operation with their teachers and with other students in co-operative learning, classroom discourse and interactive instruction (Vermunt, 1992). Examples of the new instructional models are reciprocal teaching (Brown and Palincsar, 1989), modelling (Schoenfeld, 1985), procedural facilitation (Scardamalia and Bereiter, 1985) and cognitive apprenticeship (Collins, Brown and Newman (1989).

The implications for policy

Whatever the imperfections in the research base, though, it is clear that we have reproducible findings across countries concerning effective teaching factors, as in the studies from the USA and the Mortimore *et al.* (1988) work from the UK, that look like an understanding of 'what works'. At the moment, the great majority of the policy 'levers' being pulled in most countries are at the school level, such as school development plans and target setting, and at local education authority level (LEA), such as LEA development plans. The problems with the mostly 'school-level' orientation of contemporary policy and contemporary educational discourse as judged against the literature is, of course, that:

- within-school variation by department within secondary school and by teacher within primary school is much greater than the variation between schools on their 'mean' levels of achievement or 'value added' effectiveness (Fitz-Gibbon, 1996); and
- the effect of the classroom level in those multilevel analyses that have been undertaken, since the introduction of this technique in the mid-1980s, is probably three to four times greater than that of the school level (Creemers, 1994).

It may be that a classroom or 'learning level' orientation would be more predictive than a school level orientation of achievement gains for the following reasons:

- The departmental level in a secondary school or 'year' level in a primary school is closer to the classroom level than is the school level, opening up the possibility of generating greater change in classrooms.
- While not every school is an effective school, every school has within itself some practice that is more effective than its other practice. Many schools will have within themselves practice that is absolutely effective across all schools. With a within-school, 'learning level' orientation every school can work on its own internal conditions.
- Focusing 'within' schools may be a way of permitting greater levels of competence to emerge at the school level, since it is possible that the absence of strategic thinking at school level in many parts of the educational system is related to the overload of pressures among headteachers, who are having referred to them problems which should be dealt with by the day-to-day operation of the teachers.
- Within-school units of policy intervention, such as classes or subjects, are smaller and therefore potentially more malleable than those at 'whole school' level.
- Teachers in general, and those teachers in less effective settings in particular (Reynolds, 1991, 1996), may be more influenced by classroom-level policies that are close to their focal concerns of teaching and the curriculum, rather than by the policies that are 'managerial' and orientated to the school level.
- The possibility of obtaining 'school level to school level' transfer of good practice, plus any possible transfer from LEAs in connection with their role as monitors of school quality through their involvement in

the approval of school's development plans, may be more difficult than the possibility of obtaining 'within school' transfer of practice.

While it is clearly important to maximize both the school-level factors and the learning-level factors in their effectiveness, it is important to note that the most powerful intervention strategies, Reading Recovery (Clay, 1993) and the Education for All programme of Slavin (1996), have a pronounced focus upon pulling the lever of the 'instructional' level, as well as ensuring school-level conditions conducive to reading instruction. Indeed, in these programmes, which generate both the highest levels of achievement gain in reading ever seen in educational research *and* achievement gains that are (most unusually) higher among initially low-scoring children, the school level is seen as merely setting the conditions for effective learning to take place at the classroom or instructional level.

Given that we clearly know 'what works', in addition to a concentration upon improving the classroom it is important to ensure that all teachers have access to this knowledge base through effective teacher training.

The implications for practice

Historically, of course, the precise methods utilized by teachers in most countries have been to a great extent determined by individual teachers and schools, although clearly the 'craft' of teaching was influenced by teacher trainers in higher education as well as by changing national educational discourse about what were appropriate methods, as was probably the case with the influence of so-called 'child-centred' methods in the 1970s in the primary sector in the UK.

More recently, however, the required behaviour of teachers and the organizational forms within which these behaviours are to be exhibited have been increasingly made explicit and indeed notions about the behaviours that are effective permeate the OFSTED inspection process introduced in England and Wales from the early 1990s. The British Literacy and Numeracy Strategy represents, for all teachers in Reception (kindergarten) classes through to Year 6 (ages 4 to 11), a clear, centrally determined belief as to what should be the form and content of lessons, with in the case of Numeracy Strategy a commitment to whole-class 'mental mathematics' as the first section of a lesson, to be followed by pupils working in groups for a middle lesson section and whole-class review at the end. Using the Numeracy Strategy as a further example, certain teacher behaviours were espoused (Department for Education and Employment, 1998a and b), such as a 'whole-class interactive' style of teaching involving a high frequency of questions, and questions involving more than a recitation of factual knowledge but actually aimed at both encouraging understanding and application of knowledge and generation of 'higher-order' skills.

This prescription of teacher behaviours carries with it a difficult set of baggage for any group of teacher professionals to handle, intellectually and emotionally. Historically, the 'ownership paradigm' has held sway for the last ten to 15 years in a number of countries, in which paradigm it was believed that teachers would be more likely both to be effective and to develop as professionals if they were involved in actually creating the methods that their schools and classrooms would then reflect. However, this paradigm has been threatened by a number of realizations:

- Encouraging 'self invention' may generate a range between teachers, with effective teachers 'self inventing' more effective methods than less effective teachers.
- The 'inventing the wheel' of appropriate methods by teachers may be very time-consuming, since it may take considerable periods to 'discover' what works.
- There is some evidence from the USA that schools that have relied upon the invention of methods through belief in the value of ownership may generate less pupil growth in achievement than those that purchase one of the many 'off the shelf' designs to promote school and instructional effectiveness (Stringfield, Ross and Smith, 1997).

Rather than leaving schools and teachers to self-invent methods, and rather than leaving the system to 'discover' what may be appropriate for them, there is a view that wishes the profession resourced by the evidence about 'what works' and that wishes for a profession that is encouraged what 'good practice' to display. There are of course problems with this new paradigm too:

- Educational history shows that policy-makers have been attracted to the prescription of policies for which there is no apparent evidence of effectiveness as well as to those that are in accord with academic research (an example of this is the proposal that was floated at the time of the launch of the Numeracy Strategy to ban the use of calculators for all children from ages 5 to 11). The widespread realization among the profession that mandating has been pursued with non-rational policies as well as with rational ones leads in Britain currently to the often heard cry from individual teachers of 'Why should we believe you this time (about literacy and numeracy) when you weren't right before?', and can demoralize and make negative the profession, outweighing any gain that might have occurred if behaviours had been taken up.
- In many areas of vital importance to teachers there may be no valid 'technology' of schooling or teaching to transmit, since the knowledge base may not exist. While there are internationally considerable similarities in what makes a school effective, for example, it is clear that the behaviours of the principal or headteacher that are associated with her or his school being effective are different in different countries, and may be different in schools of different socio-economic composition,

governance structure, level of effectiveness and phase of development within countries (Teddlie and Reynolds, 2000). As a further example, while we have seen that there are many 'universals' that seem to exist in terms of sharing an association with pupil achievement, such as high expectations, structure, active teaching and time management, it is likely that what is necessary to be an effective teacher of art, or physical education, may be different in terms of attributes, skills and knowledge from what is necessary to be an effective teacher of mathematics or science.

- The 'technology' or knowledge base that exists may be considerably stronger in certain areas of educational life than in others. As an example, students' social development is increasingly being argued to be an essential goal for teachers, given the needs of a future society (e.g. Stoll and Fink, 1996). Studies of academic and social development, however, have found that while the impact upon the child of the teacher and the school may be as great in the area of social outcomes as in the academic, the teaching and schooling factors associated with the effect were smaller in number than those that could be discovered related to academic achievement (e.g. Mortimore *et al.,* 1988).
- It would indeed be overly optimistic to expect governments to behave at all times as 'rational actors', both capable and willing to use best research evidence, particularly in the light of pressures to constantly initiate new change initiatives.
- Furthermore, an overly prescriptive approach could stifle innovation.

All these factors suggest that there may need to be a rather large 'health warning' attached to any mandated set of teacher behaviours that may emanate from educational policy-makers. It is beneficial to ensure that teachers have access to the knowledge base on effective teaching through initial teacher training and professional development. This can help ensure that the most valid methods are used by teachers, therefore maximizing the outcomes of students in their academic and social areas, and thereby enhancing the prospects of the next generation. To take British educational practice as an example, the self-determination of teachers' methods that has characterized British educational history led to primary school lessons that involved perhaps only 20–25 per cent of total lesson time being utilized for whole-class teaching, and to a predominance of time being utilized for individual students to self-learn, often involving utilization of heavily differentiated 'schemes'. Research into teacher effectiveness strongly suggests that whole-class instruction of perhaps 50 per cent of total lesson time is optimal for high levels of achievement in basic skills at the junior stage (Creemers, 1994). As another example, very few British lessons in either the primary or the secondary stage have involved a 10-minute period of review for the whole class at the end of the lesson, since the 'review' at the end of the lesson in British schools has historically tended to be a very brief social form of closure rather than an academic one. As a further example, British teachers have not been using truly collaborative group work methods extensively, even though they are enormously powerful in the generation of 'higher-order' skills (Slavin, 1996). These practices need to be taught, as there is frankly no suggestion that British teachers would, or maybe could, 'discover' the utility of these methods if left to their own devices.

Giving all teachers access to the effective teaching knowledge base methods can speed professional development by saving the considerable amount of time that would otherwise be utilized while professionals 'invent' their good practice. Precise estimates of time must be a matter of considerable conjecture but it may be that the 'standard' instructional effectiveness material that featured historically within many American initial teacher education would represent three or four years' worth of professional development for a median teacher or school. Utilizing the material may give a substantial advantage to the individuals and/or institutions exposed to it.

This can also aid the consistency, cohesion and predictability of schooling, thereby ensuring that students receive a more structured and reliable organizational experience. There is a considerable volume of hints in the school and teacher effectiveness literature that ineffective schools and teachers with low student 'value added' exhibit greater variance in behaviours over set time periods than their more effective peers (Teddlie and Reynolds, 2000). Children appear to respond well to a restricted range of behaviours and to predictability in terms of the teacher behaviours and the organization of a lesson, although of course they respond to variety in terms of intellectual stimuli within it.

It is important to stress that the provision of a foundation of knowledge on effective methods should not be regarded as *sufficient* for professional development to occur, only as most likely *necessary*. For the medium- to long-term development of teachers as individuals and indeed of a teaching profession, it is likely that the things that would promote improvement may be different to the 'foundational' needs of having basic competencies in place. Long-term professional growth would probably involve teachers being able actively to utilize high quality management information systems to create both more valid and more advanced knowledge than the necessarily simple foundations that they were given through initial training in effective behaviours. However, it seems likely that the provision of the foundational knowledge about 'good practice' and the routinization of that knowledge into day-to-day professional practice will further the generation of a competent profession more than it will disable it from intellectual advance.

The need for blend

As well as being alert to the danger that the quite understandable desire of governments to mandate the use of effective methods of teaching does not prevent teachers from making progress in their own long-term professional development, we need to be aware of the need for an international reach to discussions about teaching methods. There has historically been a rather mystifying combination of extreme ethnocentrism in education, typified by the belief that British primary education was the best in the world, that has existed hand in hand with occasional spasms of policy borrowing from other countries, typically from the Pacific Rim. Rather than lurching from one extreme, so-called progressive methods, to the other, so-called traditional methods, it is important that countries blend together approaches in methods. As an example, at just the same time as some in the West have decided the future lies in the adoption of Eastern methods, the East has decided that their future lies in trying out Western methods. These societies are well aware of what their systems of education have done for them. Taiwan, for example, possesses children who do well in international surveys despite having mostly semi-literate grandparents and parents with little secondary education. Their technology of education is a relatively simple one, involving much instruction in large classes. The technology is given to all teachers through their initial teacher education and subsequent in-service training. It involves mechanisms to eradicate any trailing edge of low-achieving pupils, and studies pupils by frequent testing.

However, this system is now much more criticized than before. Whole-class teaching is now agreed to involve costs for the extremes of the achievement range, since teachers have to teach 'to the middle'. While the less able may be caught up, the more able may remain unstimulated. Situations where there is high control over children's learning may not produce children who can work independently. They may discourage the generation of new ideas, and creativity may not be that easy to achieve in such ordered settings. Children who are used to working in one large group are unused to the collaborative small group work that modern industrialists want.

For all these reasons, there is now a belief in societies like Taiwan that Western traditions need to be blended with their own. A British visitor will be plied with more questions about the progressive school Summerhill during a week in Taiwan than in a lifetime on the British conference circuit. Enthusiasm is high for what they label open education, based upon a rapid growth of open-plan schools and associated team teaching in Japan.

Taiwan has some pilot 'open education' schools. Japan is said to have reduced the customary very high percentage of time that pupils are taught in whole classes to 60 per cent. Taiwan has just held its first government sponsored conference on open education, with speakers from the USA, Japan and the UK.

There is a world of difference, though, in how these societies are approaching the task of changing their educational system, compared with how others have behaved. First, they are searching the world for people and evidence that they can cherry-pick to give their system a new blend. They are aware that more is known about how to affect and alter the academic outcomes of education than the social ones. They are seeking the technology for new outcomes before they begin any reforms, whereas in Britain we have always assumed that we could make it up as we went along – the equivalent of trying to build a plane in flight.

Second, policy-makers are aware that other countries have attempted to change a wide range of things at the same time, involving curriculum, class organization, educational goals, school organization and pupil experience, generating considerable overload. They intend to phase reform and concentrate on root changes rather than on branch or peripheral ones.

Third, the Pacific Rim countries are aware of the need for clarity in what they are attempting to do. Vague British concepts such as 'the whole child' will have little place in their vocabulary. They will ensure that the changes that they want will be generated by all teachers being given the technology that is necessary, in terms of appropriate teaching behaviours and understandings. As befits a country in which uttering the phrase 'teaching is an art not a science' generates embarrassed concern for the mental health of the speaker, initial teacher education and in-service education will reflect the new methodologies that teachers will be expected to use. The reformers will insist that changes in individual classrooms are faithful to national designs, viewing a strong technology of instruction – whether progressive or traditional – as the friend of the disadvantaged, the slow learning and the needy.

What the Pacific Rim countries are particularly interested in is the power of collaborative group work to deliver vastly improved traditional outcomes, plus some new ones. They know the American research literature and the huge learning gains that properly implemented group work can bring – especially if the group has responsibility for the task, if individuals have additional individual tasks and if material is properly differentiated to ensure it is appropriate. Taiwanese classrooms will erode the proportion of whole-class interactive teaching from its present 90 per cent or so at primary school to perhaps 70 per cent, with group work taking up 20 per cent and individual work continuing at the present 10 per cent of total time.

Two things seem to be important. First, Pacific Rim societies are seeking a new blend. It would be foolish to return to their basics just at the time that they themselves are aware of the need to change. As they search for a blend of traditional and innovative practices, our own search must likewise involve a desire to keep what we do well, in addition to recognizing areas where we have much to learn. Indeed, it is possible that while British investigative methods may be inappropriate with some subject areas, they explain the superiority over much of the rest of the world in science. For the West, as well as Taiwan and the others, the answer is a blend, not a slavish cult worship, of what others do.

Second, the importance of the Pacific Rim societies is that they have an agreed technology of practice. It is clear that enormous advantages accrue to those societies which can possess 'strong systems', rather than rely heavily on 'strong people' or 'unusual persons' to run their schools. Strong systems minimize the variance in the quality of education provided, whereas systems that rely on persons to generate their own methods, inevitably of different levels of competence, will generate variance according to how much 'strength' persons have. Strong systems can generate a higher proportion of educational professionals with the requisite skills to run effective schools, whereas systems that rely on personal characteristics are restricted to the number of persons who possess the personal characteristics.

A new vision

We have no doubt that any desire for teachers to be seen as technologists, rather than as philosopher kings, has limited appeal in many countries of the world. In defence, one can point to the success of another profession, the medical profession, which in the decades of the early part of this century reminded one of what teachers may be close to being now – they were relatively poor, demoralized and self destructive, attempting to get their emotional and professional satisfaction out of inventing their own, often ineffective, methods. Everyone tried to invent their own cure for tuberculosis, few did so. Now they use methods which research has established as valid and, based upon an audit of the patient, obtain their professional fulfilment and emotional satisfaction from seeing the sick become well and the lame become whole. The few that did find the cure for tuberculosis have had that discovery given to all.

Teachers need, similarly, to reject the demoralizing nonsense that they should daily reinvent the teaching wheel, and that their professional satisfaction is linked to their exhausting yet doomed attempt at educational and instructional do-it-yourself (DIY), the educational equivalent of the invention of a cure for tuberculosis. Instead, they should be encouraged to use known to be valid methods outlined in this book, while at the same time always enquiring as to how they can make them better. They should be encouraged to gain their satisfaction not from the DIY but from seeing children learn and from seeing the educationally lame then walk. The result would be a more self-respecting and emotionally fulfilled teaching profession, more educated children and more prosperous and cohesive societies.

All this is achievable if we continue to develop the science of teacher effectiveness outlined in this book.

References

Adams, M. (1990) *Beginning to Read: Thinking and Learning about Print*. Cambridge, MA: MIT Press.

Adey, P. and Shayer, M. (1994) *Really Raising Standards: Cognitive Intervention and Academic Achievement*. London: Routledge.

Ager, R. (1999) *Information and Communications Technology in Primary Schools. Children or Computers in Control?* London: David Fulton.

Aiex, N. K. (1993) *A Communicative Approach to Observation and Feedback*. ERIC Clearinghouse on Disabilities and Gifted Education, ERIC Digest ED364926.

American Association of Mental Retardation (AAMR) (2000) *Definition of Mental Retardation*. http://www.aamr.org/policies/faqmentalretardation.html

American Psychological Association (APA) (1994) *Diagnostic and Statistical Manual of Mental Disorders*, 4th edn. Washington, DC: APA.

Anghileri, J. (ed.) (1995) *Children's Mathematical Thinking in the Primary Years: Perspectives on Children's Learning – Children, Teachers and Learning*. London: Cassell.

Arends, R. I. (1998) *Learning to Teach*. Boston, MA: McGraw-Hill.

Askew, M., Rhodes, V., Brown, M., William, D. and Johnson, D. (1997) *Effective Teachers of Numeracy: Report of a Study Carried Out for the Teacher Training Agency*. London: King's College London, School of Education.

Askew, M. and William, D. (1995) *Recent Research in Mathematics Education 5–16*. London: Office For Standards in Education, p. 53.

Aubrey, C. (1993) An investigation of the mathematical competencies which young children bring into school. *British Educational Research Journal*, 19(1), 27–41.

Ausubel, D. P. (1968) *Educational Psychology: A Cognitive View*. New York: Holt, Rinehart & Winston.

Badger, E. and Thomas, B. (1992). *Open-Ended Questions in Reading*. ERIC Clearinghouse on Disabilities and Gifted Education, ERIC Digest ED355253.

Banerji, M. and Dailey, R. A. (1995). A study of the effects of an inclusion model on students with learning disabilities. *Journal of Learning Disabilities*, 28(8), 511–22.

Basic Skills Agency (1997) *International Numeracy Survey: A Comparison of the Basic Numeracy Skills of Adults 16–60 in Seven Countries*. London: Basic Skills Agency, p. 26.

Battistich, V., Solomon, D. and Delucchi, K. (1993). Interaction processes and student outcomes in cooperative learning groups. *Elementary School Journal*, 94(1), 19–32.

Baum, S. (1990) *Gifted but Learning Disabled: A Puzzling Paradox*. Reston, VA: The ERIC Clearinghouse on Disabilities and Gifted Education, Digest E479.

Baumrind, D. (1991) The influence of parenting style on adolescent competence and substance use. *Journal of Early Adolescence*, 11(1), 56–95.

Begley, S. and Rogers, A. (1998) You're OK, I'm terrific: 'self-esteem' backfires. *Newsweek*, January.

Beirne-Smith, P., Patton, J. R. and Ittenbach, R. (1994) *Mental Retardation*. Riverside, NJ: Macmillan.

Benbow, C. P. (1991) Meeting the needs of gifted students through use of acceleration. In M. C. Wang, M. C. Reynolds and H. J. Walberg (eds) *Handbook of Special Education: Research and Practice*. Oxford: Pergamon Press.

Bennett, N., Desforges, C., Cockburn, A. and Wilkinson, B. (1981) *The Quality of Pupil Learning: Interim Report*. Lancaster: University of Lancaster, Department of Education.

Benzwie, T. (1987) *A Moving Experience*. Tucson, AZ: Zephyr Press.

Berends, M. (1995) Educational stratification and students' social bonding to school. *British Journal of Sociology of Education*, 16(3), 327–51.

Black, P. and William, D. (1998) Inside the black box: raising standards through classroom assessment. *Phi Delta Kappan*, 79(10), 139–50.

Black, S. (1997) Doing our homework on homework. *American School Board Journal*, 183(2), 48–51.

Blagg, N., Ballinger, M. and Gardner, R. (1988) *Somerset Thinking Skills Course*. Oxford: Blackwell.

Boers, D. and Caspary, P. (1995) Real-life homework. *Executive Educator*, 17(3), 37–8.

Borich, G. (1996) *Effective Teaching Methods*. 3rd edn. New York: Macmillan.

Brody, L. E. and Stanley, J. C. (1991) Young college students: assessing factors that contribute to success. In W. T. Southern and E. D. Jones (eds) *The Academic Acceleration of Gifted Children*. London: Teachers College Press.

Bronzheim, S. (1994) *An Educator's Guide to Tourette's Syndrome*. Bayside, NJ: Tourette Syndrome Association Inc.

Brookover, W. B., Beady, C., Flood, P., Schweitzer, J. and Wisenbaker, J. (1979) *Schools, Social Systems and Student Achievement: Schools Can Make a Difference*. New York: Praeger.

Brophy, J. (1981) Teacher praise: a functional analysis. *Review of Educational Research*, 88(2), 5–32.

Brophy, J. (1992) Probing the subtleties of subject matter teaching. *Educational Leadership*, 49(7), 4–8.

Brophy, J. (1996) *Teaching Problem Students*. New York: Guildford.

Brophy, J. E. and Good, T. L. (1986) Teacher behaviour and student achievement. In M. C. Wittrock (ed) *Handbook of Research on Teaching*. New York: Macmillan.

Brown, A. L. and Palincsar, A. S. (1989) Guided, cooperative learning and individualised knowledge acquisition. In L. B. Resnick (ed.) *Knowing, Learning and Instruction*. Hillsdale, NJ: Lawrence Erlbaum Associates.

Brown, S. (1990) *Getting the Most from Observing Teaching*. Spotlights, the Scottish Council for Research in Education. *http://www.scre.ac.uk/spotlight/spotlight32.html*

Brualdi, A. (1998). Implementing performance assessment in the classroom. *Practical Assessment, Research and Evaluation*, 6(2), 31–48.

Bryan, T. and Sullivan-Burstein, K. (1997) Homework how-to's. *Teaching Exceptional Children*, 29(6), 32–7.

Bryant, P. (1994) Children and arithmetic. *Journal of Child Psychology and Psychiatry*, 36(1), 3–32.

Bryant, P. (1997) Mathematical understanding in the nursery school years. In T. Nunes and P. Bryant (eds) *Learning and Teaching Mathematics: An International Perspective*. Hove: Psychology Press.

Bucher, K. T. (1998) *Information Technology for Schools*. Worthington, OH: Linworth.

Burns, R. B. (1979) *The Self-Concept in Theory, Measurement and Behaviour*. London: Longman.

Bynner, J. and Parsons, S. (1997) *Does Numeracy Matter? Evidence From the National Child Development Study on the Impact of Poor Numeracy on Adult Life*. London: Basic Skills Agency, p. 48.

Bynner, J. and Steedman, J. (1995) *Difficulties with Basic Skills. Findings from the 1970 British Cohort Study*. London: Basic Skills Agency.

Byrne, B. M. and Shavelson, R. J. (1986) On the structure of adolescent self-concept. *Journal of Educational Psychology*, 78(6), 478–81.

Caldwell, B. (1997). *Educating Children Who Are Deaf or Hard of Hearing: Cued Speech*. Reston, VA: ERIC Clearinghouse on Disabilities and Gifted Education, ERIC Digest E555.

Canter, L. (1976) *Assertive Discipline: A Take Charge Approach for Today's Educator*. Seal Beach, CA: Canter and Associates.

Canter, L. (1989). Assertive discipline: more than names on the board and marbles in the jar. *Phi Delta Kappan*, 70(9), 57–61.

Carlberg, C. and Kavale, K. (1980) The efficacy of special placement for exceptional children: a meta-analysis. *Journal of Special Education*, 14(31), 295–309.

Carnine, D. W., Silbert, J. and Kameenui, E. J. (1996) *Direct Instruction Reading*. Englewood Cliffs, NJ: Prentice Hall.

Cassidy, S. (1999) 'Startling' findings on primary homework. *Times Educational Supplement*, 2 July.

Center, Y., Wheldall, K., Freeman, L. and Outhred, L. (1995). An Evaluation of Reading Recovery. *Reading Research Quarterly*, 30(2), 240–263.

Centra, J. A. (1975) Colleagues as raters of classroom instruction. *Journal of Higher Education*, 46(3), 237–337.

Centre for Academic Practice, University of Warwick (2000). *Observing Teaching, Guidance Notes for Departments*. http://www.warwick.ac.uk

Chall, J. (1995) *Stages of Reading*. New York: Wadsworth.

Chapman, J. W. and Tunmer, W. E. (1995) Development of young children's reading self-concepts: an examination of emerging subcomponents and their relationship with reading achievement. *Journal of Educational Psychology*, 87(1), 154–67.

Chen, M. and Ehrenberg, T. (1993) Test scores, homework, aspirations and teachers' grades. *Studies in Educational Evaluation*, 19(4), 403–19.

Church, S. (1994) *Is Whole Language Really Warm and Fuzzy? Facts on Myths about Whole Language Education*. http://toread.copm/myths.html

Clay, M. M. (1993) *Reading Recovery. A Guidebook for Teachers in Training*. Portsmouth, NH: Heinemann.

Cohen, L. (1999) The power of portfolios. *Early Childhood Today*, February, 13–27.

Collins, A., Brown, J. S. and Newman, S. E. (1989) Cognitive apprenticeship: teaching the crafts of reading, writing and mathematics. In L. B. Resnick (ed.) *Knowing, Learning and Instruction*. Hillsdale, NJ: Lawrence Erlbaum Associates.

Cooper, H. (1989) Synthesis of research on homework. *Educational Leadership*, 47(3), 58–91.

Cooper, H. (1994) *The Battle over Homework: An Administrator's Guide to Setting Sound and Effective Policies*. London: Corwin Press.

Cooper, J. O., Heron, T. E. and Heward, T. L. (1987) *Applied Behavior Analysis*. Upper Saddle River, NJ: Merrill/Prentice Hall.

Coopersmith, S. (1967) *The Antecedents of Self-Esteem*. San Francisco: W. H. Freeman.

Cotton, K. (1997). *Educating for Citizenship*. Portland, OR: Northwest Regional Education Laboratory.

Covington, M. C. and Beery, R. G. (1976) *Self-Worth and School Learning*. New York: Holt, Rinehart & Winston.

Creemers, B. P. M. (1994) *The Effective Classroom*. London: Cassell.

Creemers, B. P. M. and Reezigt, G. J. (1999) The role of school and classroom climate in elementary school learning environments. In H. J. Freiberg (ed.) *School Climate: Measuring, Improving and Sustaining Healthy Learning Environments*. London: Falmer Press.

Croll, P. (1996) Teacher–pupil interaction in the classroom. In P. Croll and N. Hastings (eds) *Effective Primary Teaching*. London: David Fulton.

Davis, G. A. and Rimm, S. B. (1988) *Education of the Gifted and Talented*. Englewood Cliffs, NJ: Prentice Hall.

De Corte, E., Greer, B. and Verschaffel, L. (1996). Mathematics teaching and learning. In D. C. Berliner and R. Calfee (eds) *Handbook of Educational Psychology*. New York: Macmillan.

Deno, S., Maruyama, G., Espin, C. and Cohen, C. (1990) Educating students with mild disabilities in general education classrooms: Minnesota alternatives. *Exceptional Children*, 57(2), 150–161.

Department for Education and Employment (DfEE) (1998a). *Numeracy Matters: The Preliminary Report of the Numeracy Task Force*. London: DfEE.

Department for Education and Employment (DfEE) (1988b). *The Implementation of the National Numeracy Strategy*. London: DfEE.

Department for Education and Employment (DfEE) (1999). *The Structure of the Literacy Hour*. http://www.standards.dfee.gov.uk/literacy/literacyhour

Department for Education and Employment (2000). *Definition of SEN*. http://www.dfee.gov.uk/sen/sengloss.htm.

DeRosier, M. E., Kupersmidt, J. B. and Patterson, C. J. (1994). Children's academic and behavioral adjustment as a function of the chronicity and proximity of peer rejection. *Child Development*, 65(6), 1799–813.

Dietel, R. J., Herman, J. L. and Knuth, R. A. (1991) *What Does Research Say about Assessment?* Oak Brook: North Central Regional Education Laboratory.

Dodge, K., Petit, G., McClaskey, C. and Brown, M. (1986) *Social Competence in Children*. Monographs of the Society for Research in Child Development, 51(2).

Dunlap, G., DePerzel, M., Clarke, S., Wilson, D., Wright, S., White, R. and Gomez, A. (1994) Choice making and proactive behavioral support for students with emotional and behavioral challenges. *Journal of Applied Behavior Analysis*, 27(3), 505–18.

Dunlap, G. and Fox, L. (1999) *Teaching Students with Autism*. Reston, VA: ERIC Clearinghouse on Disabilities and Gifted Education, ERIC Digest E582.

Dunn, R. and Dunn, K. (1978) *Teaching Students Through Their Individual Learning Styles*. Reston, VA: Reston Publishing.

Dunn, R., Dunn, K. and Price, A. (1985) *Learning Styles Inventory*. Reston, VA: Reston Publishing.

Easterbrooks, S. and Baker-Hawkins, S. (1994) *Deaf and Hard of Hearing Students: Educational Service Guidelines*. Alexandria, VA: National Association of State Directors of Special Education.

Edelman Borden, M. (1997) *Smart Start. The Parents' Guide to Preschool Education*. Washington, DC: Facts-on-File Publications.

Edwards, C., Gandini, L. and Foorman, G. (1993) *The Hundred Languages of Children: The Reggio Emilia Approach to Early Childhood Education*. Norwood, NJ: Ablex.

Edwards, J. (1991) The direct teaching of thinking skills. In G. Evans (ed.) *Learning and Teaching Cognitive Skills*. Hawthorn, Victoria: Australian Council for Educational Research.

Egertson, H. A. (1997) *The Shifting Kindergarten Curriculum*. Reston, VA: ERIC Clearinghouse on Early Years Education, ERIC Digest 643.

Elliott, S. N. (1995) *Creating Meaningful Performance Assessments*. Reston, VA: ERIC Clearinghouse on Disabilities and Gifted Education, ERIC Digest ED381985.

Emmer, E., Evertson, C., Clements, B. and Worsham, M. (1997) *Classroom Management for Secondary Teachers*. Upper Saddle River, NJ: Prentice Hall.

ERIC Clearinghouse on Disabilities and Gifted Education (1993). *Behavioral Disorders: Focus on Change*. Reston VA: ERIC Clearinghouse on Disabilities and Gifted Education, ERIC Digest E518.

Erlbaum, B. and Vaughn, S. (1999) *Can School-Based Interventions Enhance the Self-Concept of Students with Learning Disabilities?* http://www.ncld.org/summit99/osep2.htm

Erlbaum, B., Watson Moody, S., Vaughn, S., Shumm, J. S. and Hughes, M. (1999) *The Effects of Instructional Grouping Format on the Reading Outcomes of Students with Disabilities: A Meta-Analytic Review*. http://www.ncld.org/summit99/osep2.htm

Everston, C. (1997) *Classroom Management for Elementary Teachers*. Needham, MA: Allyn & Bacon.

Evertson, C. and Emmer, E. (1982) Effective management at the beginning of the school year in junior high classes. *Journal of Educational Psychology*, 74(4), 485–98.

Faulkner, J. and Blyth, C. (1995). Homework: is it really worth all the bother? *Educational Studies*, 21(3), 447–54.

Feuerstein, R., Rand, Y. Hoffman, M. and Miller, M. (1980) *Instrumental Enrichment: An Intervention Programme for Cognitive Modifiability*. Baltimore, MD: University Park Press.

Fitz-Gibbon, C. T. (1996) *Monitoring Education: Indicators, Quality and Effectiveness*. London: Cassell.

Fitzpatrick, K. A. (1982) The effect of a secondary classroom management training program on teacher and student behavior. Paper presented at the AERA Annual Meeting, New York.

Foorman, B. R., Fletcher, J. and Francis, D. (1996) *A Scientific Approach to Reading Instruction*. http://www.ldonline.org/ld_indepth/reading/cars.html

Foyle, H. C. and Bailey, G. D. (1988). Research on homework experiments in social studies: implications for teaching. *Social Education*, 52(4), 292–8.

Fraser, B. J. (1994) Research on classroom and school climate. In D. Gabel (ed.) *Handbook of Research on Science Teaching and Learning*. New York: Macmillan.

Fraser, B. J. (1999) Using learning environment assessments to improve classroom and school climates. In H. J. Freiberg (ed.) *School Climate: Measuring, Improving and Sustaining Healthy Learning Environments*. London: Falmer Press.

Freiberg, H. J. (1999) Three creative ways to measure school climate and next steps. In H. J. Freiberg (ed.) *School Climate: Measuring, Improving and Sustaining Healthy Learning Environments*. London: Falmer Press.

Freiberg, H. J. and Stein, T. A. (1999) Measuring, improving and sustaining healthy learning environments. In H. J. Freiberg (ed.) *School Climate: Measuring, Improving and Sustaining Healthy Learning Environments*. London: Falmer Press.

Fulk, B. (2000) 20 ways to make instruction more memorable. *Intervention in School and Clinic*, 35(3), 183–4.

Furtwengler, B. (1987) *Classroom Climate Inventory*. Wichita, KS: RSI.

Gagne, R. M. (1965) *The Conditions of Learning*. New York: Holt, Rinehart & Winston.

Gagne, R. M., Yekovick, C. W. and Yekovick, F. R. (1993). *The Cognitive Psychology of School Learning*. New York: HarperCollins.

Gallagher, J. J. (1985) *Teaching the Gifted Child*. Boston: Allyn & Bacon.

Galloway, D. (1985) *Schools, Pupils and Special Educational Needs*. Beckenham: Croom Helm.

Galton, M. and Croll, P. (1980) Pupil progress in the basic skills. In M. Galton and B. Simon (eds) *Progress and Performance in the Primary Classroom*. London: Routledge.

Gardner, H. (1983) *Frames of Mind: The Theory of Multiple Intelligences*. New York: Basic Books.

Gardner, H. (1993) *Multiple Intelligences: The Theory in Practice*. New York: Basic Books.

Gartner, A. and Lipsky, D. K. (1987) Beyond special education: toward a quality system for all students. *Harvard Educational Review*, 57(4), 367–95.

Geeke, P. (1988) *Evaluation Report on the Reading Recovery Field Trial in Central Australia*. Australia: Centre for Studies in Literacy, University of Wollongong.

Geers, A. and Moog, J. (1989) Factors predictive of the development of literacy in profoundly hearing-impaired adolescents. *Volta Review*, 91 (69–86).

Gersten, R., Baker, S., Marks, U. S. and Smith, S. B. (1999) *Effective Instruction for Learning Disabled or At-Risk English-Language Learners*. At http://www.ncld.org/summit99/osep3.htm

Gipps, C. and McGilchrist, B. (1999) Primary school learners. In P. Mortimore (ed.) *Understanding Pedagogy and its Impact on Learning*. London: Paul Chapman Publishing.

Goldberg, D. (ed.) (1994) Auditory-verbal philosophy: a tutorial. *Volta Review*, 95(3), 181–262.

Goldberg, D. (1997). *Educating Children Who Are Deaf or Hard of Hearing: Auditory-Verbal*. Reston, VA: ERIC Clearinghouse on Disabilities and Gifted Education, Digest E552.

Good, T. L. and Grouws, D. (1979) The Missouri Mathematics Effectiveness Project: an experimental study in fourth grade classrooms. *Journal of Educational Psychology*, 71(3), 355–62.

Good, T. L., Grouws, D. A. and Ebmeier, D. (1983) *Active Mathematics Teaching*. New York: Longman.

Goodenow, C. (1993) Classroom belonging among early adolescent students. *Journal of Early Adolescence*, 13(1), 21–43.

Goodman, K. S. and Goodman, Y. (1982). A whole language comprehension centred view of reading development. In L. Reed and S. Louis (eds) *Basic Skills: Issues and Choices*. St Louis, MO: CEMREL.

Gould, S. J. (1996) *The Mismeasure of Man*. New York: Norton.

Gravemeijer, K. (1997). Mediating between concrete and abstract. In T. Nunes and P. Bryant (eds) *Learning and Teaching Mathematics. An International Perspective*. Hove, Psychology Press.

Green, D. (1998) IT provision in English schools. *Mathematics in School*, 27(3), 9–12.

Griffin, G. A. and Barnes, S. (1986). Using research findings to change school and classroom practice: results of an experimental study. *American Educational Research Journal*, 23(4), 572–86.

Gronlund, N. E. (1991) *Constructing Achievement Tests*. Englewood Cliffs, NJ: Prentice Hall.

Grugnett, L. and Jaquet, F. (1996) Senior secondary school practices. In A. J. Bishop, K. Clements, C. Keitel, J. Kilpatrick and C. Laborde (eds) *International Handbook of Mathematics Education*. Dordrecht: Kluwer.

Gustasson, G. (1997) *Educating Children Who Are Deaf or Hard of Hearing: English-Based Sign Systems*. Reston, VA: ERIC Clearinghouse on Disabilities and Gifted Education, ERIC Digest E556.

Haen, J. F. (2000) Reading recovery: success for how many? Paper presented at the Annual Meeting of the American Educational Research Association, New Orleans, April.

Hallam, S. and Cowan, R. (1999) *What Do We Know about Homework?* London: Institute of Education, Viewpoint no. 9.

Hallinan, M. T. and Sorensen, A. B. (1985) Ability grouping and student friendship. *American Educational Research Journal*, 22(4), 485–99.

Hallinan, M. T. and Williams, R. A. (1990) Student characteristics and the peer influence process. *Sociology of Education*, 63(2), 122–32.

Hallinger, P. and Murphy, J. (1985) Assessing the instructional leadership behavior of principals. *Elementary School Journal*, 86(2), 328–55.

Hansell, S. and Karweit, N. (1983). Curricular placement, friendship networks and status attainment. In J. L. Epstein and N. Karweit (eds) *Friends in School, Patterns of Selection and Influence*. New York: Academic Press.

Hansford, B. C. and Hattie, J. A. (1982) The relationship between self and achievement/performance measures. *Review of Educational Research*, 52(1), 123–42.

Hargreaves, D. H. (1967) *Social relations in a secondary school*. London and Henley: Routledge & Kegan Paul.

Harris, M. J., Rosenthal, R. and Snodgrass, S. E. (1986) The effects of teacher expectations, gender and behavior on pupil academic performance and self-concept. *Journal of Educational Research*, 79(3), 173–9.

Hart, B. and Risley, T. R. (1995) *Meaningful Differences in the Everyday Experience of Young American Children*. Baltimore, MA: Paul Brookes.

Hartup, W. W. and Moore, S. G. (1990) Early peer relations: developmental significance and prognostic implications. *Early Childhood Research Quarterly*, 5 March, 1–17.

Hawkins-Shepard, C. (1994). *Mental Retardation*. Reston, VA: ERIC Clearinghouse on Disabilities and Gifted Education, EC Digest 528.

Hembree, R. (1992). Experiments and relational studies in problem-solving: meta-analysis. *Journal for Research in Mathematics Education*, 23(3), 242–73.

Hembree, R. and Dessart, D. J. (1986) Effects of hand-held calculators in precollege mathematics education: a meta-analysis. *Journal for Research in Mathematics Education*, 27(2), 83–99.

Hembree, R. and Dessart, D. J. (1992) Research on calculators in mathematics education. In T. Fey and C. R. Hirsch (eds) *Research on Calculators in Mathematics Education*. Reston, VA: NCTM.

Hiebert, J. and Carpenter, T. P. (1992) Learning and teaching with understanding. In D. A. Grouws (ed.), *Handbook of Research on Mathematics Teaching and Learning*. New York, Macmillan.

Higgins, S. and Muijs, R. D. (1999) ICT and numeracy in primary schools. In I. Thompson (ed.) *Issues in Teaching Numeracy in Primary Schools*. Ballmoor, Bucks: Open University Press.

High/Scope (2000) *The High/Scope Approach*. High/Scope Educational Research Foundation. http://www.high/scope.org

Hirsh-Pasek, K., Hyson, M. and Recorla, L. (1990) Academic environments in preschool: do they pressure or challenge young children? *Early Education and Development*, 1(6), 401–23.

Hodges, H. (1994) A consumer's guide to learning style programs. *School Administrator*, 51(1), 14–18.

Hoge, D. R., Smit, E. K. and Crist, J. T. (1995) Reciprocal effects of self-concept and academic achievement in sixth and seventh grade. *Journal of Youth and Adolescence*, 24(3), 295–314.

Hoover Dempsey, K. V., Bassler, O. C. and Burow, R. (1995) Parents' reported involvement in students' homework: Strategies and practices. *Elementary School Journal*, 95(5), 435–50.

Horcones, J. (1991). Walden two in real life: behavior analysis in the design of the culture. In W. Ishaq (ed.) *Human Behavior in Today's World*. New York: Praeger.

Horcones, J. (1992). Natural reinforcement: a way to improve education. In W. Ishaq (ed.) *Journal of Applied Behavior Analysis*. Boston: Christopher Gordon.

Hyson, M. C. and Van Trieste, K. (1987) *The Shy Child*. ERIC Clearinghouse on Elementary and Early Childhood Education, ED295741.

Janos, P. M. and Robinson, N. M. (1985) The performance of students in a radical acceleration at the university level. *Gifted Child Quarterly*, 29(4), 175–80.

Jenkins, J. R., Jewell, M., Leicester, N., O'Connor, R., Jenkins, L. M. and Troutner, N. M. (1994) Accommodations for individual differences without classroom ability groups: an experiment in school restructuring. *Exceptional Children*, 60(4), 344–58.

Johnson, D. W. and Johnson, R. T. (1989). Cooperative learning: what special educators need to know. *The Pointer*, 33(2), 5–10.

Johnson, D. W. and Johnson, R. T. (1994) *Joining Together: Group Theory and Group Skills*. Englewood Cliffs, NJ: Prentice Hall.

Johnson, D. W. and Johnson, R. T. (2000) Cooperative learning. Presentation given at the Annual Meeting of the American Educational Research Association, New Orleans, April.

Johnsson-Smaragdi, U. and Jonsson, A. (1995) Self-evaluation in an ecological perspective: neighbourhood, family and peers, schooling and media use. In K. E. Rosengren (ed.) *Media Effects and Beyond*. London: Routledge.

Joyce, B. and Weil, M. (1996) *Models of Teaching*. 5th edn. Boston: Allyn & Bacon.

Kantrowitz, B. and Wingert, P. (1992) An 'F' in world competition. *Newsweek*, 17 February, p. 57.

Katz, L. G. (1997) Tomorrow begins today: implications from research. *ERIC/EECE Newsletter*, 9(4), 14.

Katz, L. G. (1999) Another look at what young children should be learning. *ERIC/ EECE Newsletter*, 11(2), 1–3.

Keith, T. Z. (1987) Children and homework. In A. Thomas and J. Grimes (eds) *Children's Needs: Psychological Perspectives*. Washington, DC: National Association of School Psychologists.

Keltikangas-Jarvinen, L. (1992) Self-esteem as a predictor of future school achievement. *European Journal of Psychology of Education*, 7(2), 123–30.

Kemple, K. M. (1992) *Understanding and Facilitating Preschool Children's Peer Acceptance*. ERIC Clearinghouse on Elementary and Early Childhood Education, EC Digest ED345866.

Knoblauch, B. (1998) *Teaching Children with Tourette's Syndrome*. Reston, VA: ERIC Clearinghouse on Disabilities and Gifted Education, EC Digest 570.

Kolb, D. (1973) *Toward a Typology of Learning Styles and Learning Environments: An Investigation of the Impact of Learning Styles and Discipline Demands on the Academic Performance, Social Adaptation and Career Choices of MIT Seniors*. Cambridge, MA: MIT Press.

Kounin, J. (1970) *Discipline and Groups Management in the Classroom*. New York: Holt, Rinehart & Winston.

Kulik, J. A. (1992) *An Analysis of Research on Ability Groupings: Historical and Contemporary Perspectives*. Storrs, CT: The National Research Center on the Gifted and Talented, University of Connecticut.

Kupersmidth, J. B. and Coie, J. D. (1990) Preadolescent peer status, aggression, and school adjustment predictors of externalising problems in adolescence. *Child Development*, 61(5), 1350–62.

Lacey, C. (1970) *Hightown Grammar. The School as a Social System*. Manchester: Manchester University Press.

LaConte, R. T. (1981) *Homework as a Learning Experience: What Research Says to the Teacher*. Washington, DC: NEA.

Laird, R. D., Pettit, G. S., Mize, J., Brown, E. G. and Linsey, E. (1994) Parent-child conversations about peer relationships: contributions to competence. *Family Relations*, 43(4), 425–32.

Lavoie, R. D. (1997) *The Teacher's Role in Developing Social Skills*. LDA-CA. http:// www.kidsource.com/LDA-CA/teacher.html

Lester, K. K. Jr (1994) Musings about mathematical problem-solving research: 1970–1994. *Journal for Research in Mathematics Education*, 25(6), 660–75.

Lewis, C. and Tsuchida, I. (1997) Planned educational change in Japan: the case of elementary science instruction. *Journal of Educational Policy*, 12(5), 313–31.

Lindsey, E. W., Mize, J. and Pettit, G. S. (1997) Mutuality in parent–child play: consequences for children's peer competence. *Journal of Social and Personality Relationships*, 37(9), 634–61.

Linn, M. C. and Burbules, N. C. (1993) Construction of knowledge and group learning. In K. Tobin (ed.) *The Practice of Constructivism in Science Education*. Washington, DC: American Association for the Advancement of Science.

Linn, M. C., Lewis, C., Tsuchida, I. and Butler Songer, N. (2000) Beyond fourth-grade science: why do US and Japanese students diverge? *Educational Researcher*, 29(3), 4–14.

Lipsky, D. K. and Gartner, A. (1997) *Inclusion and School Reform: Transforming America's Classrooms*. Baltimore, MD: Paul H. Brookes.

Litzinger, M. E. and Osif, B. (1993) Accommodating diverse learning styles: designing instruction for electronic information sources. In L. Shirato (ed.) *What is Good Instruction Now? Library Instruction for the 90's*. Ann Arbor, MI: Pierian Press.

Lyon, G. R. (1994) *Research in Learning Disabilities at the NICHD*. Bethesda, MD: NICHD Technical Document/Human Learning and Behavior Branch.

Lyon, G. R. (1999) *The NICHD Research Program in Reading Development, Reading Disorders and Reading Instruction*. NICHD: Keys to Successful Learning Summit. http://www.nichd.org/summit99/keys99-nichd.htm

Lyon, G. R. and Kameenui, E. J. (2000) *National Institute of Child Health and Development (NICHD) Research Supports America Reads Challenge.* http://www.ed.gov/inits/americareads/nichd.html

Macklem, G. L. (1990) Measuring aptitude. *Practical Assessment, Research and Evaluation,* 2(5), 4.

Madaus, G. F. and O'Dwyer, L. M. (1999) A short history of performance assessment. *Phi Delta Kappan,* 80(9), 688–95.

Madden, N.A. and Slavin, R. E. (1983) Mainstreaming students with mild handicaps: academic and social outcomes. *Review of Educational Research,* 53(4), 519–69.

Madden, N. A., Slavin, R. E., Karweit, N. L., Dolan, L. J. and Wasik, B. A. (1993) Success for all: longitudinal effects of a restructuring program for inner-city elementary schools. *American Educational Research Journal,* 30(1), 123–48.

Mandeville, G. K. and Liu, Q. (1997) The effect of teacher certification and task level on mathematics achievement. *Teaching and Teacher Education,* 13(4), 397–407.

Mann, D. (2000) *Research evidence of learning technology and its meaning for ICSEI participants.* Paper presented at the International Congress of School Effectiveness and Improvement, Hong Kong, January.

Manset, G. and Semmel, M. I. (1997) An inclusive program for students with mild disabilities: a comparison review of model programs. *Journal of Special Education,* 31(2), 155–80.

Maqsud, M. and Rouhani, S. (1991). Relationships between socio-economic status, locus of control, self-concept and academic achievement of Bophutatswana adolescents. *Journal of Youth and Adolescence,* 20(1), 107–13.

Marcon, R. A. (1992) Differential effects of three preschool models on inner-city 4-year-olds. *Early Childhood Research Quarterly,* 7(4), 517–30.

Marsh, H. W. (1990). Causal ordering of academic self-concept and academic achievement: a multiwave, longitudinal panel analysis. *Journal of Educational Psychology,* 82(4), 646–56.

Marsh, H. W., Parker, J. and Barnes, J. (1985) Multidimensional adolescent self-concepts: their relationship to age, sex and academic measures. *American Educational Research Journal,* 22(3), 422–44.

Marsh, H. W., Relich, J. D. and Smith, I. D. (1983) Self-concept: the construct validity of interpretations based on the SDQ. *Journal of Personality and Social Psychology,* 45(1), 213–31.

McElgunn, B. (1996) *Critical Discoveries in Learning Disabilities: A Summary of Findings by NIH Research Programs in Learning Disabilities.* Research Centres Report at the LDA Conference. At http://www.ncld.org/summit99/osep3.htm

Mead, G. H. (1934) *Mind, Self and Society from the Standpoint of a Social Behaviorist.* Chicago: Chicago University Press.

Mehrens, W. A. (1998) Consequences of assessment: what is the evidence? *Education Policy Analysis Archives,* 6(13).

Merttens, R. (ed.) (1996) *Teaching Numeracy: Maths in the Primary Classroom.* Primary Professional Bookshelf. Leamington Spa: Scholastic.

Miles, P. L. (1989) A communication based strategy to improve teaching: the continuous feedback technique. Paper presented at the Annual Meeting of the Speech Communication Association, ED 314 787.

Miller, L. B. and Bizzell, R. P. (1983) Long-term effects of four preschool programs: sixth, seventh and eighth grades. *Child Development,* 54(3), 727–41.

Moats, L. C. (1995) *Spelling: Development, Disabilities and Instruction.* Timonium, MS: York Press.

Moats, L. C. (1996). Neither/nor: resolving the debate between whole language and phonics. Lecture given at the 1996 Washington Summit Conference of Learning Disabilities, transcript from http://www.greenwoodinstitute.org/resources/resnor.html

Moran, P. B. and Eckenrode, J. (1991) Gender differences in the costs and benefits of peer relations during adolescence. *Journal of Adolescent Research*, 6(4), 396–409.

Mortimore, P., Sammons, P., Stoll, L., Lewis, D. and Ecob, R. (1988). *School Matters*. Wells, Somerset: Open Books.

Moskal, B. M. (2000) Scoring rubrics: what, when and how? *Practical Assessment, Research and Evaluation*, 7(3), 10–15.

Mosley, J. (1996) *Quality Circle Time*. Wisbech: LDA.

Muijs, R. D. (1997) *Self, School And Media. A Longitudinal Study of the Relationship Between Self-Concept, School Achievement, Peer Relations and Media Use among Flemish Primary School Children*. Leuven: K.U.Leuven, Department of Communication Science.

Muijs, R. D. (1998) The reciprocal relationship between self-concept and school achievement. *British Journal of Educational Psychology*, 67(3), 263–776.

Muijs, R. D. (1998b) The relationship between KS test results in HRS schools and the CAT. Unpublished research paper, Newcastle University, Education Dept.

Muijs, R. D. (2000) *Three Innovative Uses of ICT in the Primary Classroom*. Loughborough: Educational Effectiveness Centre.

Muijs, R. D. and Reynolds, D. (1999) School effectiveness and teacher effectiveness: some preliminary findings from the evaluation of the Mathematics Enhancement Programme. Presented at the American Educational Research Association Conference, Montreal, Quebec, 19 April.

Muijs, R. D. and Reynolds, D. (2000a). *Teaching Effectiveness Distance Learning Modules*. London: CfBT.

Muijs, R. D. and Reynolds, D. (2000b). School effectiveness and teacher effectiveness: some preliminary findings from the evaluation of the Mathematics Enhancement Programme. *School Effectiveness and School Improvement*, 11(3), forthcoming.

Muijs, R. D. and Reynolds, D. (2000c). Effective mathematics teaching: year 2 of a research project. Paper presented at the International Conference on School Effectiveness and School Improvement, Hong Kong, 8 January.

National Center for Learning Disabilities (2000) *General Tips for Parents*. http://www.ncld.org/tips/tip5

National Institute of Child Health and Development (2000) *National Reading Panel Reports Combination of Teaching Phonics, Word Sounds, Giving Feedback on Oral Reading, Most Effective Way to Teach Reading*. National Institutes of Health News Release, 13 April. http://www.nichd.nih.gov/new/releases/nrp.htm

National Institute of Mental Health (NIMH) (1995) *Learning Disabilities*. Washington, DC: NIMH.

Nattiv, A. (1994) Helping behaviors and math achievement gain of students using cooperative learning. *Elementary School Journal*, 94(3), 285–97.

Ness, B. and Latessa, E. (1979) Gifted children and self-teaching techniques. *Directive Teacher*, 2(1), 10–12.

Newcomb, A. F. and Bagwell, C. L. (1996) The developmental significance of children's friendship relations. In W. M. Bukowski, A. F. Newcomb and W. W. Hartup (eds) *The Company They Keep: Friendship in Childhood and Adolescence*. Cambridge: Cambridge University Press.

Nunes, T. and Bryant, P. (1996) *Children Doing Mathematics*. Oxford: Blackwell.

Nunn, G. D. and Parrish, T. S. (1992) The psychological characteristics of at-risk high school students. *Adolescence*, 27(106), 435–40.

Office for Standards in Education (OFSTED) (2000) Literacy and numeracy are key to higher standards in all schools, says chief inspector. OFSTED press release, 8 February.

Organization for Economic Co-Operation and Development (OECD) (1994) *Teacher Quality: Synthesis of Country Studies*. Paris: OECD.

Ornstein, A. C. (1994) Homework, studying and role-taking: essential skills for students. *NASSP Bulletin*, 78(558), 58–70.

Orr, E. and Dinur, B. (1995) Social setting differences in self-esteem: kibbutz and urban adolescents. *Journal of Youth and Adolescence*, 24(1), 3–27.

Orton, A. (1992) *Learning Mathematics: Issues, Theory and Classroom Practice*. 2nd edn. London: Cassell.

Palincsar, A. S. and Brown, A. L. (1984) The reciprocal teaching of comprehension-fostering and comprehension-monitoring activities. *Cognition and Instruction*, 1(2), 117–75.

Palincsar, A. S. and McPhail, J. C. (1993) A critique of the metaphor of distillation in 'Toward a Knowledge Base for School Learning'. *Review of Educational Research*, 63(3), 327–34.

Parke, B. (1992) *Challenging Gifted Students in the Regular Classroom*. ERIC, EC Digest E513.

Parker, J. G. and Asher, S. R. (1987) Peer relations and later social adjustment: are low-accepted children at risk? *Psychological Bulletin*, 102(3), 357–89.

Parker, J. G. and Asher, S. R. (1993) Friendship and friendship quality in middle childhood: links with peer group acceptance and feelings of loneliness and social dissatisfaction. *Developmental Psychology*, 29(4), 611–21.

Pekrun, R. (1990) Social support, achievement evaluations and self-concepts in adolescence. In L. Oppenheimer (ed.) *The Self-Concept. European Perspectives on Its Develoment, Aspects and Applications*. Berlin: Springer.

Perkins, D. N. and Salomon, G. (1989) Are cognitive skills context bound? *Educational Researcher*, 18(1), 16–25.

Pressley, M., Goodchild, F., Fleet, J. and Zajchowski, R. (1989) The challenges of classroom strategy instruction. *Elementary School Journal*, 58(3), 266–78.

Purkey, W. W. (1970) *Self-Concept and School Achievement*. Englewood Cliffs, NJ: Prentice Hall.

Rand, Y., Mintzker, R., Hoffman, M. B. and Friedlander, Y. (1981) The Instrumental Enrichment programme: immediate and long-term effects. In P. Mittler (ed.) *Frontiers of Knowledge: Mental Retardation*, vol. 1. Baltimore, MD: University Park Press.

Reis, S. M., Westberg, K. L, Kulikowich, J. M. and Purcell, J. H. (1998) Curriculum compacting and achievement test scores: what does the research say? *Gifted Child Quarterly*, 42(2), 123–9.

Resnick, L. B. (1987) *Education and Learning to Think*. Washington, DC: National Academy Press.

Reynolds, D. (1991) Changing ineffective schools. In M. Ainscow (ed.) *Effective Schools for All*. London: David Fulton.

Reynolds, D. (1992) School effectiveness and school improvement: an updated review of the British literature. In D. Reynolds and P. Cuttance (eds) *School Effectiveness. Research, Policy and Practice*. London: Cassell.

Reynolds, D. (1996) Turning around ineffective schools: some evidence and some speculations. In J. Gray, D. Reynolds, C. FitzGibbon and D. Jesson (eds) *Merging Traditions: The Future of School Effectiveness and School Improvement*. London: Cassell.

Reynolds, D., Sammons, P., Stoll, L., Barber, M. and Hillman, J. (1996) School effectiveness and school improvement in the United Kingdom. *School Effectiveness and School Improvement*, 7(2), 133–58.

Reynolds, D., Creemers, B.P.M., Nesselrodt, P. S., Schaffer, E. C., Stringfield, S. and Teddlie, C. (1994) (eds) *Advances in School Effectiveness Research and Practice*. Oxford: Pergamon Press.

Reynolds, D. and Farrell, S. (1996) *Worlds Apart? A Review of International Studies of Educational Achievement Involving England*. London: HMSO.

Reynolds, D. and Muijs, R. D. (1999a). The effective teaching of mathematics: a review of research. *School Leadership and Management*, 19(3), 273–88.

Reynolds, D. and Muijs, R. D. (1999b) Numeracy matters: contemporary policy issues in the teaching of mathematics. In I. Thompson (ed.) *Issues in Teaching Numeracy in Primary Schools*. Ballmoor, Bucks: Open University Press.

Reynolds, D. and Sullivan, M. (1979) Bringing schools back in. In L. Barton (ed.) *Schools, Pupils and Deviance*. Driffield: Nafferton.

Robinson, N. M. and Noble, K. D. (1991). Social-emotional development and adjustment of gifted children. In W. T. Southern and E. D. Jones (eds). *The Academic Acceleration of Gifted Children*. London: Teachers College Press.

Roe, K. (1983) *Mass Media and Adolescent Schooling: Conflict or Coexistence*. Stockholm: Almquist & Wiksell International.

Roeber, E. D. (1996) Guidelines for the development and management of performance assessments. *Practical Assessment, Research and Evaluation*, 5(7), 1–13.

Rogers, C. R. (1967) Some observations on the organisation of personality. In R. S. Lazarus and E. M. Opton (eds) *Personality, Selected Readings*. Harmondsworth: Penguin Books.

Rogers, K. B. (1991) *The Relationship of Grouping Practices to the Education of the Gifted and Talented*. Storrs, CT: National Research Center on the Gifted and Talented, University of Connecticut.

Rosenberg, M., Schooler, C. and Schoenbach, C. (1989) Self-esteem and adolescent problems: modelling reciprocal effects. *American Sociological Review*, 54 (December), 1004–18.

Rosenberg, M., Schooler, C., Schoenbach, C. and Rosenberg, F. (1995) Global self-esteem and specific self-esteem: different concepts, different outcomes. *American Sociological Review*, 60(4), 141–56.

Rosenshine, B. (1979) Content, time and direct instruction. In P. L. Peterson and H. J. Walberg (eds) *Research on Teaching*. New York: Macmillan.

Rosenshine, B. (1980) How time is spent in elementary classrooms. In C. Denham and A. Lieberman (eds) *Time to Learn*. Washington, DC: US Department of Education.

Rosenshine, B. and Furst, N. (1973) The use of direct observation to study teaching. In R. W. M. Travers (ed.) *Second Handbook of Research on Teaching*. Chicago: Rand McNally.

Rosenshine, B. and Stevens, R. (1986) Teaching functions. In M. C. Wittrock (ed.) *Handbook of Research on Teaching*. Upper Saddle River, NJ: Merrill/Prentice Hall.

Rosenthal, R. and Jacobson, L. (1968) *Pygmalion in the Classroom. Teacher Expectations and Pupils' Intellectual Growth*. New York: Holt, Rinehart & Winston.

Rotheram, M. J. (1987) Children's social and academic competence. *Journal of Educational Research*, 80(4), 206–11.

Rowe, M. B. (1986) Wait time: slowing down may be a way of speeding up. *Journal of Teacher Education*, 37(1), 43–50.

Ruthven, K., Rousham, L. and Chaplin, D. (1998) The long-term effects of a 'calculator aware' number curriculum on pupils' mathematical attainments and attitudes in the primary phase. *Research Papers in Education*, 12(3), 249–81.

Rutter, M., Maughan, B., Mortimore, R. and Ouston, J. (1979) *Fifteen Thousand Hours. Secondary Schools and their Effects on Children*. London: Open Books.

Rutter, M. and Rutter, M. (1992) *Developing Minds. Challenge and Continuity Across the Life Span*. New York: Basic Books.

Salomon, G. and Perkins, D. N. (1989) Rocky roads to transfer: rethinking mechanism of a neglected phenomenon. *Educational Psychologist*, 24(2), 113–42.

Sanders, W. L. and Horn, S. P. (1994) The Tennessee value-added system: mixed model methodology in educational assessment. *Journal of Personnel Evaluation in Education*, 8(3), 299–311.

Sanders, W. L. and Horn, S. P. (1995) Educational assessment reassessed: the usefulness of standardised and alternative measures of student achievement as indicators for the assessment of educational outcomes. *Educational Policy Analysis Archives*, 3(6).

Scardamalia, M. and Bereiter, C. (1985) Development of dialectical processes in composition. In D. R. Olson, N. Torrance and A. Hildyard (eds) *Literacy, Language and Learning*. Cambridge: Cambridge University Press.

Schaffer, E. (1997) Interviews with the author, University of Newcastle, autumn.

Schaffer, E. C., Muijs, R. D., Kitson, C. and Reynolds, D. (1998) *Mathematics Enhancement Classroom Observation Record.* Newcastle upon Tyne: Educational Effectiveness and Improvement Centre.

Schaffer, E. C., Nesselrodt, P. S. and Stringfield, S. (1994) The contributions of classroom observation to school effectiveness research. In D. Reynolds, B.P.M. Creemers, P. S. Nesselrodt, E. C. Schaffer, S. Stringfield and C. Teddlie (eds) *Advances in School Effectiveness Research and Practice.* Oxford: Pergamon.

Scheerens, J. and Creemers, B. P. M. (1996) School effectiveness in the Netherlands: the modest influence of a research programme. *School Effectiveness and School Improvement,* 7(2), 181–95.

Schoenfeld, A. H. (1985). *Mathematical Problem Solving.* New York: Academic Press.

Schoenfeld, A. H. (1987) What's all the fuss about metacognition? In A. H. Schoenfeld (ed.) *Cognitive Science and Mathematics Education.* Hillsdale, NJ: Lawrence Erlbaum Associates.

Schoenfeld, A. H. (1992) Learning to think mathematically: problem solving, metacognition and sense making in mathematics. In D. A. Grouws (ed.) *Handbook of Research on Mathematics Teaching and Learning.* New York: Macmillan.

Schulte, A. C., Osborne, S. S. and McKinney, J. D. (1990) Academic outcomes for students with learning disabilities in consultative and resource room programs. *Exceptional Children,* 57(2), 162–72.

Schweinhart, L. J. and Weikart, D. P. (1997) *Lasting Differences: The High/Scope Preschool Curriculum Comparison Study through Age 23.* (High/Scope Educational Research Foundation Monograph no. 12). Ypsilanti, MI: High/Scope Press.

Scriven, M. (1999) The nature of evaluation. *Practical Assessment, Research and Evaluation,* 11(6), 1–4.

Secada, W. G. (1992) Race, ethnicity, social class, language, and achievement in mathematics. In D. A. Grouws (ed.) *Handbook of Research on Mathematics Teaching and Learning.* New York: Macmillan.

Shavelson, R. and Baxter, G. (1992) What we've learnt about assessing hands-on science. *Educational Leadership,* 49.

Shavelson, R. J. and Bolus, R. (1982). Self-concept: the interplay of theory and methods. *Journal of Educational Psychology,* 74(1), 3–17.

Shavelson, R. J., Hubner, J. J. and Stanton, G. C. (1976) Self-concept: validation of construct interpretations. *Review of Educational Research,* 46(3), 407–41.

Shayer, M. and Beasley, F. (1989) Does instrumental enrichment work? *British Educational Research Journal,* 13(2), 101–19.

Shore, K. (1998) *Special Kids Problem Solver: Ready-to-Use Interventions for Helping Students with Academic, Behavioural and Physical Problems.* Upper Saddle River, NJ: Prentice Hall.

Silverman, L. K. (1992) *How Parents Can Support Gifted Children.* Reston, VA: The ERIC Clearinghouse on Disabilities and Gifted Education, ED Digest E515.

Siraj-Blatchford, I. (1999) Early childhood pedagogy: practice, principles and research. In P. Mortimore (ed.) *Understanding Pedagogy and its Impact on Learning.* London: Paul Chapman Publishing.

Skaalvik, E. M. and Hagtvet, K. A. (1990) Academic achievement and self-concept: an analysis of causal predominance in a developmental perspective. *Journal of Personality and Social Psychology,* 58(2), 292–307.

Slavin, R. E. (1983) *Cooperative Learning.* New York: Longman.

Slavin, R. E. (1993) *Student Team Learning: An Overview and Practical Guide.* Washington, DC: National Education Association.

Slavin, R. E. (1995) A model of effective instruction. *Educational Forum,* 59(2), 166–76.

Slavin, R. E. (1996) *Education for All.* Lisse: Swets & Zeitlinger.

Slavin, R. E. and Madden, N. A. (1986) The integration of students with mild academic handicaps in regular classrooms. *Prospects,* 16(4), 443–61.

Slavin, R. E., Madden, N., Dolan, L., Wasik, B., Ross, S., Smith, L. and Dianda, M. (1996) Success for all: a summary of research. *Journal for the Education of Children Placed at Risk*, 1(1), 44–76.

Somekh, B. and Davis, N. (1997). *Using Information Technology Effectively in Teaching and Learning*. London: Routledge.

Sosniak, L. A. and Ethington, C. A. (1994) When teaching problem solving proceeds successfully in US 8th grade classrooms. In I. Westbury, C. A. Ethington, L. A. Sosniak and D. P. Baker (eds) *In Search of Effective Mathematics Education*. Norwood, NJ: Ablex.

Southern, W. T. and Jones, E. D. (1991) Academic acceleration: background and issues. In W. T. Southern and E. D. Jones (eds) *The Academic Acceleration of Gifted Children*. London: Teachers College Press.

Stahl, S. A. (1999) Different strokes for different folks? A critique of learning styles. *American Educator*, 23(3), 27–31.

Stahl, S. A., Duffy-Hester, A. M. and Stahl, K. A. D. (1998). Everything you wanted to know about phonics but were afraid to ask. *Reading Research Quarterly*, 35(8), 338–55.

Stallings, J. and Kasowitz, D. (1974) *Follow Through Classroom Observation Evaluation*. Menlo Park, CA: SRT International.

Stas, J. and De Wever, H. (1985) *Self-concept en Schoolsucces: Empirisch Onderzoek in het ASO en het TSO*. Leuven: Licentiaatsverhandeling Pedagogische Wetenschappen, K. U. Leuven.

Stevens, C. J. and Sanchez, K. S. (1999) Perceptions of parents and community members as a measure of school climate. In H. J. Freiberg (ed.) *School Climate. Measuring, Improving and Sustaining Healthy Learning Environments*. London: Falmer Press.

Stevens, S. H. (1997) *Classroom Success for the LD and ADHD Child*. Stephen H. Blair, publisher.

Stiggins, R. J. (1987) *Profiling Classroom Assessment Environments*. Paper presented at the Annual Meeting of the National Council on Measurement in Education, San Francisco.

Stoll, L. and Fink, D. (1996) *Changing our Schools*. Buckingham: Open University Press.

Stone, P. (1997) *Educating Children Who Are Deaf or Hard of Hearing: Auditory-Oral*. Reston, VA: Eric Clearinghouse on Disabilities and Gifted Education, EC Digest E551.

Stringfield, S., Ross, S. and Smith, A. (1997) *Bold Plans for School Restructuring*. New York: Lawrence Erlbaum Associates.

Swanson, H. L. (1999) *Intervention Research for Students with Learning Disabilities: A Meta-Analysis of Treatment Outcomes*. http://www.ncld.org/summit99/osep2.htm

Tashakkori, A. and Teddlie, C. (1998) *Mixed Methodology: Combining Qualitative and Quantitative Approaches*. Applied Social Research Methods Paper 46. Newbury Park, CA: Sage.

Teddlie, C. and Reynolds, D. (2000) (eds) *The International Handbook of School Effectiveness Research*. London: Falmer Press.

Thompson, I. (1997) The early years curriculum tomorrow. In I. Thompson (ed.) *Teaching and Learning Early Number*. Buckingham: Open University Press.

Tierney, R. J. and Readence, J. E. (2000) *Reading Strategies and Practices. A Compendium*. Needham Heights, MA: Allyn & Bacon.

Times (1999). Mathematics degree leads to higher earnings. *The Times*, 30 November.

Torgesen, J. K. (1993) Variations on theory in learning disability. In G. R. Lyon, D. B. Gray, J. E. Kavanagh and N. A. Krasnegor (eds) *Better Understanding of Learning Disabilities: New Views from Research and Their Implications for Education and Public Policies*. Baltimore, MD: Brookes.

Van Schie, E., Wiegman, O., Kuttschreuter, M. and Boer, H. (1996). Speelfrequentie, vrijetijdsbesteding en sociale integratie bij computerspelen. *Tijdschrift voor Communicatiewetenschap*, 24(1), 29–39.

Van Tassel-Baska, J. (1992) Educational decision making on acceleration and grouping. *Gifted Child Quarterly*, 36(2), 68–72.

Van Tassel-Baska, J. (1994) *Comprehensive Curriculum for Gifted Learners*. Boston: Allyn & Bacon.

Veenman, S. (1992) Effectieve instructie volgens het directe instructiemodel. *Pedagogische Studien*, 69(4), 242–69.

Vermunt, J. (1992). *Leerstijlen en Sturen van Leerprocessen in het Hoger Onderwijs: Naar Procesgerichte Instructie in Zelfstandig Denken*. Amsterdam/Lisse: Swets and Zeitlinger.

Verschaffel, L. and De Corte, E. (1993) A decade of research on word problem solving in Leuven: theoretical, methodological and practical outcomes. *Educational Psychology Review*, 5(3), 239–56.

Vygotsky, L. (1973) *Thought and Language*. Cambridge, MA: MIT Press.

Walberg, H. J. (1993) Learning 'disabilities' revisited. *European Journal of Special Needs Education*, 8(3), 289–302.

Wang, M. C. and Baker, E. T. (1986) Mainstreaming programs: design features and effects. *Journal of Special Education*, 19(4), 503–21.

Wang, M. C., Haertel, G. D. and Walberg, H. J. (1990). What influences learning? A content analysis of review literature. *Journal of Educational Research*, 84(1), 30–43.

Wang, M. C., Haertel, G. D. and Walberg, H. J. (1993). Toward a knowledge base for school learning. *Review of Educational Research*, 63, 249–94.

Wang, M. C., Haertel, G. D. and Walberg, H. J. (1997) Learning influences. In H. J. Walberg and G. D. Haertel (eds) *Psychology and Educational Practice*. Berkeley, CA: McCutchan.

Wasik, B. A. and Slavin, R. E. (1993) Preventing early reading failure with one-to-one tutoring: a review of five programs. *Reading Research Quarterly*, 28(2), 179–200.

Watson, D. (ed.) (1993) *The Impact Report. An Evaluation of the Impact of Information Technology on Children's Achievement in Primary and Secondary Schools*. London: King's College.

Weaver, C. (1990) *Understanding Whole Language: From Principles to Practice*. Portsmouth, NH: Heinemann.

Webb, N. M. (1991) Task-related verbal interaction and mathematics learning in small groups. *Journal for Research in Mathematics Education*, 22(2), 366–89.

Webb, N. M. and Moore Kendersky, C. M. (1984) Student interaction and learning in small-group and whole-class settings. In P. L. Peterson, M. Wilkinson and M. Hallinan, M. (eds) *The Social Context of Instruction*. Orlando, FL: Academic Press.

Weinstein, C. E. & Mayer, R. E. (1986). The teaching of learning strategies. In M. C. Wittrock (ed.) *Handbook of Research on Teaching*. New York: MacMillan.

West, C. K., Fish, J. A. and Stevens, R. J. (1980) General self-concept, self-concept of academic ability and school achievement: implications for 'causes' of self-concept. *Australian Journal of Education*, 24(2), 194–213.

Westerhof, K. J. (1992) On the effectiveness of teaching: direct versus indirect instruction. *School Effectiveness and School Improvement*, 3(3), 204–15.

Whitmore, J. and Maker, J. (1985) *Intellectual Giftedness Among Disabled Persons*. Rockville, MD: Aspen Press.

Wiggins, G. P. (1989) A true test: toward more authentic and equitable assessment. *Phi Delta Kappan*, 70(9), 703–13.

Williams, P. (1993) Integration of students with moderate learning difficulties. *European Journal of Special Needs Education*, 8(3), 303–20.

Williams, G. A. and Asher, S. R. (1993) Children without friends. In C. M. Todd (ed.) *Day Care Connections*. Urbana-Champaign, IL: University of Illinois Cooperative Extension Service.

Winebrenner, S. and Devlin, B. (1996) *Cluster Grouping of Gifted Students: How to Provide Full-Time Services on a Part Time Budget.* Reston, VA: ERIC Clearinghouse on Disabilities and Gifted Education, Digest E538.

Wood, D. (1998) *The UK ILS Evaluation: Final Report.* Coventry: British Educational Communications and Technology Agency.

Wood, E. and Bennett, N. (1999) Progression and continuity in early childhood education: tensions and contradictions. *International Journal of Early Years Education,* 7(1), 5–16.

Woolfolk, A. (1997) *Educational Psychology.* Needham, MA: Allyn & Bacon.

Wragg, C. (1995) Classroom management: the perspectives of teachers, pupils, and researcher. Paper presented at the Annual Meeting of the American Educational Research Association, San Francisco.

Wubbels, T., Brekelmans, M. and Hooymayers, H. (1991) Interpersonal teacher behavior in the classroom. In B. J. Fraser and H. J. Walberg (eds) *Educational Environments: Evaluation, Antecedents and Consequences.* Oxford: Pergamon Press.

Wylie, C. (1998) *Six Years Old and Competent: The Second Stage of the Competent Children Project – a Summary of the Main Findings.* Wellington, NZ: New Zealand Council for Educational Research.

Wylie, R. C. (1974) *The Self-Concept, a Critical Survey of Pertinent Research Literature.* Lincoln, NE: University of Nebraska Press.

Zigmond, N. and Baker, J. M. (1997) Inclusion of pupils with learning disabilities in general education settings. In S. J. Peijl, C. J. W. Meyer, and S. Hegarty (eds) *Inclusive Education: A Global Agenda.* London: Routledge.

Index

The index includes the Introduction and the Conclusion. Book titles are given in italics. Added to the page number, f denotes a figure.